CW00747149

BARROW BUILT SUBMARINES
An Art Collection

First published in the United Kingdom in 2010 by the Barrow-in-Furness
Submarine Heritage Centre Paintings Committee.

Republished in 2017 by NavyBooks

© Copyright 2017

All rights reserved. No part of this publication may be reproduced, stored in a retrieval system, or transmitted in any form, or by any means, electronic, mechanical, photo-copying, recording or otherwise, without the prior written permission of the publisher and copyright holder.

NavyBooks, Unit 6B, Heathlands Business Park, Liskeard, Cornwall, PL14 4DH

Contents

Contents continued

FOREWORD

by Rear Admiral Niall Kilgour CB

President of the Submariners Association

'Barrow Built Submarines' is an excellent book. It is not just about Barrow, although that connection is paramount, but it also provides a historical review of all the submarines operated by the Royal Navy since the first introduction of the 'Holland' class submarine in 1901. The details of each class are here together with short pithy summaries of the background to each class, their strengths or weaknesses and their fortunes in war and peace. It is immensely readable.

Barrow of course is at the centre of all this. The submarines I served in and went on to command, HMS PORPOISE and HMS COURAGEOUS were both 'Barrow Boats'. The collective view amongst the various ships' companies was of reliability, technical excellence and absolute trust in the product. What a tribute that is to the dedicated work force at Barrow who over the years and generations have created and built these hugely complex machines.

Barrow is now the only submarine building yard left in the UK. The work force who put together our latest nuclear attack submarine, the Astute class, have had to tackle one of the most complicated jigsaws known to man; to me they are wizards in their own right and must rightly be regarded as a truly national asset. This book is a tribute to their work and an easily read capsule of the Submarine Service over the years. I commend it to you.

The Submariners Association is an Association of ex and serving Submariners which seeks to maintain the special bonds of friendship, loyalty and comradeship, together with a pride in the Submarine Service, formed during service in Her Majesty's Submarines.

All royalties from this book will be shared between the Submariners Association and the Barrow-in-Furness Branch of the Submariners Association.

INTRODUCTION

This book forms a part of the NavyBooks series on warships built at the many shipyards around UK, joining the first two - Devonport Built Warships and Cammell Laird Built Warships in our list. However, it is also slightly different in both its genesis and development – most of our books are based on black and white photographic images of the ships referenced in them, alongside relevant technical details and specifications of the vessels. In this case, while the technical details and specifications are all included, as well as much interesting history of the employment and operations of the submarines pictured, and the men that served in them, every image is a painting and not a photograph.

The book began life as a fund raising effort for what was to be a 'Submarine Heritage Centre' based in Barrow-in-Furness with the de-commissioned submarine ONYX as its centrepiece. The paintings in the book were intended to be displayed at the centre and the original book was sold to a limited, mostly local Barrow-in-Furness and submariner audience, to raise funds for the centre and the Barrow-in-Furness Branch of the Submariners Association.

Disappointingly, the Heritage Centre project folded in 2010, ONYX left Barrow for the breaker's yard and the charity behind the project was wound up in 2014. Thus there is now, nowhere to display these paintings and the bulk remain in storage in the Dock Museum in Barrow and the Town Hall; a few are on display in the Town Hall, in the Mayor's Parlour. Two are on loan to the Barrow Sea Cadets and one is on display in the Navy Club on Barrow Island. Some others are privately owned. This book is therefore the only place where the entire collection can be seen in one place.

Copyright to the original book passed to The Barrow-in-Furness Branch of the Submariners Association. NavyBooks has, with the assistance and support of The Barrow-in-Furness Branch, revised and reprinted the book.

The submarine was deemed '*underhand, unfair and damned un-English*' by Admiral Sir Arthur Wilson, then Controller of the Navy, after the idea was brought to him. Nonetheless, the Royal Navy, recognising the vessel's massive military potential, secretly placed an order with submarine pioneer John Philip Holland. The book starts in 1900 when 'Vickers Sons and Maxim Ltd' of Barrow-In-Furness took the order to build the first submarine for the Royal Navy – a Holland class, built on licence from the Electric Boat Company of Groton, USA. Remarkably, HOLLAND 1 still exists. It sank while under tow to the scrapyard but was discovered in 1981, salvaged and is now the centrepiece of the Royal Navy Submarine Museum in Gosport, Hampshire. It concludes with a painting of HMS ASTUTE leaving Barrow for sea trials in 2010. The book includes an index of every 'Barrow Built Boat' from 1901 to 2017 and goes on to provide, under 'Miscellaneous', paintings of submarines built in Barrow for other nations or otherwise associated with the Royal Navy. The book concludes with thirteen 'Decade Paintings' which cover all types of ships built at Barrow as well as a useful index of Barrow built ships that are not specifically covered in those paintings.

Thus the book is not only a fine work of art, fit to grace any library or coffee table but it is also a very useful reference for anyone interested in the history of submarines and, indeed, the history of the Barrow-in-Furness shipyard.

Ian Whitehouse

ABOUT THE ARTIST

Mr. Tom Murphy

Tom Murphy was born in Barrow-in-Furness in 1935 and attended school at Walney Juniors and then Walney Modern (Seniors). On leaving school at fifteen Tom went into the then Vickers Armstrong where he served his time as an apprentice Fitter. On completion of his apprenticeship Tom's love of the sea led him to joining the Merchant Marine as an Engineering Officer. Tom served with such lines as Ellerman's and Esso and on such ships as the CITY OF STAFFORD and ESSO PEMBROKESHIRE - Esso's Flagship of the day. Tom has always had a great passion for drawing and painting and with this natural connection with the sea it was to be expected many of Tom's finest works would be connected with ships and the sea.

On leaving the Merchant Marine, Tom returned to his trade within the Shipyard in Barrow and worked on submarines from HMS WARSPITE onwards, his work also took him to all the major shipyards/dockyards where submarines where refitted. Tom retired from the Shipyard in 1992. At the time of his retirement Tom was working as a foreman in SMITE (Submarine Machinery Installation and Test Establishment) in the then Vickers Shipbuilding and Engineering Works.

Tom was very pleased to be approached by the Barrow-in-Furness Submarine Heritage Collection Appeal Committee and without his full support, co-operation and hard work the paintings and this book would not exist. Our deepest thanks go to Tom Murphy - who has spent a great deal of time researching each painting prior to being able to start the actual work.

Acknowledgements

The Barrow-in-Furness Submariners Association, for their support of this revised edition of their original book.

The Submariners Association and Rear Admiral N S R Kilgour CB for the Foreword

Finally, we thank YOU for purchasing this book and hope you enjoy our efforts in telling the history of that unique machine called – SUBMARINE.

Section One
Submarine Paintings

HM SUBMARINE TORPEDO BOAT "HOLLAND" CLASS
HOLLAND 1

The Painting and the HOLLAND 1 Story

The main picture (a watercolour) has a centrepiece that shows the launch of HOLLAND No.1. It is surrounded by views of HOLLAND Nos. 1, 2, 3, 4 and 5. On the lower left side is John P. Holland, the inventor and on the right hand side is Captain Reginald Bacon, the first 'Inspecting Captain of Submarines' for the Admiralty. The lower mount shows a pencil profile drawing of a "Holland" class submarine.

HOLLAND No.1 was the first submarine to be built for the Royal Navy and was intended as the first of a Class of five, built under licence and supervision from the Electric Boat Company of Groton, USA, using American parts.

Holland No.1 was employed in coastal defence duties, training and exercises for her entire career. Sold for scrap in 1913 and whilst under tow to the scrap yard, she sank off Plymouth (near the Eddystone Lighthouse) and lay undiscovered until 1981. She was salvaged in 1982 and taken to the Royal Navy Submarine Museum at Gosport for restoration and public display.

Class Information

John P. Holland, schoolteacher, submarine enthusiast and fervently anti-British, emigrated from Ireland to America in 1873. He saw submarines, transported across the Atlantic in merchant ships and launched close to Britain, as an effective way of attacking the British fleet. An Irish patriotic group (the Fenian Brotherhood) financed the construction of several of his designs, each better than the last but all of which sank at one time or another. In 1893 he won a competition for a US Navy submarine, which was unsuccessful through Navy interference in the design. To prove his concept and supported by an anonymous gift, he produced for the US Navy at his own expense what he called HOLLAND VIII, which the US Navy purchased in 1900 for $150,000 and immediately ordered seven more. Two years

before, unable to pay his creditors, he had to merge his company with that of Isaac L. Rice, his battery supplier, into the Electric Boat Company. Though Holland was appointed Chief Engineer, Rice held the financial and management reins and by 1899 had acquired Holland's patents. Within a few years, in ill-health, Holland became merely a figurehead and left the company in 1904 for obscurity.

This submarine, HOLLAND VIII, was the ancestor of every submarine in the world since. For the first time, a single design combined a successful underwater weapon system, teardrop hull optimised for underwater performance, relatively reliable depth control (by hydroplanes using full ballast tanks - previous designs varied depth by adjusting the ballast water, a recipe for instability, as they found), and an 'at-sea' ability to recharge batteries through separate surfaced and submerged propulsion units that could flexibly divide engine output between propeller and battery charging.

France, then seen as a likely enemy, was also developing considerable expertise in building and using submarines of their own design. The Admiralty could not have a situation in which the US, France and possibly other nations (Russia was also active) had a means of naval warfare denied to the world's biggest navy.

By the time a British decision was taken, the US Navy, in association with Electric Boat, had developed its slightly larger "A" (Adder) class which was bought by Russia and Japan. The Admiralty also bought this and named it "Holland" class, of which HOLLAND No.1 was the first.

Captain Bacon became frustrated over problems with the design documents for the class and set up a design team with Vickers to resolve them. They made such rapid and wide-ranging progress that a sixth Submarine was actually designed and built as the first of a new submarine class - the "A" class.

HOLLAND No1 DATA

Builder:	Vickers, Sons and Maxim Ltd, Barrow-in-Furness, England	Yard Number: 280	Cost: £35,000
Significant Dates:	Ordered: December 1900; Laid Down: 4th February 1901; Launched: 2nd October 1901		
Dimensions:	Length: 63 feet 10 inches; Beam: 11 feet 10 inches; Draught: 9 feet 11 inches		
Displacement:	Surfaced: 113 tons; Dived: 122 tons		
Machinery:	Surfaced: Single cylinder petrol engine 160 bhp; Dived: Single electric motor of 70 bhp; Single shaft		
Speed:	Surfaced: 7.4 knots; Dived: 6 knots		
Endurance:	Surfaced: 235 nautical miles @ full speed; Dived: 20 nautical miles at 5 knots.		
Armament:	1 x 14-inch torpedo tube		
Complement:	7 crew (2 Officers & 5 Ratings)		

John .P. Holland

Captain Bacon,
Father of the Submarine Service.

The Mayor of Barrow-in-Furness, Councillor David Pidduck (2002-03) and the Borough Council have pleasure in sponsoring the painting of Submarine Torpedo Boat Number 1 (Holland class) - the first submarine built for the Royal Navy at Barrow-in-Furness. *"This was the start of a long connection between Barrow-in-Furness, its people and the Royal Navy's Submarine Service."*

HM SUBMARINES
SUBMARINE A1

The Painting and the A1 Story

The main picture (a watercolour) shows A1 at sea. On the horizon is the Castle Line ship BERWICK CASTLE. The lower mount shows a pencil drawing of an "A" class submarine and mice that were used to check for toxic fumes within the submarine.

Submarine A1 became the Royal Navy's first submarine casualty, accidentally rammed by the BERWICK CASTLE whilst on exercise in the Eastern Solent on 18th March 1904. Since that day more than 5,000 Royal Navy submariners have perished in war and in accidents. These were the first:

Lieutenant Loftus Mansergh (in Command), Sub Lieutenant John Churchill, Chief Engine Room Artificer William Parkinson, Petty Officers George Baker, William Dudgeon, Vivian Roberts, Engine Room Artificer Clinton Bayly, Able Seamen Charles King, Peter Wallace, Chief Stoker Albert Fleming, Stoker Albert Ellis.

The submarine sank in only 39 feet of water but with the loss of all hands. She was struck on the starboard side near the conning tower. This led to the fitting of a second watertight hatch at the base of conning tower as an additional safety measure for later vessels, a practice that continues to this day. In April 1904 she was raised, re-commissioned, and eventually scrapped in 1911.

Class Information

The Admiralty and Vickers made such progress in their development plans with the "Holland" class that a sixth Submarine was built to a new design and became A1, the first of the "A" class, 40 feet longer than the "Holland", with a more powerful petrol engine. Though this was a recognisable class of thirteen submarines there was continuous development within the class. A2 to A13 had larger hulls, there were progressive increases in engine and electric motor powers and from A5 onwards, two torpedo tubes were fitted with more reloads. The last, A13, was fitted with an experimental 'heavy oil' engine, an interim step to a true diesel, to overcome the dangers associated with petrol engines in confined spaces, though it

was some years before the fruits of this experiment were realised. The class of 13 submarines was built between 1902 and 1905. It was regarded as a success by the Admiralty and gave a strong basis for the build-up of a submarine force. Almost all the officers and ratings qualifying in submarines before WW1, and some qualifying during the early years of the war, were trained in this class.

The "A" class was an unlucky class. A4 was very nearly lost from flooding during exercises in the Solent early on 16th October 1905 but recovered safely to the surface only to sink later on the same day as the submarine was being taken into dock for survey and repair. Luckily no one was lost in either accident. A5 had a petrol vapour explosion on 16th February 1905 alongside the submarine tender HMS HAZARD at Queenstown, Ireland. Six crew were killed and two injured - as were four of a rescue crew caught in a second explosion. A8 sank in Plymouth Sound on 8th June 1905 after an internal explosion. Fourteen of the eighteen crew and trainees onboard died.

A9 was hit on the conning tower by the steamer COATH off Penlee Point near Plymouth in February 1906 however, following A1's fatal accident, A9 had been fitted with a secondary hatch which, despite damage to the main hatch, remained watertight and all survived. A1, whilst refuelling alongside at 'Petrol' Pier in HMS DOLPHIN on 6th August 1910 had an explosion of petrol vapour. Although no one was killed the Commanding Officer and six of his crew were injured. A3 was lost with all hands on 2nd February 1912 after collision with the submarine tender HMS HAZARD off the Isle of Wight. A7 was lost with all hands after a diving accident in Whitsand Bay off Plymouth on 16th January 1914. A10 sank after accidental flooding at Ardrossan, Scotland on 17th March 1917 whilst alongside with no crew onboard.

The surviving nine "A" class submarines were paid off by the end of WW1 and most quickly went to the scrap yard except that A2 kept up the accident tradition by sinking in 1920 on the way to the breakers' yard. She remained on the bottom until recovered in 1925 and broken up.

Sᴜʙᴍᴀʀɪɴᴇ **A**1 Dᴀᴛᴀ

Builder:	Vickers, Sons and Maxim Ltd, Barrow-in-Furness	Yard Number: 285	Cost: £41,000
Significant Dates:	Laid Down: 19 February 1902; Launched: 9 July 1902; Completed: 23 July 1903		
Dimensions:	Length: 103 feet 3 inches; Beam: 12 feet 8 inches; Draught: 10 feet 1 inch		
Displacement:	Surfaced: 190 ton; Dived: 207 tons		
Machinery:	Surfaced: Single Wolseley petrol engine of 160 bhp; Dived: Single electric motor of 150 bhp; One shaft		
Speed:	Surfaced: 9 knots; Dived: 6 knots		
Endurance:	Surfaced: 500 nautical miles at 9 knots; Dived: 20 nautical miles at 5 knots		
Armament:	1 x 18-inch forward torpedo tube (three torpedoes carried)		
Complement:	11 (2 Officers and 9 Ratings)		

This painting was commissioned by Lieutenant Tony (Florrie) Ford, RN - Staff Officer (Operations), Captain Faslane Flotilla, HM Naval Base Clyde.

HM SUBMARINES "B" CLASS
SUBMARINE B11

The Painting and the B11 Story

The main picture (a watercolour) shows B11 passing through one of five minefields to sink the Turkish coastal defence ship MESUDIYE, which can be seen in the distance, along with many local craft going about their daily business. The lower mount shows (from left to right) Lieutenant Norman Douglas Holbrook who was awarded the Victoria Cross for this action, the Turkish battleship MESUDIYE and a stern view of a "B" class submarine.

At the outbreak of hostilities with Turkey the Allies imposed a blockade of the Dardanelles. By December 1914, a large flotilla of ships of all types was gathered at the Greek island of Lemnos. Amongst them were three "B" class submarines – B9, B10 and B11. Under the command of Lieutenant Norman Holbrook B11 entered the Dardanelles on 13th December 1914. Notwithstanding the very difficult currents he dived his boat under five rows of mines into Sari Siglar Bay and torpedoed the Turkish coastal defence ship MESUDIYE, which was guarding the minefield. Although attacked by both shore gunfire and torpedo boats, Lieutenant Holbrook brought his boat back safely having been submerged for nine hours. He was awarded the Victoria Cross and his First Lieutenant (Lieutenant Sydney Winn), the Distinguished Service Order. The rest of the ship's company were each awarded the Distinguished Service Medal.

Class Information

The "B" class comprised eleven submarines – all built by the Barrow shipyard and launched between 1904 and 1906. Although similar in layout to the "A" class, they were significantly larger, with a more substantial casing which improved performance on the surface and made deck activities easier for the crew. Unlike the "A" class, they also had an additional pair of hydroplanes mounted on the conning tower to improve underwater control. From this class onwards, forward hydroplanes became standard on RN submarines, but never again on the conning tower, always at the bow.

In 1911, "B" class submarines formed the first two 'Overseas' Submarine Flotillas in the RN, with three based at Gibraltar and three at Malta. Submarine B2 was lost before the outbreak of WW1 when a collision on 4th October 1912 with the Hamburg-Amerika Liner AMERIKA practically cut the submarine in half. The Commanding Officer (Lieutenant Percy O'Brien) and all but one of his crew were lost. In September 1915 B11, with the five other "B" class boats of the Mediterranean Flotilla was based on the Italian submarine depot ship MARCO POLO at Venice. From here they patrolled in the Adriatic. Submarine B10 was sunk at Venice following an air raid by Austrian aircraft. Recovered, she was deliberately sunk again to put out a fire caused by a shipyard worker. Again recovered, she was declared a 'write off'. By late 1916 five remained usable but became ineffective as submarines through lack of spare parts. They were converted into surface patrol craft (S6 – S11). Fitted with deck guns at Venice they were used to patrol the Otranto Barrage.

B11, with the rest of the "B" class submarines of the Mediterranean Flotillas, was sold in Malta in 1919 for scrap. The four remaining "B" class submarines, which had remained in home waters during WW1 for coastal and training duties, were sold for breaking up between 1919 and 1921.

B11 DATA (TYPICAL OF THE CLASS)

Builder:	Vickers, Sons and Maxim Ltd, Barrow-in-Furness. Yard Number: 329
Significant Dates:	Ordered: 1904; Launched: 24th February 1906; Completed: 11th July 1906
Dimensions:	Length: 142 feet 2½ inches; Beam: 13 feet 7 inches; Draught: 11 feet 2 inches
Displacement:	Surfaced: 287 tons; Dived: 316 tons
Machinery:	Surfaced: Single 6 cylinder petrol engine 600 bhp; Dived: Single electric motor of 180 bhp Single shaft
Speed:	Surfaced: 13 knots; Dived: 7 knots
Endurance:	Surfaced: 1,000 nautical miles at 8½ knots; Dived: 50 nautical miles at 4½ knots
Armament:	2 x 18-inch bow torpedo tubes (four torpedoes carried)
Complement:	16 (2 officers and 14 ratings)

This painting was sponsored by the personal contributions of the National Management Committee (2003) of the Submariners Association.

HM SUBMARINES "C" CLASS
HMS C3

The Painting and the C3 Story

The main picture is a watercolour showing two "C" class submarines underway in Portsmouth Harbour in 1922. They are passing a fleet of Royal Navy vessels including HMS VICTORY which was then still afloat. The lower mount shows C1 in a floating dock and a "C" class submarine at sea.

C3, a typical vessel of this class, was deliberately expended in the St George's Day Raid on Zeebrugge in 1918, the intention of which was to bottle up the German submarines and surface craft which operated from there. As part of the raid a viaduct joining the Mole at Zeebrugge to the mainland was to be destroyed by ramming C3 - packed with 5 tons of Amatol explosives - into the viaduct's supports and then exploding the charge. The submarine (with a reduced crew of six) was towed to the general area and then made its way under the viaduct under its own power. The Commanding Officer then lit the fuse and the crew made good their escape in a skiff and were picked up offshore by a picket boat. The Commanding Officer (Lieutenant Sandford) managed to position C3 perfectly. The explosives did their job and destroyed the viaduct. Lieutenant Sandford was awarded the Victoria Cross and all the crew were decorated.

Class Information

This remains the largest class of submarine built for the Royal Navy in peacetime, running to thirty-eight vessels. Most of the main characteristics were the same as the preceding "B" class but the "C" class did not have midships hydroplanes and there were also improvements in detail. This was the last class of petrol engined submarines in the Royal Navy. The first order was in 1906 for eleven submarines; a further seven were ordered in the 1906/07 Estimates, another twelve in the following year and the final eight were announced in the 1908/09 Estimates. All thirty-eight submarines had been completed by the end of 1910 - a remarkable rate of production that often saw two submarines being launched on the same day. The size of the class was perhaps an indication that the Admiralty was becoming more convinced of the submarine weapon and the need for a strong submarine service.

Seven of thirty eight of the class were built at Chatham.

Three "C" class submarines (C36, 37, 38) formed an Overseas Flotilla at Hong Kong in 1911, making the journey partly under their own power and partly towed. Departing on 8th February 1911 under their respective Commanding Officers (Lieutenants Godfrey Herbert, Athelstan Fenner and John Codrington) the passage from Devonport took three months. They remained there for the duration of WW1.

During WW1 the remainder of the class was mainly based on North Sea ports, providing coastal patrols. Four served in the Baltic with a flotilla based in Russian ports. These submarines were partly dismantled, towed to North Russia and then transported on barges through rivers and canals to St. Petersburg where they were re-assembled and put into service. C32 was blown up by her crew after running aground on 24th October 1917. The remaining three were scuttled at Helsingfors in 1918 to prevent their capture and use by Germany.

The "C" class had a number of peacetime accidents. Commanding Officer Lieutenant Guy Hart was killed in C8 on 13th June 1907 in an explosion, the engine back-firing into the crank pit. On the 14th of July 1909 C11 collided with the steamer SS EDDYSTONE near Haisborough Light off Cromer. The EDDYSTONE struck C11 aft and appears to have cut off the stern of the submarine, which immediately heeled over and sank; thirteen of the crew were lost. C14, commanded by Lieutenant George W.E. Naper, collided with Admiralty Hopper Number 29 in Plymouth Sound on the 10th December 1913, was holed and sank but not before all the crew had been saved. The wreck was later salvaged, refitted and returned to service. The Commanding Officer (Lieutenant Thomas C Meryon) was lost overboard from C21 in poor weather on 28th November 1913 when returning to Dundee after carrying out an exercise in St. Andrews Bay, the submarine heeled over in a sudden squall. He lost his balance, fell overboard from the bridge and was not recovered.

Twenty six of the "C" class submarines survived the war. All were disposed of for scrap between 1919 and 1922.

C3 Data (Typical of the Class)

Builder:	Vickers, Sons & Maxim, Barrow-in-Furness	Yard Number: 336	Cost: £47,000

Significant Dates:	Ordered: 1905; Launched: 3rd Oct 1906; Completed: 23rd Feb 1907
Dimensions:	Length: 142 feet 2½ inches; Beam: 13 feet 7 inches; Draught: 11 feet 2 inches
Displacement:	Surfaced: 287 tons; Dived: 316 tons
Machinery:	Surfaced: Single 16 cylinder petrol engine 600 bhp; Dived: Single electric motor of 180 bhp; One shaft
Speed:	Surfaced: 13 knots; Dived: 7½ knots
Endurance:	Surfaced: 1300 nautical miles at 9 knots; Dived: 50 nautical miles at 4½ knots
Armament:	2 x 18-inch bow torpedo tubes (four torpedoes carried)
Complement:	16 (2 Officers and 14 Ratings)

This painting was sponsored by Graham and Bambi Spencer of McGrath Cove, Nova Scotia, Canada, who said: *"We have chosen to sponsor this class of submarine to commemorate Canada's involvement in the "C" class with their first submarines CC1 & CC2."* Soon before the start of WW1, the Premier of British Columbia purchased CC1 and CC2. They were built in Seattle and resembled the British "C" class submarines.

HM SUBMARINES "D" CLASS
HMS D1

The Painting and the D1 Story

The main picture (an acrylic) shows Submarine D1 passing between Piel Island and Roa Island. Also shown is the Lifeboat Station as it was in 1912 with the lifeboat THOMAS FIELDEN on the slipway.

The lower mount (left hand side) is a tinted pencil drawing depicting Roa Island in 1912 showing the Lifeboat Station and the same lifeboat with a Morecambe Bay prawner, a classic local working boat, sailing past. To the right is a steam locomotive leaving the island, which was connected by a causeway to the mainland. The centre of the lower mount shows the Royal National Lifeboat Institution logo c.2000 whilst, on the right hand side, is the "D" class inflatable inshore lifeboat D-567 c.2000.

The "D" class submarines were considered to be so innovative that D1 was built in the utmost secrecy in a securely guarded building shed and launched in secrecy in the presence of only departmental heads and a few officers from the 3,730 ton cruiser HMS MERCURY which was in Barrow at the time. When moved to the fitting out berth the submarine was kept screened from public view.

Class Information

The "D" class had significant improvements over all the earlier British classes of submarine and was the Admiralty's first attempt to produce submarines that could carry out extended patrols away from coastal areas. They were fitted with diesel engines, which made for more crew safety, saddle ballast tanks which increased buoyancy and watertight bulkheads giving increased survivability in an accident. Two shafts and two engines were an important feature given the poor reliability of engines at that time, a wireless transmitter and, on D4, probably the first gun to be fitted during construction to any submarine in the world (a 12-pounder in a disappearing mount).

They had over twice the propulsive power of the preceding "C" class and used two shafts for the first time. Their increased displacement gave greater internal space and the innovative use of saddle tanks to hold the main ballast water externally also provided additional inboard space although, following on the A13 experiment, the two diesel engines driving the twin propellers, the additional torpedo tube aft and an increased complement probably left little space for improved habitability. With their enlarged bridge structure, these boats had a profile that became that of the classic conventional submarine. Six of the class were built by Vickers whilst two (D7 and D8) were built at HM Dockyard, Chatham.

Successful and relatively reliable, the "D" class was worked very hard during WW1 patrolling the North Sea, the Heligoland Bight and protecting the cross channel troop ships.

During WW1 four of the class – D2, D3, D5 and D6 were lost. D5 was sunk after hitting a mine in the North Sea on 3rd November 1914. Only the Commanding Officer (Lieutenant Commander Godfrey Herbert) and four of his crew survived. D2 (Lieutenant Commander Clement Head) vanished without trace in the North Sea on 25th November 1914. D3 (Lieutenant William Maitland-Dougall, RCNVR) was lost with all hands after being bombed by a French air ship in the Channel on 25th March 1918 and D6 was torpedoed off Northern Ireland on 26th June 1918. The Commanding Officer (Lieutenant Samuel Brookes) and his First Lieutenant were the only survivors.

D1 was sunk as a gunnery target on 23rd October 1918. The three remaining "D" class submarines, D4, D7 and D8, were paid off in July 1919 and, on 19th December 1921, all three submarines were sold to Pounds of Portsmouth for breaking up.

D1 DATA

Builder:	Vickers, Sons and Maxim Ltd, Barrow-in-Furness	Yard Number: 350	Cost: £79,910
Significant Dates:	Ordered: 21st January 1907; Launched: 16th May 1908; Completed: 17th September 1909		
Dimensions:	Length: 163 feet; Beam: 20 feet 6 inches; Draught: 10 feet 6 inches		
Displacement:	Surfaced: 483 tons; Dived: 595 tons		
Machinery:	Surfaced: 2 x Voight diesels = 1,200 bhp; Dived: 2 x Vickers electric motors = 550 bhp; Twin shafts		
Speed:	Surfaced: 14 knots; Dived: 9 knots		
Endurance:	Surfaced: 1,750 nautical miles at 11.2 knots; Dived: 50 nautical miles at 5 knots; Fuel: 29 tons		
Armament:	3 x 18-inch torpedo tubes (2 x bow and 1 x stern) six torpedoes carried.		
Complement:	30 (2 Officers and 28 Ratings)		

Lifeboats

This painting was sponsored by the Management Committee of the RNLI - Barrow Lifeboat Station. The RNLI Lifeboat Station at Roa Island operates an 'All Weather' lifeboat and an inshore "D" class inflatable so the "D" class submarine is the ideal portrait to represent both the Station and its volunteer crews."

HM SUBMARINES "E" CLASS
HMS E14

The Painting and the E14 Story

The main picture is a watercolour showing E14 passing the invasion fleet at Mudros on her way to the Dardanelles. It is noted that the cargo vessel to the left is the RIVER CLYDE adapted for landing troops by having access openings cut into the hull and walkways fitted to enable troops to embark onto landing craft. On the right hand side can be seen the four funnels of the hospital ship BRITANNIC – at the time the largest ship ever built. The lower mount shows the German Battleship SMS GOEBEN - a prime target for British submarines; Lieutenant Commander Geoffrey Saxton White, VC; Commander Edward Courtney-Boyle VC; and Lieutenant Commander Martin Eric Nasmith, VC of the Submarine E11.

During the Gallipoli Campaign of 1915 submarines were sent into the very dangerous Dardanelles and the Sea of Marmora to disrupt Turkish sea traffic. E14 arrived in the Sea of Marmora on the 29th April 1915 having safely completed the 12 hour passage through the heavily mined and netted Dardanelles, supporting other boats, including Barrow built E11 (Lt. Cdr. Martin E Nasmith, VC). Under the command of Lt. Cdr. Edward C Boyle, E14 completed three patrols and a total of seventy days in the Sea of Marmora and accounted for a considerable amount of Turkish shipping including two gunboats and three troop transports - which included the 5,000 ton GUL-DJEMEL carrying 6,000 troops and a battery of artillery to Gallipoli. For his endeavours Edward Boyle was awarded the Victoria Cross.

On 27th January 1918 E14 was again sent into the Dardanelles to sink the German battle-cruiser GOEBEN, which was aground off Nagara Point. Now under the command of Lt. Cdr. Geoffrey S. White, E14 arrived off Nagara only to find that the GOEBEN had been towed away. With nothing left to do she reversed course to make her way out and on the way down the strait fired at a large merchantman. However the torpedo exploded prematurely, badly damaging the submarine. Nevertheless E14 continued her dived passage towards the open sea for two hours, becoming so heavily flooded that she became uncontrollable. This forced Geoffrey White to surface in the hope of escaping but E14 was hit by gunfire from shore batteries. With no hope of escape he then headed E14 towards the shore to give his ship's company a chance of safety. He was killed in the attempt, as were his other officers and the majority of his crew. The seven survivors were made Prisoners of War. For his selfless sacrifice Lt. Cdr. White was awarded the Victoria Cross.

E14 is the only submarine in which two different Commanding Officers won Victoria Crosses in two separate events separated by some two years.

Class Information

Completed between 1913 and 1916, the "E" class was the most successful Royal Navy submarine class of WW1 and served in all areas of operations including the North Sea, the Baltic, the Mediterranean, the Pacific and, famously, Turkish waters. It was in this class that many Royal Navy submariners, who rose to high rank, learned their trade.

"E" class submarines were enlarged and improved versions of the earlier "D" class, the most evident difference being the addition of beam torpedo tubes, the first in Royal Navy submarines. Eighteen orders had been placed before war was declared, progressively increased to fifty eight, of which twenty were built at Barrow. Such was the urgent need for submarines that once war was declared the work to build the class was shared between thirteen different shipyards. Of the fifty eight ordered only fifty five were completed. One (E28 ordered from Yarrows) was cancelled and two (E57 and E58 ordered from Vickers) were completed as the lead boats of the new "L" class.

One of the class, E5 suffered an accident on 8th June 1913 in which one officer and two ratings were killed and nine others injured following a diesel engine crankcase explosion. Twenty eight "E" class were lost during WW1, to enemy action, wrecked or scuttled to prevent capture. E4 and E41, sank after colliding with each other in an exercise but both were later recovered and continued in service. In all fifty six officers and five hundred and forty one ratings were killed in action or died from accident or illness whilst serving in the "E"class; in addition one officer and thirteen ratings died as prisoners of war.

All the RN "E" class submarines that survived WW1 were sold for scrap between 1921 and 1923, except for E48 which was sunk as a target in 1921 but later (1928) was raised and scrapped.

Two of the class, Yard Nos. 419 and 420 were built for the Royal Australian Navy - their first submarines. HMAS AE1 was launched on 22nd May 1913 and lost in unknown circumstances on 14th September 1914 in the Pacific. HMAS AE2 was launched on 18th June 1913 and was sunk in the Sea of Marmora on 30th April 1915. (See also 'Australian Submarines' pages 122 & 123)

E14 DATA (TYPICAL OF THE CLASS)

Builder:	Vickers Limited, Barrow-in-Furness	Yard Number: 438	Cost: £105,700
Significant Dates:	Ordered: 14th October 1912; Launched: 7th July 1914; Completed: 10th December 1914		
Dimensions:	Length: 181 feet; Beam: 22 feet 8 inches; Draught: 12 feet 6 inches		
Displacement:	Surfaced: 667 tons; Dived: 807 tons		
Machinery:	Surfaced: Twin diesel engines, total 1,600 bhp; Dived: Twin electric motors, total 840 bhp Two shafts		
Speed:	Surfaced: 15 knots; Dived: 10 knots		
Endurance:	Surfaced: 3,225 nautical miles at 10 knots		Fuel: 40 tons
Armament:	5 x 18-inch torpedo tubes (2 x bow, 2 x beam, 1 x stern); ten torpedoes carried; 1x12-pounder gun		Complement: 30 (3 Officers and 27 Ratings)

24

This painting was sponsored by Mr. Peter Dismore, MBE, a member of the Submariners Association, Barrow-in-Furness Branch. Peter was a Warrant Officer when he retired from the Submarine Service.

HM SUBMARINES NAUTILUS CLASS
HMS NAUTILUS

The Painting and the NAUTILUS Story

The main picture (in acrylic) shows HMS NAUTILUS, the first Royal Navy Submarine to be given a name, leaving Barrow with Blackpool Tower to the right and the Barrow-based passenger ship LADY MOYRA in the background. The lower mount (in pencil and watercolours) shows from left to right:

(a) An earlier NAUTILUS designed by Campbell & Ash and built by Wolseley & Lyon. It was propelled by electric motors, had a length of 60 feet and displaced 50 tons. This NAUTILUS was trapped on the bottom whilst on trials in Tilbury Docks, London in 1886 together with her crew and the Royal Navy's Chief Constructor, Sir William White onboard, but eventually was safely recovered to the surface.

(b) The Pearly Nautilus or Argonaut (Nautilus Pompilius) – a cephalopod or mollusc found deep in the Indian Ocean.

(c) USS NAUTILUS – the world's first nuclear submarine seen here returning to New York after being the first ship ever to reach the geographical North Pole on 3rd August, 1958.

(c) Fulton's NAUTILUS – built by Robert Fulton in 1799/1800. It was 21 feet 4 inches long with a copper sheathed hull. It had sails for surface propulsion and had two hand cranked screws for underwater propulsion.

Class Information

In 1900 the Admiralty supported the licence with Electric Boat that gave Vickers a monopoly of Holland patents in Britain and Europe, but by 1910, they were unhappy with only a single supply source and were concerned over Vickers production performance. In 1911 they gave notice that they intended to terminate the company's (monopoly) contract to supply the RN. They also established their own group, the Submarine Design Committee, to recommend future designs.

One outcome was the requirement for a large submarine able to operate overseas with a displacement of around 1,000 tons, a surfaced speed of 20 knots (to keep up with the battle-fleet) and a double hull. This was the first Naval Requirement for a Fleet Submarine, something many navies pursued with only limited success until the advent of nuclear power. Both Vickers and Scott's of Greenock, Scotland, were invited to tender. Although the Scott's Italian design was more liked and promised a higher speed, an order went to Vickers, in part because they were thought to have more experience in large diesel engines, then viewed with misgivings by the Admiralty. That order was for HMS NAUTILUS. The Italian (Laurenti) design submitted by Scott's of Greenock also resulted in an order for HMS SWORD-FISH – originally intended to be diesel powered but completed as the first steam powered RN submarine.

HMS NAUTILUS' design was significant for reasons other than its size - at the time it was twice the size of any existing submarine. It put Vickers under notice of the Admiralty's determination to distance the direction of RN submarine development from the Company, replacing the somewhat informal joint arrangements until then. It also showed their willingness to consider other designers and builders. Although Vickers was awarded this order and many others subsequently, their submarine monopoly had ended.

The long construction time of HMS NAUTILUS was due to the Admiralty stopping work on the boat due to the engines being experimental and the war effort preventing full shop trials being conducted and, in part, to allow work to be carried out on more urgent submarine construction. HMS NAUTILUS was renamed Submarine N1 on 5th June 1917. There were considerable teething troubles and she never became fully operational. Moved to Portsmouth in 1918 she ended her days as a battery charging boat for other submarines. On 9th June 1922 HMS NAUTILUS was sold for breaking up at Cashmore's at Newport on the Isle of Wight.

NAUTILUS DATA

Builder:	Vickers Limited, Barrow-in-Furness	Yard No: 436	Cost: Estimated at £203,850
Significant Dates:	Ordered: 23rd Apr 1913; Laid Down: 13th Mar 1913; Launched: 16th December 1914; Completed: October 1917		
Significant Data:	Length: 258 feet 4½ inches; Beam: 26 feet; Draught: 22 feet 6½ inches		
Displacement:	Surfaced: 1,270 tons; Dived: 1,694 tons		
Machinery:	Surfaced: Twin 12 cylinder Vickers diesels (3,700 bhp); Dived: Two electric motors (1,000 bhp) Twin shafts		
Speed:	Surfaced: 17 knots (designed); Dived: 9 knots (designed)		
Endurance:	Surfaced: 5,300 nautical miles at 11 knots; Dived: 72 miles at 5 knots		
Armament:	2 x 18-inch bow torpedo tubes; 4 x 18-inch beam torpedo tubes; 2 x 18-inch stern torpedo tubes' 1 x 3-inch High Angle gun		
Complement:	42 (5 Officers and 37 Ratings)		

This painting was sponsored by Mr. David Cole who served his time as an electrical apprentice in the Barrow shipyard from 1976 to 1980. Mr. Cole comments *"This painting is dedicated to my parents Bill and Joan Cole. My dad served in submarines during the Cold War from 1966 to 1987. On his retirement from the Royal Navy he worked in the Barrow shipyard for a further 15 years."*

"My mother worked in the Barrow shipyard for most of her working life and worked at many different types of jobs in the yard. She took early retirement in 1995."

HM SUBMARINES "V" CLASS
SUBMARINES V1 to V4

The Painting and the V3 Story

The main picture (a watercolour) shows Submarine V3 passing HMS VICTORY on passage through Portsmouth Harbour. The lower mount shows a view of the Barrow Shipyard - Devonshire Dock (circa 1915) and part of the Barrow-in-Furness landscape showing the Iron and Steelworks and Corn Silo along with many other local industrial sites. Submarine V3 was typical of the class being used as a training vessel operating around the east and south coasts of England. V3 did not see active war service and was scrapped in 1920.

Class Information

In 1912/13 the Submarine Design Committee sought designs for coastal submarines. Designs were submitted by several companies and by the Admiralty. Scott's of Greenock submitted a concept for an "S" class submarine based on an Italian 'Laurenti' design and received orders for three of the type. Whitworth's submitted a bid based on the French 'Labeuf' design and received orders for four "W" class submarines of two different types.

Despite having a lot of submarine work in hand, and perhaps, mindful of that they no longer had monopoly for submarine business the Vickers' concept for a coastal submarine resulted in orders for four submarines designated the "V" class – the V was taken from the first letter of the Vickers' name. All four of the "V" class were built between 1914 and 1915.

The "V" class had a hull form which gave a good underwater speed but offset by poor underwater endurance. Overall the "V" class was a not successful submarine. In consequence the class was employed mainly as training submarines and they saw no active service. However, the 'V' class design was the basis of the subsequent, Admiralty designed, "F" class. This Admiralty design received eight orders but only three were built. All of the "V" class submarines were taken out of service in July 1919 and were sold for breaking up in 1920/21.

Note: Submarine V1 differed from the other 3 in the Class being 3 feet 6 inches shorter, 4 tons less displacement and had 300 bhp electric motors rather than 380bhp.

Submarine V3 Data

Builder:	Vickers Limited	Yard Number: 450	Cost: Estimated at £76,100
Significant Dates:	Ordered: August 1913; Laid Down: 17th Jan 1914; Launched: 1st April 1915; Completed 22nd Jan 1916		
Dimensions:	Length: 147 feet 6 inches; Beam: 16 ft 3 inches; Draught: 11 feet 6 inches		
Displacement:	Surfaced: 391 tons; Dived: 457 tons		
Machinery:	Surfaced: 2 x Vickers 8 cylinders diesels (900bhp); Dived: 2 electric motors (380bhp)		
Speed:	Surfaced: 14 knots; Dived: 9 knots.		
Endurance:	Surfaced: 2,800 nautical miles at 9 knots; Dived: 50 nautical miles at 5 knots		
Fuel:	16.5 tons		
Armaments:	2 x 18-inch torpedo tubes; two spare torpedoes carried; 1 x 12-pounder deck gun		
Complement:	20 (2 Officers and 18 Ratings)		

This painting was commissioned by a kind donation from the Barrow and District Licensed Victuallers Association. The payment for the painting was presented by the Chairman of the Association, Mr. Mike Fallon, in May 2004.

HM SUBMARINES "G" CLASS
HMS G13

The Painting and the G13 Story

The Main Picture (a watercolour) shows Submarine G13 on the surface, engaged in action with a German Zeppelin. The action is shown just as the sun is rising on the right hand side of the painting. The lower mount includes an ink and wash drawing of Submarine G10 and a portrait of the Commanding Officer - Lieutenant Commander George Bradshaw, RN.

Zeppelins of the German Navy regularly patrolled the Heligoland Bight - the main approach to the German naval bases on their North Sea coast - and made regular sorties across the North Sea to bomb eastern England and London. Initially several British submarines carried 2-pounder or 12-pounder guns primarily to fire at Zeppelins which, at least over the North Sea, enjoyed undisputed monopoly of the air.

However, in the encounters between Zeppelins and British submarines, no Zeppelin was ever brought down - in fact they generally succeeded in forcing submarines to dive. In one instance late in 1917 Submarine G13 (Lieutenant Commander G.F. Bradshaw), whilst diving at sunrise, sighted a Zeppelin patrolling to the North. Surface gun action was ordered, opening with five rounds of rapid fire whilst the boat got underway. The Zeppelin took up station off the submarine's stern where the submarine's gun could not be brought to bear, forcing it to dive. Attempts by G13 to surface were greeted by the dropping of one or two bombs to keep her down. Towards sunset several bombs were dropped by the Zeppelin which then disappeared landward, allowing G13 finally to surface.

Earlier, on 10th March 1917 G13, under the command of Lieutenant Commander Bradshaw, sank the German U-Boat UC-43 (Leutnant zur See Sebelin) off Muckle Flugga (north of the Shetland Islands), for which he was awarded the Distinguished Service Order.

Class Information

In 1913 the Admiralty became aware of an extensive German programme for long range submarines. In response they created a requirement for a new class of submarine, one outcome of which was the "G" class, to be built by Vickers, Chatham Dockyard, Armstrong-Whitworth, Scott's and White. Fifteen were ordered, of which fourteen were completed. Vickers built six (G8 to G13).

These were the first British submarines to be fitted with a 21-inch torpedo fired from a stern tube. Living conditions were considered to be a great improvement on the previous classes - particularly in the provision of an electric oven. Some builders were encouraged to fit their own choice of diesel engines, with the aim of widening the British experience and knowledge of what was still an almost experimental engine form. Four sources were foreseen - Vickers, MAN (Germany), Fiat (Italy) or Sulzer (Switzerland). With WW1 starting, MAN became impossible, Fiat also temporarily so and Sulzer deliveries became uncertain. Because of these problems all except Scott's used Vickers engines (Scott's were already Fiat licencees and used their engines).

During WW1 the "G" class operated mainly in the North Sea and North Russia. Three of the class were lost in the war but others sank two U-boats. G7 was lost with all hands in the North Sea on 1st November 1918 and G8 on 14th January 1918. G9 was sunk in error off the Norwegian coast by HMS PASLEY with only one survivor - a Stoker named Drake.

Submarine G11 was wrecked of Howick, Northumberland on 22nd November 1918 and two of the crew were drowned whilst attempting to reach the shore. The temporary Commanding Officer of G11 at the time was Lieutenant Commander Bradshaw – formerly Commander of Submarine G13.

The surviving ten submarines of the class were paid off in January 1919.

SUBMARINE G13 DATA

Builder:	Vickers Limited, Barrow-in-Furness	Yard Number: 468	Cost: Estimated at £125,000

Significant Dates: Ordered: 4th November 1914; Laid Down: 9th April 1915; Launched: 18th July 1916; Completed: 23rd September 1916

Dimensions: Length: 187 feet; Beam: 22 feet 8 inches; Draught: 13 feet 4 inches

Displacement: Surfaced: 703 tons; Dived: 837 tons

Machinery: Surfaced: 2 x Vickers 8 cylinder diesels (1,600 bhp); Dived: 2 x electric motors (840 bhp); Twin shafts

Speed: Surfaced: 14.25 knots; Dived: 9 knots.

Endurance: Surfaced: 1,650 nautical miles at14 knots; Dived: 95 nautical miles at 3 knots

Armaments: 4 x 18-inch Torpedo Tubes (2 x bow, 2 x beam); 1 x 21-inch Torpedo Tube (stern); 1 x 3-inch disappearing High Angle Quick Firing Gun; 1 x portable 2-Pdr

Complement: 30 (3 Officers and 27 Ratings)

This painting was sponsored by Lieutenant Commander Barrie Downer, RN (Retired) - a Member of the Submariners Association, Barrow-in-Furness Branch. Barrie joined the Royal Navy in 1962 as a Radio Electrical Apprentice. He joined the Submarine Service in 1966 and served in submarines HMS VALIANT, HMS SPARTAN, briefly in HMS SUPERB and HMS SCEPTRE and also in submarine related appointments until his retirement from the service in May 1994. Barrie now lives in Barrow-in-Furness. After working with the Ministry of Defence as part of the Astute Project Team in the Shipyard he retired in 2013.

HM SUBMARINES "IMPROVED K" CLASS
HMS K26

The Painting and the K26 Story

The main picture (a watercolour) shows submarine K26 at sea. The lower mount shows pencil drawings of the earlier "K" class boats. K26 was an 'improved' version of the earlier "K" class boats. She was launched at Barrow in 1919 but was only completed at Chatham in 1923. K26 was longer than the earlier vessels and carried more armament but the machinery was the same. As a result she was half a knot slower than the earlier "K" class. During 1924, K26 successfully cruised to Colombo, Ceylon (Sri Lanka) and back. K26 survived without incident until March 1931 when she was scrapped at Malta.

Class Information

The "K" class submarines were designed to maintain station with the Grand Fleet to counteract a rumoured German ocean-going high surface-speed submarine. Seventeen of the class were built out of twenty one projected, ordered from a variety of shipbuilders and built in great secrecy.

The Admiralty's (well-founded) low level of confidence in large diesel engines but continued desire for fast submarines inevitably led them into their ill-starred steam-powered submarine adventures. The belief being that surface ship turbine technology was the only reliable means of achieving high sustained surface speeds and could be readily fitted in submarines - a very mistaken belief. The first British steam-powered submarine was SWORDFISH, an Italian design built by Scott's and ordered at the same time as the Vickers NAUTILUS (see page 26). Despite some good features the design was not a success.

However, the Royal Navy still wanted a submarine class with high surface speed, ideally 24 knots. This speed would have required eight of the biggest diesel engines then available - clearly not possible - or steam-turbine propulsion. The choice was inevitable and the outcome was the infamous "K" class. *The only good thing about the "K" boats was they never engaged the enemy*" said Rear Admiral Ernest Leir (Captain of K3) in 1961. To remedy the worst characteristics of the class, an "Improved K" was designed. Six were ordered but only one was built - K26.

Ironically, turbine propulsion (via gearing or electric motors) was and remains the best way of achieving high sustained speed in submarines. The defect lay in the manner of making steam. Suitable technology simply did not exist until the German Type XVIIB of WW2 made steam through chemical decomposition and later the Americans used nuclear power. These two lines were represented in the RN by the experimental "Explorer" class submarines of the 1950's and the nuclear-powered submarines, beginning with DREADNOUGHT in 1963.

These "submersible K class Destroyers" were the largest, heaviest and fastest submarines in the world at that time. In fact, they proved to be so fast that no WW2 submarine could have outstripped them. Conversely, no modern warship in any Navy ever suffered so many calamities.

They were involved in sixteen major accidents and countless minor mishaps. K1 was badly damaged in a collision with K4 in November 1917 and had to be sunk. K13 sank on trials but was later raised and refitted as K22. On 31 January 1918, nine "K" class were on exercises with surface ships near May Island in the Firth of Forth. At night and with all travelling at high speed K14's steering jammed, initiating a sequence of collisions in which K4 and K17 were sunk, three more "K's" were damaged and over 100 lives lost. K5 disappeared in the Western Approaches in January 1921. Another, K15, sank accidentally in Portsmouth Harbour on 25 June 1921 when alongside the cruiser HMS CANTERBURY - luckily without casualties.

SUBMARINE K26 DATA

Builder:	Vickers Limited	Yard Number: 564
Significant Dates:	Ordered: April 1918; Laid Down: June 1918; Launched: 26th August 1919; Completed at H.M. Dockyard Chatham 28th June 1923	
Dimensions:	Length: 351 feet; Beam: 28 feet; Draught: 16 feet 10 inches	
Displacement:	Surfaced: 2,140 tons; Dived: 2,530 tons	
Machinery:	Surfaced: 2 x Yarrow 235 psi oil fired boilers; 2 x geared steam turbines; 10,000 bhp; Twin shafts; Dived: 4 electric motors (1,440 bhp);	
	1 x auxiliary diesel (800bhp)	
Speed	Surfaced: 23½ knots; Dived: 8 knot	
Fuel:	300 tons (later quoted as 267 tons)	
Armament:	6 x 21-inch bow torpedo tubes; 4 x 18-inch beam torpedo tubes; 3 x 4-inch guns	
Complement:	59 (5 Officers and 54 Ratings)	

David and Fiona Barlow and Bob and Helen Wishart of the Scottish Branch of the Submariners Association have sponsored this painting. Three of the "K" class were lost in Scottish waters due to accidents. Having attended Annual Memorial Ceremonies over the years for the loss of these boats the sponsors have established a close affinity with the "K" class of submarine.

HM SUBMARINES "H21" CLASS
HMS H28

The Painting and the H28 Story

The main picture is a watercolour showing H28 at sea in company with other "H" class submarines and also HMS SUPERB. They are shadowed by a Royal Navy Blimp. The lower mount depicts H28 leaving Barrow-in-Furness with Vickers Ltd. Shipyard in the distance and also H28 passing Piel Island and Walney lighthouse. H28 was typical of the British built version of the "H" class and saw action during WW2 at Brest but was mainly used for training purposes. She was sold for scrap in 1944.

Class Information

Shortly after the outbreak of WW1 the First Sea Lord, Admiral 'Jackie' Fisher, ordered twenty "H" class submarines from Bethlehem Steel in America, identical to the US Navy's "H" class. Because of American neutrality, it was arranged that H1 to H10 would be assembled by Canadian Vickers from American parts. H11 to H20 would be built by Bethlehem Steel, it being assumed that by then the war would be over and American neutrality no longer an issue. The first ten "H" class boats were delivered quickly and in time for some to serve in the Dardanelles and in the Sea of Marmora. H1 to H4 were the first ever submarines to cross the Atlantic.

The war did not finish quickly. In consequence, the neutrality of the United States prevented the American built boats being completed until America joined the war in 1917. In the event only two of the second batch (H11 & H12) saw Royal Navy service. Two of the others (CH14 and CH15) were transferred to the Canadian Navy and the other six were ceded to Chile.

The "H" class was highly regarded by the Royal Navy. They were quick to submerge, stable, had good sea-going characteristics and were easy to control. There were four watertight bulkheads, a powerful attack potential through four bow tubes and reliable propulsion machinery. The first ten were heavily used during the war.

The success of the class led to a British improved version – the H21 class. The main update was replacing the 4 x 18-inch bow torpedo tubes with 4 x 21-inch. These boats were 21 feet longer. Thirty four "H21" class submarines were ordered, twelve from Vickers at Barrow-in-Furness, six from Cammell Laird at Birkenhead, eight from Armstrong Whitworth at Newcastle, four from Beardmore at Glasgow and two each from HM Dockyard at Pembroke Dock and HM Dockyard. Ten of these were later cancelled.

The majority of the twelve Vickers built boats were completed too late to see action in WW1. Of these, H29 accidentally sank in Devonport Dockyard in August 1926, was raised and scrapped in 1927. Eight others, including H21 were scrapped between 1926 and 1935.

Nine boats of the class survived to see action in WW2. Three of these were Vickers-built – H28, H31 and H32. Although employed mainly as Anti-Submarine training boats they did form part of the 'Ring of Steel' around the French port of Brest whilst the German battleships SCHARNHORST, GNEISENAU and LÜTZOW were there after their Atlantic sorties of 1940/1941. H31 was lost, believed mined, in the Bay of Biscay on the 24th December 1941. H28 and H32 were sold for scrap in 1944.

SUBMARINE **H28** DATA

Builder:	Vickers Limited, Barrow-in-Furness	Yard Number: 528	Cost: No cost figures yet identified
Significant Dates:	Ordered: January 1917; Laid Down: 8th January 1917; Launched: 12th March 1918; Completed: 29th June 1919		
Dimensions:	Length: 171 feet 9 inches; Beam: 15 feet 4 inches; Draught: 13 feet 2½ inches.		
Displacement:	Surfaced: 438 tons; Dived: 504 tons		
Machinery:	Surfaced: Twin 8 cylinder 4-stroke S.A. diesels (480 bhp); Dived: Twin electric motors (620 bhp); Twin shafts		
Speed:	Surfaced: 11½ knots; Dived: 9 knots		
Endurance:	Surfaced: 1,600 nautical miles at 10 knots; Dived: 70 miles at 3 knots		
Fuel:	16 tons		
Armaments:	4 x 21-inch bow torpedo tubes		
Complement:	22 (3 Officers and 19 Ratings)		

This painting was commissioned by Dorothy Moody and family in memory of Bob Moody, who served in this class of submarine and who was a Founder Member of the Submarine Old Comrades Association – Barrow-in-Furness Branch.

HM SUBMARINES "L" CLASS
HMS L4

The Painting and the HMS L4 Story

The main picture is a watercolour showing submarine L4 on the South China Station with HMS TITANIA and Chinese junks sailing by. The lower mount has two pencil drawings showing, on the left, an "L" class submarine at sea and, on the right, L3 under construction at Vickers Ltd., Barrow-in-Furness.

Submarine L4 was completed during the last few months of WW1. She served in the North Sea before being transferred to Hong Kong and the South China Station in the early 1920's. Whilst serving there on 21st October, 1927, L4 foiled a pirate attack on the SS IRENE by firing a shot through the vessel's hull. 238 passengers were rescued and the pirates were caught. L4 was scrapped in 1934 being sold to Wards of Grays.

Class Information

The "L" class was a key element of the RN submarine force in the 1920's. The class started out as a larger development of the "E" class, the last two of which were constructed as the first two of the "L" class. Subsequently the class was further developed and came to form four distinct groups-the basic "L", the "L9" variant, the minelayer "L" variant and the "L50" variant. Although the culmination of the class, the L50 variant, was developed before L1 was launched. There was no L13, perhaps from superstition?

This was a projected class of seventy three submarines of which only thirty three were built. Of these Vickers built eighteen - four of the basic "L" class, eight of the "L9" variant and six of the minelayer variant - between May 1917 and October 1919. They were the first Royal Navy submarines to carry a proportion of their diesel fuel in external ballast tanks. Although initially only 20 tons was carried externally, this started a practice that was to continue until the phasing out of the 'conventional' submarine in the Royal Navy during the 1980's.

The basic "L" class submarine was 50 feet longer than its progenitor "E" class, with further small increases for the variants; all had the same beam and draught. They all had substantially increased diesel and electric power compared to "E" Class, and "L1" bow torpedo tubes were doubled to four, two beam tubes were kept but stern tubes were deleted. The "L9" variant had the bow tubes changed from 18-inch to 21-inch, an extra watertight bulkhead, the pressure hull lengthened and more fuel was carried. The minelayers had a vertical chute each side amidships. A total of 16 mines were carried and the beam torpedo tubes were removed. The final "L50" variant concentrated its torpedo armament in six bow tubes, with no beam or stern tubes. Gun armament varied across the entire class. Some had none, some a single gun on a disappearing mount and three had guns mounted on the bridge (conning platform).

Specifically intended for North Sea service the Admiralty, of course, based some in Hong Kong in the 1920's. Three went to the Baltic in 1919, as part of Britain's involvement in the aftermath of the Russian revolution. One, L55 hit a British mine and sank with loss of all the crew. Despite having been sent to support anti-Soviet forces, the Soviet Navy recovered her in 1928, treated the dead with ceremony and returned the bodies for burial at Haslar Royal Naval Cemetery. They kept the submarine and commissioned her into service with the Soviet Baltic Fleet.

Some "L" class were active in WW1. In the North Sea; Barrow-built L10 was the only war loss - sunk with all hands off the Texel by German destroyers on 24th Jan 1918. Other Barrow-built losses were L9 and L24. During a typhoon at Hong Kong in 1923 L9 broke free from its moorings, was driven against the Harbour Wall and was wrecked. There were no casualties. L24 was accidentally sunk with all hands in a collision with the battleship RESOLUTION off Portland on 14th January 1924.

Almost all the class was scrapped between 1927 and the late 1930's. However three served through WW2. Of the Barrow built submarines of the class, L26 and L27 lasted the longest and were sent to Canada in 1944 for training purposes. L26 was sunk there as an anti-submarine target on 25th September 1945 and L27 was scrapped in Canada in 1947. Two of the cancelled "L" class were later completed by the Armstrong Yard in 1927 and were sold to Yugoslavia as HRABI and NEBJOŠA.

HMS L4 Data

Builder:	Vickers Limited, Barrow-in-Furness Yard Number: 496
Significant Dates:	Ordered: May 1916; Laid Down: 21st June 1916; Launched: 17th November 1917; Completed: 26th February 1918
Dimensions:	Length: 231 feet; Beam: 23 feet 6 inches; Draught: 13 feet 3 inches
Displacement:	Surfaced: 891 tons; Dived: 1,074 tons
Machinery:	Surfaced 2 x 12 cylinder SA Vickers diesels (2,400 bhp); Dived: 2 x electric motors (1,600 bhp); Twin shafts
Speed:	Surfaced: 17½ knots; Dived: 10½ knots
Endurance:	Surfaced: 2,800 nautical miles at 17½ knots; Dived: 14 nautical miles at 10.5 knots
Fuel:	78 tons
Armament:	6 x 18-inch torpedo tubes (4 bow, 2 beam); 10 torpedoes carried; 1 x 4-inch gun.
Complement:	35 Officers and Ratings

This painting is dedicated by Captain John Green, Merchant Navy (Retired), in memory of Hubert 'Bert' Thompson, who served with the Royal Navy as an Engine Room Artificer in WW1. He subsequently joined the ranks of the Royal Air Force and eventually retired as Wing Commander. He fought for his country during two World Wars, was 'Mentioned in Despatches' and was awarded the MBE.

HM SUBMARINES "M" CLASS
SUBMARINES M1, M2 and M3

The Painting

The main picture (a watercolour) shows from left to right M3 configured as a minelayer, M2 modified with a hangar to carry aircraft and M1, as originally designed, with a 12-inch gun. The lower mount has pencil drawings of M1 and M2, whilst the upper mount has a pencil drawing of M3.

Class Information

By the outbreak of war in 1914 the majority of navies with submarines wanted a gun, both as an alternative to torpedoes and also to attack land targets. It was the Royal Navy which sent the largest gun to sea in a submarine – in the "M" class.

The thinking behind such a weapon was made clear by Rear Admiral, Submarines: *"The object was to supplement torpedo attacks against surface ships, which could often elude a torpedo. A 12-inch projectile fired at fairly close range should be difficult to elude. Furthermore, fifty shells could be carried instead of a few torpedoes."*

The "M" class was intended to be a class of four submarines (originally ordered as submarines K18 to K21). All carried a 12-inch gun but M2 was eventually converted to carry a sea-plane and M3 to a minelayer; M4 was cancelled when part-built and scrapped. The guns were taken from "Majestic" class pre-Dreadnought Battleships

awaiting the breakers yard. The gun and mounting weighed 129 tons, which collectively enhanced the class diving qualities – the weight helped to keep the boat down, whilst the volume stabilised the boat at periscope depth and in rough weather. Diving time was very short for so large a submarine - 90 seconds is reputed. The hull was a new design but the propulsion machinery was that of the "L" class. M1 and M2 were built at Barrow and M3 at Armstrong-Whitworth, Newcastle.

Submarine M1 served briefly in the Mediterranean 1918 during WW1 and also served in the Mediterranean and Home Waters in the 1920's. M1 was sunk with the loss of all hands in collision with the Swedish collier VIDAR whilst on exercise off Start Point, Devon, on 12th November 1925.

Submarine M2 was completed too late to see war service. In 1927-28 she was converted to a sea-plane carrier, the 12-inch gun being replaced with an aircraft hangar and a small Parnell Peto spotter aircraft. Trials showed that the submarine could surface from periscope depth, open the hangar door, fly off the aircraft, shut the hangar door and dive again in five minutes. M2 was lost with all hands, cause unknown but probably during flying off exercises in the English Channel on 26th January 1932.

Submarine M3 was also converted, with the 12-inch gun being replaced with a modified casing and mine laying rails enabling the Submarine to carry 100 mines. M3 was sold for scrap in 1933.

SUBMARINE **M1 & M2** DATA

Builder: M1 and M2:	Vickers Limited, Barrow-in-Furness Yard Numbers: 491 & 494 Cost: No cost figures yet identified
Significant Dates:	M1 Ordered: February 1916; Laid Down: 13th July 1916; Launched: 9th July 1917; Completed: 17th April 1918
	M2 Ordered: May 1916; Laid Down: 13th July 1916; Launched: 15 April 1919; Completed: 14th February 1920
Dimensions:	Length: 296 feet 9 inches; Beam: 24 feet 8 in; Draught: 18 feet 8 in
Displacement:	Surfaced: 1,594 tons; Dived: 1,946 tons
Machinery:	Surfaced: Twin diesel engines total 2,400 bhp; Dived: Twin electric motors total 1,600 bhp; Twin shafts
Speed:	Surfaced: 15 knots; Dived: 9 knots
Endurance:	Surfaced: 3,800 nm at 10 knots; Dived: 80nm at 2 knots
Fuel:	97.5 tons
Armament:	Single 12-inch BL 30 calibre Mark XI gun; Single 3-inch gun; Single 0.303 Machine gun; 4 x 18-inch bow torpedo tubes
Complement:	64 (6 Officers and 58 Ratings)

The Rotary Club of Barrow-in-Furness are pleased to sponsor this painting as it celebrates the endeavours of the people of Barrow-in-Furness, and note that these vessels were in operation at the time this Rotary Club was founded in the early thirties of the 20th century.

HM SUBMARINES "R" CLASS
HMS R7 and R8

The Painting and the Story

The main picture (a watercolour) portrays the diving trials of submarine R8 off the Cumbrian coast with Black Coombe hill in the left background. Submarine R7 is acting as 'Guard Ship' along with a destroyer of the period - HMS PHOENIX - and overhead is the Airship R80. HMS PHOENIX was built in the Vickers Shipyard as part of the 1910/1911 Programme. One reason for her building was that Vickers wished to retain their surface warship skills as the Shipyard had embarked on a major submarine build programme at that time. The Airship R80 was the first British airship to be streamlined. Designed by Barnes Wallis and built by Vickers on Walney Island this airship first flew on 19th July 1920 and was dismantled in 1925.

The events shown are fictitious. However, they have been incorporated to show three units that have their own individual niche in history and demonstrate that Barrow shipyard was even then at the forefront of technology.

Class Information

The "R" class was an important and farsighted design. It was the first submarine in any Navy specifically intended to hunt and kill other submarines - the original 'Hunter Killer' - a role that we now take for granted with nuclear submarines. Whilst war experience was showing the RN that submarines then in service stood a good chance at periscope depth of locating enemy submarines, they found it very difficult to mount successful attacks. It was thought that the way to overcome this was a design with high underwater speed, extensive underwater detectors and a powerful torpedo outfit of six 18-inch torpedo bow tubes. They were completed very late during WW1 and only one actually carried out an attack on a U-boat - firing a full salvo of six torpedoes – all of which missed! They were known in the Submarine Flotillas as the 'Little Arthur's' – a play on their size and the "R" designation.

These boats were streamlined and had no external ballast tanks, no gun and only a bow casing and a faired casing around the conning tower for superstructure. The hull tapered away finely to the stern to the single propeller shaft. Designed as they were for a high underwater speed their machinery (propulsion arrangements) caused manoeuvrability problems whilst running on the surface. However, underwater the two rudders, single propeller and fine hull form gave them very good manoeuvrability and performance. They were the first submarine class in which speed underwater was greater than on the surface.

The diesel engine was the same as in the "H" class but built in the UK; two electric motors drove the single shaft, with another, of low power, for slow speed underwater use, to conserve battery energy - another "first". There were five acoustic (sonar) sensors at the bow as well six torpedo tubes - heavy armament for such a small submarine (and the first RN submarine so fitted). It has been frequently remarked that the design was 40 years ahead of its time. A design diving depth of 250ft has been quoted but these vessels were restricted to 150 ft in service.

This was a projected class of twelve submarines (two were cancelled) of which Vickers built two – R7 and R8 during 1918. The majority of the class of ten completed boats had been scrapped by 1923 although R4 did survive as a fast underwater target at the Portland Anti-Submarine School until 1934. In hindsight, the failure to develop this concept was very short-sighted given future events.

HMS R7 & HMS R8 Data

Builder:	Vickers Limited, Barrow-in-Furness	Yard Numbers: 549 & 550	Costs: No costs yet identified
Significant Dates:	R7 Ordered: October 1917; Laid Down: 14th November 1917; Launched: 14th May 1918; Completed: 29th June 1918		
	R8 Ordered: October 1917; Laid Down: 14th November 1917; Launched: 28th Jun 1918; Completed: 26th July 1918		
Dimensions:	Length: 163 feet 9 inches; Beam: 15 feet 9 inches; Draught: 11 feet 6 inches		
Displacement:	Surfaced: 410 tons; Dived: 503 tons		
Machinery:	Surfaced: Single 8 cylinder NELSECO diesel engine licence-built by HM Dockyard Chatham: 240 bhp: Dived: Two electric motors total 1200 bhp and a single 25 bhp electric motor for slow speeds; Single shaft		
Speed:	Surfaced: 9.5 knots; Dived: 15 knots		
Endurance:	Surfaced: 2,000 nautical miles at 9 knots; Dived: 15 nautical miles at 15 knots or 240 nautical miles at 4 knots		
Fuel:	13.5 tons		
Armaments:	6 x 18-inch bow torpedo tubes; Twelve reloads carried		
Complement:	22 Officers and Ratings		

This painting was sponsored by Mr. Tommy Snaith and his wife in memory of both their fathers who served in the British Armed Forces during WW2.

HM SUBMARINES "ODIN" CLASS
HMS OSIRIS

The Painting and the HMS OSIRIS Story

The main picture is a watercolour showing HMS OSIRIS departing from the Vickers Armstrong shipyard in Barrow-in-Furness. She is escorted by two tugs – the left hand one is a Barrow based tug and the other is a REA tug from Liverpool. In the background can be seen the High Level (Roller) Bridge. HMS MEDWAY is shown being fitted out with the help of the heavy lift crane beneath which is the long dark building known as the North Shop designed for the production of heavy guns for the Royal and other Navy's. The lower mount shows the launch of HMS OSIRIS in May 1928 and the badges of HM Submarines OSIRIS, OSWALD and OTUS. On the right is HMS OXLEY (1937).

On commissioning, HMS OSIRIS was sent with the rest of the class to Hong Kong to join other Submarines of the 4th Submarine flotilla. She stayed there until 1940 when they all returned to the Mediterranean to join the 1st Submarine Flotilla at Alexandria. On the 14th August 1940 HMS OSIRIS, one of the two Vickers-built boats of the class to survive WW2, sank the Italian steamship LEOPARD (3,296 tons) and in September 1940, the Italian torpedo-boat PALESTRO (890 tons). She also sank several smaller vessels. In 1943 she was sent to Durban as an anti-submarine training boat and scrapped there in September 1946.

Class Information

The Anglo-Japanese Co-operation Treaty ended in 1922 causing Britain to review its military future in the Far East. The Admiralty, amongst other things, decided upon a new type of overseas patrol submarine whose design would be focussed on Far Eastern operation. Compared to existing submarines, they sought improved habitability, greater diving depth and longer endurance.

The outcome was the "O" class of submarines. First, HMS OBERON in the nature of a prototype, then a variant for the Royal Australian Navy (HMS OTWAY and HMS OXLEY) developed by Vickers Barrow from HMS OBERON. These were followed by the "Odin" class, adopting lessons learned from HMS OBERON (six built) and finally three boats for

Chile, often called the "Capitan O'Brien" class.

The requirement for deep diving and long range was difficult to meet and obliged the carriage of fuel oil externally. The external tanks were initially riveted but leaked at depth, leaving a surface trail. They were replaced by welded tanks. The large quantity of fuel, relative to boat size resulted in diving being quick. Following usual British practice, they all had a 4-inch trainable gun at the forward end of the bridge superstructure. Whilst militarily an effective placing, the consequence was a long and high "fin" which made the class very visible on the surface and added to drag when submerged. Of the six "Odin" class, three were built at Barrow – HM Submarines OSIRIS, OSWALD and OTUS. The lead submarine of the class – HMS ODIN - was built at the Royal Dockyard in Chatham. The other two, HMS OLYMPUS and HMS ORPHEUS, were built by the Beardmore Yard on the Clyde.

The second Vickers built war survivor was HMS OTUS which was sold for scrap in 1945 and was scuttled off Durban The third Vickers built submarine of the class - HMS OSWALD (Lieutenant Commander D.A. Fraser) - was sunk on 1st August 1940 having been rammed by the Italian destroyer UGOLINO VIVALDI off Calabria. Fifty two of the crew of fifty five were taken prisoner of war – the other three were lost in the sinking.

Both of the Beardmore submarines were lost. HMS ORPHEUS (Lieutenant Commander J.A.S. Wise) sank with all hands after being depth-charged by the Italian TURBINE in the Eastern Mediterranean on 27th June 1940. HMS OLYMPUS (Lieutenant Commander H. G. Dymott) was lost on 8th May 1942 with large loss of life in particularly sad circumstances. Just before sailing personnel from other submarines, mainly HMS PANDORA, P36 and P39, embarked for the passage home. An hour after sailing from Malta the submarine hit a mine and sank within 10 minutes. It is thought that ninety out of the ninety eight onboard got out of the submarine safely but only nine survived, some after swimming several miles back to Malta. Three survivors were from OLYMPUS, six from P39 but none from P36. Chatham built ODIN (Lieutenant Commander K.M. Woods,) was lost with all hands on 13th June 1940 after attacks by the Italian Torpedo Boats STRALE and BALENO off Taranto.

HMS OSIRIS DATA (TYPICAL OF THE CLASS)

Builder:	Vickers Armstrong Ltd Barrow-in-Furness	Yard Number: 633	Cost: £280,000
Significant dates:	Ordered: 2nd December 1926; Launched: 19th May 1928; Completed: 27th February 1929		
Dimensions:	Length: 283 feet 6 inches; Beam: 29 feet 11 inches; Draught: 16 feet 1 inch.		
Displacement:	Surfaced: 1,781 tons; Dived: 2,038 tons.		
Machinery:	Surfaced: Twin diesel engines total 4,400 bhp; Dived: Twin electric motors total 1,320 bhp; Two shafts		
Speed:	Surfaced: 17½ knots; Dived: 9 knots		
Fuel:	78 tons		
Endurance:	Surfaced: 8,500 nm at 10 kts, 11,400 nm at 8 kts; Dived: 52 nautical miles at 4 knots		
Armament:	8 x 21-inch torpedo tubes (6 bow & 2 stern); 14 torpedoes carried; 1 x 4-inch Deck Gun and 2 x Machine Guns		
Complement:	53 (5 Officers and 48 Ratings)		

Commander Julian Beauchamp, RN, who was the second Commanding Officer of the more modern conventional submarine HMS OLYMPUS, sponsored this painting.

HM SUBMARINES "P" CLASS
HMS PANDORA

The Painting and the Story

The main picture of this painting is a gouache depicting HMS PANDORA sailing in the South China Sea. The lower mount is a pencil drawing of a "P" class submarine with the submarine badges of HMS PERSEUS, HMS POSEIDON, HMS PROTEUS and HMS PANDORA. It had been intended to name one of the class PYTHON but a member of the Admiralty's Naming Committee pointed out that a number of RN vessels named after snakes had had unsuccessful, in some cases disastrous, careers. So PYTHON became PANDORA.

On 31st March 1942 HMS PANDORA arrived in Malta with supplies for the beleaguered island including torpedoes for the Fleet Air Arm. Having discharged oil at Marsamxett the submarine then moved alongside at Hamilton Wharf to discharge cargo. This had to be done during the day so she could sail that night. During a heavy air raid on the 1st April the submarine received two direct hits and sank in less than four minutes, taking twenty-five of her Ship's Company with her.

Class Information

The previous "O" class (see HMS ODIN) had shortcomings, particularly poor underwater manoeuvrability, which could only be remedied by modifying the design. The result was the "P" class, focussed on the same Far Eastern overseas patrol needs. The whole class was sent to the China Station on commissioning in 1931 - to be based with the 4th Submarine Flotilla at Hong Kong. Originally outfitted with the MkIV** torpedo, this class was the first to carry the Mark VII (later the Mk VIII Mod 4**) torpedo which was to remain in service for over 50 years. This torpedo's last victim was the Argentinean cruiser ARA GENERAL BELGRANO in the Falklands War.

The six boats of the class were laid down in 1928 and launched in 1929. Four were built by Vickers Armstrong, Barrow-in-Furness. These were HM Submarines PERSEUS, PROTEUS, PANDORA and POSEIDON. The two others – HMS PARTHIAN and HMS PHOENIX - were built by Chatham Dockyard and Cammell Laird respectively.

On 9th June 1931 whilst manoeuvring on the surface 20 miles north of Wei Wei HMS POSEIDON was in collision with the Chinese steamer SS YUTA. The Submarine sank in under two minutes. Some of the ship's company escaped before she sank and six of the crew escaped from the forward end of the submarine using the then new Davis Submarine Escape Apparatus (DSEA). No one escaped from the after ends. In all twenty two lives were lost. In 1940 the remaining five of the class were sent to the Mediterranean to join the 1st Flotilla at Alexandria. As well as carrying out patrols against Axis shipping, the boats carried much needed supplies to the besieged island of Malta.

On 10th July 1940 HMS PHOENIX (Lieutenant Commander G.H. Nowell) was lost with all hands after a depth charge attack by the Italian Torpedo Boat ALBATROS off Augusta, Sicily. On 6th December 1941, returning from Malta to Alexandria, HMS PERSEUS struck a mine off western Greece and sank. Of the ship's company of fifty-five only four remained alive in the after-ends. They all escaped using DSEA but only one, Leading Stoker John Capes survived after swimming five or so miles to the shore of Cephalonia. He was rescued and looked after for eighteen months by Greek villagers, until taken off by an allied caique on the 1st May 1943. He was awarded the British Empire Medal.

HMS PARTHIAN (Lieutenant Commander M.G. Rimmington) was lost with all hands on 7th August 1943 after striking a mine in the Southern Adriatic.

The only submarine in the class to survive the war was HMS PROTEUS. She served for three years in the Mediterranean (from 1940 to 1943) where she sank twelve Axis transports. She was later employed as a training boat in Home Waters and was finally broken up at Troon in Scotland in 1946.

HMS PANDORA DATA (TYPICAL OF THE CLASS)

Builder:	Vickers Armstrong, Barrow-in-Furness	Yard Number: 641	Cost: No costs have yet been identified
Significant Dates:	Ordered: 1929; Laid Down: 9th July 1928; Launched: 22nd August 1929; Completed: 30th June 1930		
Dimensions:	Length: 289 feet; Beam: 29 feet 11 inches; Draught: 16 feet 1 inch.		
Displacement:	Surfaced: 1,760 tons; Dived: 2,040 tons		
Machinery:	Surfaced: Twin diesels total (4,640 bhp); Dived: Twin electric motors total (1,320 bhp); Twin shafts		
Speed Surfaced:	17½ knots; Dived: 8½ knots*		
Endurance:	Surfaced: 10,750 nautical miles at 8 knots; Dived: 60 at 4 knots;		
Fuel:	159 tons		
Armaments:	8 x 21-inch torpedo tubes (6 bow, 2 stern); Fourteen torpedoes carried; 1 x 4-inch deck gun; 2 Machine guns.		
Complement:	53 (5 Officers and 48 Ratings)		

*Parthian had higher-energy cells fitted giving a better underwater performance

This painting was commissioned by Captain Patrick J Walker, Royal Navy, in memory of his uncle, Sub Lieutenant John Timothy Ryder Walker, Royal Navy Volunteer Reserve, who was lost with HMS PARTHIAN in the Mediterranean in 1943.

HM SUBMARINES "RAINBOW" CLASS
HMS ROVER

The Painting and the HMS ROVER Story

The main picture is a watercolour showing HMS ROVER in Malta harbour 'dipping her ensign' to HMS RAINBOW. The lower mount shows HMS ROVER at sea and the badges of HMS REGENT, HMS REGULUS and HMS ROVER.

On commissioning all the class were sent to the Far East to join the 4th Submarine Flotilla at Hong Kong where they served until the outbreak of WW2. In 1940 the class was sent to the Mediterranean to join the 1st Submarine Flotilla, patrolling from Alexandria. HMS ROVER was the only submarine of the class to survive the war. She was paid off after the war and was sold for scrap at Durban 30th July 1946.

Class Information

The "Rainbow" class was intended as a follow-on 'improved' "P" class, carrying out the same roles. Six were planned but only four were built. Rearrangement of equipment and spaces reduced the pressure hull and so overall length by 2 feet, compared to the "P" class. The 4-inch gun was also located at lower level. They were the first British submarines to be fitted with a bathroom for the Officers although there was no increase in overall fresh water capacity.

Three of the four submarines were built at Barrow-in-Furness but the 'Lead' boat of the class, HMS RAINBOW, was built at Chatham Dockyard. The Barrow built boats, HM Submarines REGENT, REGULUS and ROVER, were all launched on the same day - 11th July 1930. Two other submarines of the class, RUPERT (Cammell Laird) and ROYALIST (Beardmore), were ordered but were cancelled in 1929.

As with the "P" class, the war losses were high and only one "R" class submarine survived the war. The other three were lost in the Mediterranean. HMS RAINBOW (Lieutenant Commander L.P. Moore) was lost with all hands on 19th October when she was torpedoed by the Italian Submarine ENRICO TOTI off Calabria.

On the 7th December 1940 HMS REGULUS (Lieutenant Commander F.B. Currie) was listed as overdue in the Strait of Otranto. The submarine was lost with all hands and it is thought that she hit a mine. HMS REGENT (Lieutenant W.N.R. Knox) was reported as lost on 18th April 1943 whilst patrolling near the port of Monopoli. It is believed that the submarine hit a mine and was lost with all hands.

HMS Rover Data (Typical of the class)

Builder:	Vickers Armstrong Ltd, Barrow-in-Furness	Yard Number: 655	Cost: No costs identified
Significant Dates:	Ordered: 26th February 1929; Laid Down: 24th July 1929; Launched: 11th June 1930; Completed: Jan 1931		
Dimensions:	Length: 287 feet 2 inches; Beam: 29 feet 11 inches; Draught: 16 feet 1 inch		
Displacement:	Surfaced: 1,763 tons; Dived: 2,030 tons		
Machinery:	Surfaced: Twin 8 cylinder diesel engines (4,640 bhp); Dived: Twin electric motors (1,320 bhp); Twin shafts		
Speed:	Surfaced: 17½ knots; Dived: 8¾ knots*		
Endurance:	Surfaced: 10,900 nautical miles at 8 knots; Dived: 60 nautical miles at 4 knots		
Armament:	8 x 21-inch torpedo tubes (6 bow, 2 stern); 14 torpedoes carried; 1 x 4.7-inch deck gun later replaced by 1 x 4-inch		
Complement:	53 (5 Officers and 48 ratings)		

*Rainbow alone had higher-energy cells fitted, giving a better underwater performance

This painting was sponsored by Chief Radio Supervisor (CRS) Terry (Nobby) Hall, Chairman of the Derbyshire Branch of the Submariners Association.

HM SUBMARINES "PORPOISE" CLASS
HMS PORPOISE

The Painting and the HMS PORPOISE Story

The main picture (in watercolour and chalk) shows HMS PORPOISE in the Indian Ocean accompanied by dhows and dolphins. The lower mount is a pencil drawing showing the stern view of the submarine and a view of the later HMS PORPOISE of 1956.

HMS PORPOISE was built at Barrow-in-Furness. During 1940 HMS PORPOISE laid mines off Norway and escorted East Coast convoys. In January 1941 the submarine was transferred to the North Atlantic and escorted UK/Halifax convoys. In October 1941 she was transferred to the 1st Submarine Flotilla at Alexandria, stopping at Malta on the way with supplies that included aviation spirit carried in special containers under the mine casing. Between then and December 1942 HMS PORPOISE patrolled the Eastern Mediterranean and the Aegean. This included taking supplies to beleaguered Malta on what became known as the Magic Carpet runs, on which she and HMS CLYDE were the submarines most regularly employed. The supplies carried by submarine to Malta totalled 180,000 gallons of aviation spirit/petrol, 42 tons of stores and mail, 6 tons of munitions and 126 personnel.

Refitted at Portsmouth between December 1942 and May 1944, HMS PORPOISE arrived in Trincomalee, Ceylon on 4th June 1944 to join the 4th Submarine Flotilla and then patrolled and laid mines in the Malacca Straits between Malaya and Java. During September 1944 she was involved in Operation Rimau in which twenty four Australian Special Forces personnel were landed to sink Japanese shipping in Singapore Harbour using submersible canoes known as 'Sleeping Beauties'. They were to be picked up after the operation by HMS PORPOISE but she was diverted to other duties. The submarine detailed to pick them up failed to make the rendezvous; as a result 14 Australians were killed and 10 captured who, after interrogation by the Japanese, were executed by their captors. On 19th January 1945, HMS PORPOISE was sunk with all hands in the Malacca Straight off Penang by Japanese aircraft - the last Royal Navy submarine to be lost during WW2.

Class Information

The class had two variants – a single lead vessel, PORPOISE, and the "Grampus" variant of which there were five. All their hulls were based on the "Parthian" class, into which was incorporated a mine conveyor system which was an improved version of that tested on submarine HMS M3 after its conversion to a minelayer. They all carried 50 standard mines on a rail system under the casing which discharged them through doors in the stern. In HMS PORPOISE the conveyor caused the periscopes and "fin" to be offset, with balancing weights on the other side. For HMS GRAMPUS and the others rearrangements resulted in an in-line fin and casing.

HMS PORPOISE and two of the "Grampus" variant, HMS NARWHAL and HMS RORQUAL, were built at Barrow-in-Furness. The other three submarines were HMS GRAMPUS, HMS SEAL (both built at Chatham Dockyard) and HMS CACHALOT (built at Scott's, Greenock).

HMS SEAL (Lieutenant Commander R. Lonsdale) was captured by the Germans on 5th May 1940 after hitting a mine in the shallow waters of the Kattegat. One Rating was lost and the remainder taken prisoner. HMS GRAMPUS (Lieutenant Commander C.A. Rowe) was lost with all hands in the Mediterranean on 25th June 1940 after a depth charge attack by the Italian vessels CIRCE and CLIO. HMS NARWHAL (Lieutenant Commander R.J. Burch DSO) was lost with all hands off Norway on 23rd July 1940 following an aircraft attack. HMS CACHALOT (Lieutenant Commander H.R.B. Newton) was rammed and sunk by the Italian destroyer GENERAL ACHILLE PAPA off Cyrenaica in the Mediterranean on 4th August 1941 - one man was lost and the remainder taken prisoner.

The only submarine of the class to survive the war – HMS RORQUAL - was paid off and sold for scrap in 1946.

HMS PORPOISE DATA

Builder:	Vickers Armstrong Limited, Barrow-in-Furness Yard Number: 679
Significant Dates:	Ordered: 1930; Laid Down: 22nd September 1931; Launched: 30th August 1932; Completed: 11th March 1933
Dimensions:	Length: 289 feet; Beam: 29 feet 10 inches; Draught: 16 feet.
Displacement:	Surfaced: 1,768 tons; Dived: 2,053 tons
Machinery:	Surfaced: Twin diesels (3,300 bhp); Dived: Twin electric motors (1,630 bhp); Twin shafts
Speed:	Surfaced: 16 knots; Dived: 8¾ knots
Endurance:	Surfaced: 11,500 nautical miles at 8 knots; Dived: 64 nautical miles at 4 knots
Fuel:	155 tons
Armament:	6 x 21-inch torpedo tubes; Twelve torpedoes carried; 1 x 4.7-inch gun; 2 x machine guns; 50 mines
Complement:	59 (5 Officers and 54 Ratings)

This painting was sponsored by the Rutland Branch of the Submariners Association. The reason for their choice of this painting is that one of their Members served onboard this particular submarine.

HM SUBMARINES "RIVER" CLASS
HMS CLYDE

The Painting and the HMS CLYDE Story

The main picture is a gouache showing HMS CLYDE weighing anchor. The picture shows, from left to right, HMS CYCLOPS (1935), a Submarine Depot Ship, HM Paddle Tug CRACKER (1905), HMS CLYDE, HM Tug PERT (1916) and HM Tug SPRITE (1917). The lower mount shows a "River" class submarine off the Cumbrian coast, the badges of HMS SEVERN, HMS CLYDE and HMS THAMES and the launch of HMS THAMES in January 1932.

HMS CLYDE was the third and final submarine of the class to be built at Barrow. She was based in Sierra Leone but returned in 1940 to join the 2nd Submarine Flotilla based at Dundee in Scotland. She then was used during the Norwegian campaign. In 1941 HMS CLYDE and HMS SEVERN were sent to join the 1st Submarine Flotilla at Alexandria in the Mediterranean to be employed as cargo carriers for the besieged island of Malta. By September 1941 HMS CLYDE had carried a total of 1,200 tons of supplies to Malta. In 1944 both submarines were sent to the Eastern Fleet and were based on Submarine Depot Ships at Trincomalee in Ceylon. HMS CLYDE was sold on 30th July 1946 and scrapped at Durban in South Africa.

Class Information

In the late 1920's the Admiralty decided on a further attempt to develop a fleet submarine to keep up with the Battle-Fleet and fulfil the same duties as the unsuccessful "K" class, but with diesel engines for propulsion. The "River" class was the result (also known as the "Thames" class). Whilst in the 1920's their high speed would have kept them up with the Fleet, by the time the design came to be settled it was evident that the Fleet's major ships were capable of 30 knots, obliging the Admiralty finally to abandon the concept of a fleet submarine, recognising that it could never be achieved by current or foreseeable technology. Such submarines only appeared 30 years later when nuclear power gave them the sustained ability to match surface ship speeds.

The intended class of 20 was reduced to three, with changes to incorporate a capability to fulfil the overseas patrol role of the "O", "P" and "R" classes. They were, by the standards of the day, very comfortable but were lightly armed for their size.

HMS THAMES was the first diesel boat to exceed 22 knots on the surface. The class was probably faster than any other European submarine at that time. HMS THAMES was laid down first, followed by HMS SEVERN and HMS CLYDE, which were slightly larger. All were built in Barrow-in-Furness.

In 1939, having just completed a refit, HMS THAMES joined the 2nd Submarine Flotilla based at Dundee, Scotland. HMS CLYDE and HMS SEVERN were then based at Freetown, Sierra Leone but also joined the 2nd Submarine Flotilla during 1940. All three Submarines were used during the Norwegian campaign but not to their full potential as they were too large.

On 23rd July 1940 HMS THAMES (Lieutenant Commander W.D. Dunkerley,) struck a mine off Norway and was lost with all hands. HMS SEVERN was broken up at Bombay during 1946.

HMS CLYDE DATA

Builder:	Vickers Armstrong Ltd, Barrow-in-Furness Yard Number: 672 Cost: £459,886
Significant Dates:	Ordered: 1st Sep 1930; Laid Down: 15th May 1933; Launched: 5th Mar 1934; Completed: April 1935
Dimensions:	Length: 345 feet; Beam: 28 feet 3 inches; Draught: 15 feet 7½ inches
Displacement:	Surfaced: 2,165 tons; Dived: 2,680 tons
Machinery:	Surfaced: Twin 10 cylinder diesel engines (10,000 bhp); Dived: Twin electric motors (2,500 bhp)
Speed:	Surfaced: 22½ knots; Dived: 10 knots
Endurance:	Surfaced: 13,200 nautical miles at 8 knots; Dived: 118 nautical miles at 4 knots
Fuel:	216 tons
Armament:	6 x 21-inch torpedo tubes (bow); 12 torpedoes carried; 1 x 4-inch QF gun; 120 rounds carried; 1 x Machine Gun
Complement:	61 (5 Officers and 56 Ratings)

This painting was commissioned by Cameron and Beryl Douglas and their grandsons, Thomas Dent and James Irwin "In tribute to the shipwrights – past and present."

HM SUBMARINES "T" CLASS
HMS TURBULENT

The Painting and the HMS TURBULENT Story

The main picture (in gouache style) shows the WW2 "T" class submarine HMS TURBULENT entering Valetta, Malta. The lower mount shows (from left to right) the nuclear submarine HMS TURBULENT, the ship's badge, and Commander J. W. Linton VC, DSO, DSC Royal Navy.

For the whole of her short life of 15 months, HMS TURBULENT was based in the Mediterranean under Commander Linton and was very successful. In 254 days at sea she sank 100,000 tons of Axis shipping and received 254 depth charges for her pains. She sank 1 cruiser, 1 destroyer, 1 U-boat, 28 supply ships and destroyed 3 trains by gunfire.

HMS TURBULENT was lost with all hands after hitting a mine off La Maddelena, Sardinia on 23rd March 1943. This was only confirmed many years later through the discovery of identifiable wreckage.

Class Information

In the mid-1930's the Admiralty embarked on a replacement for the "O", "P" and "River" classes - none of which had quite been as successful as hoped. This had to be done within the limits of the recent London Naval Treaty, which restricted total new-build submarine tonnage. To take best advantage it was decided to limit the class displacement to 1,000 tons, which was 400 tons less than the classes it was to replace. This decision automatically limited length and diesel power, so surfaced speed was lower. Apart from this, the class was better than those it replaced in most other respects -heavier armament, better habitability and manoeuvrability. The torpedo salvo capability of up to ten ahead was the most powerful of any submarine then in service.

The "T" class submarine was an uncomplicated design with equipment and systems designed to be reliable under wartime conditions. The class had a simplified construction to reduce building time, with considerable attention paid to ease of maintenance and operation. They were very reliable and efficient submarines.

The class had three main variants – the first of class, HMS TRITON, 'Group I' boats, of which 21 were built, followed by 'Group II' boats, of which 31 were built. 'Group I' boats were slightly shorter, with lower displacement and crew than HMS TRITON. The 'Group II' boats were the first British submarines to have an all-welded hull. They had a stern torpedo tube added and the two forward beam tubes were moved and realigned to fire aft. Throughout the war, the class had many changes to armament and structure.

Seventeen of the total class of fifty five were sunk in the War. It is however for their peacetime losses that the class remains most in the public's memory. The very tragic and public losses of HMS THETIS and HMS TRUCULENT brought to every home the hazards of being a submariner. Twenty eight "T" class submarines were built at the Barrow-in-Furness shipyard. The Barrow-built first of class HMS TRITON entered service on 5th October 1937 and the last - HMS TIPTOE - was paid off on 29th August 1969. Some of this class of submarine stayed in service with foreign navies well into the 1970s.

HMS Turbulent Data (Group II)

Builder:	Vickers- Armstrong Ltd, Barrow-in-Furness Yard Number: 771
Significant Dates:	Ordered: 1940; Laid Down: 15th March 1940; Launched: 12th May 1941; Completed: 2nd December 1941
Dimensions:	Length: 273 feet 6 inches; Beam: 26 feet 6 inches; Draught: 14 feet 10 inches
Displacement:	Surfaced: 1,422 tons; Dived: 1,571 tons
Machinery:	Surfaced: 2 x Vickers 6 cylinder diesels (2,500 bhp); Dived: Twin electric motors (1,450 bhp); Twin shafts
Speed:	Surfaced: 15¾ knots; Dived: 9 knots
Endurance:	Surfaced: 8,000 nautical miles at 10 knots; Dived: 80 nautical miles at 4 knots
Armament:	11 x 21-inch torpedo tubes; 8 Bow (2 external); 2 Midships (external); 1 Stern; 17 torpedoes carried; 1 x 4-inch gun; 3 x machine guns; 1x 20mm AA
Complement:	61 (Officers and Ratings)

This painting was commissioned by the Hull and East Yorkshire Branch of the Submariners Association.

HM SUBMARINES "U" CLASS
HMS UPHOLDER

The Painting and the HMS UPHOLDER Story

This painting was the first to be commissioned for the S.H.C. Collection. The main picture (a watercolour) shows the 1940 HMS UPHOLDER leaving Malta at sunset accompanied by a second "U" class submarine. The lower mount shows a pencil profile drawing of the submarine with its badge. The right hand side shows a drawing of HMCS CHICOUTIMI which was originally the 1986 Type 2400 submarine HMS UPHOLDER, together with its badge.

HMS UPHOLDER had a short but very successful wartime career. Based in Malta with the 10th Submarine Flotilla she carried out twenty five patrols in the central Mediterranean. Not until her 6th patrol during April 1941 did HMS UPHOLDER begin to build her reputation. In her remaining nineteen patrols she sank three U-boats, one cruiser and one destroyer and damaged a further two destroyers. Equally important, she also sank 119,000 tons of enemy merchant shipping carrying vital supplies and re-inforcements to the German Afrika Korps in North Africa.

On her 25th and last patrol before going into refit HMS UPHOLDER was sunk on 14th April 1942, with the loss of all hands, by the Italian MTB PEGASO whilst carrying out an attack on a convoy off Tripoli. The Commanding Officer - Lieutenant Commander Malcolm D. Wanklyn - was awarded the Victoria Cross to add to his Distinguished Service Order and Two Bars. For her outstanding contribution to the War effort, the following Official Admiralty Communiqué was issued:

"The Board of the Admiralty regrets to announce that HM Submarine Upholder (Lt. Cdr. M. D. Wanklyn VC, DSO and double bar, RN) has been lost. Next of kin have been informed. It is seldom proper for their Lordships to draw distinction between different services rendered in the course of Navy duty, but they take this opportunity of singling out those of UPHOLDER under the Command of Lieutenant Commander Wanklyn for special mention.

She was long employed against enemy communications in the Central

Mediterranean, and she became known for the uniform high quality of her services in that arduous and dangerous duty. Such was the standard of skill and cool intrepidity set by Lt. Cdr. Wanklyn and the Officers and men under him, they and their ship became an inspiration not only in their own Flotilla, but to the fleet of which it was a part, and to Malta, where for so long it was based. The ship and her company have gone, but their example and inspiration remain."

Class Information

There was a 1936 Admiralty requirement for three small, unarmed submarines to be targets for surface ship training in anti-submarine warfare. It was important that they be cheap to build and operate. It was soon recognised that if armed they could be useful for short patrols; six bow tubes were therefore added whilst they were under construction. The outcome was the "U" class, a class with very good handling and manoeuvrability surfaced or submerged, quick and cheap to build, easy to maintain and needing only a small crew. Twelve more were ordered but after four were built, the bow tubes were reduced to four. These were all called 'Group I' boats and were followed by 34 'Group II' boats. These were the same as 'Group I' except that the stern was lengthened by five feet to improve water flow over the propellers. Of the forty-nine ordered, thirty-one were built at Barrow-in-Furness.

The class served mainly in the Mediterranean and the North Sea; twenty were sunk. Eleven were transferred to Allied navies during and after the War and the remainder were scrapped between 1946 and 1960.

'Group II' boats were initially simply designated "P-XXX" (P for Patrol) but this was changed, except for boats already sunk, to a name on the instructions of Winston Churchill, who famously decreed that no family should have to be told that their son had died in a Royal Navy vessel unworthy of a name.

HMS UPHOLDER DATA

Builder:	Vickers Armstrong Ltd, Barrow-in-Furness	Yard Number: 761
Significant Dates:	Ordered: 1939; Laid Down: 30th October 1939; Launched: 8th July 1940; Completed: 31st October 1940	
Dimensions:	Length: 190 feet 7 inches; Beam: 15 feet 9 inches; Draught: 12 feet 9 inches	
Displacement:	Surfaced: 630 tons; Dived: 730 tons	
Machinery:	Surfaced: Twin diesel engines (1230 bhp); Dived: Twin electric motors (1650 bhp)	
Speed:	Surfaced: 11¾ knots; Dived: 9 knots	
Endurance:	Surfaced: 4,050 nautical miles at 10 knots; Dived: 23 miles at 8 knots	
Armaments:	6 x 21-inch Bow torpedo tubes (4 internal, 2 external); 10 torpedoes carried	
Complement:	33 (Officers and Ratings)	

This was the first commissioned painting of this collection. When the Barrow Submarine Heritage Collection Chairman requested the Travellers Rest Social Club to sponsor a painting, the Chairman, Tommy Snaith, stated *"We were only too happy to become involved in this project. Many of our members down the years have worked in the shipyard here in Barrow. One of our committee members is also an ex-submariner and this made it all the more fitting. We wish this project every success."*

HM SUBMARINES "611" CLASS
HMS 611

The Painting and the "P-611" Story

The main picture (a watercolour) shows the Turkish Submarine ORUC REIS passing the Turkish fleet and ferries at Istanbul. The lower mount shows ORUC REIS in the Dardanelles, Turkish Navy submarine insignia and a pencil profile drawing of a "P-611" class submarine.

ORUC REIS was one of a class of four built for the Turkish Navy. The other three were MURAT REIS, BURAK REIS and ULUC ALI REIS. Completed during wartime and with Turkey a neutral country, delivery was a delicate matter. The Turkish Navy urgently required them and it suited Britain to keep Turkey as friendly as possible, though they were generally thought to be rather more pro-German than pro-British. So a compromise was reached. ORUC REIS and MURAT REIS were temporarily 'commissioned' into the Royal Navy as P-611 (Lieutenant Skelton) and P-612 (Lieutenant Pitt) with Royal Navy crews and delivered to Turkey where they were handed over to the Turkish Navy on 9th May 1942 and 16th May 1942 respectively, after which the RN crews returned home.

Class Information

These submarines were based on the Royal Navy's "S" class, which were intended for short operations in enclosed waters - exactly the Turkish situation. The "S" class is covered next in this book. Compared to these, the "P-611" class had less armament and was slightly smaller in external dimensions.

BURAK REIS and ULUC ALI REIS were renamed P614 and P615 and were fully commissioned into the Royal Navy. Both were part of the escort for the ill fated Convoy PQ17 to Russia in June 1942. Later both were dispatched to West Africa to provide ASW Training based at Freetown in Sierra Leone.

On 18th April 1943 whilst on passage to Takoradi and under escort by MMS 107, submarine P-615 (Lieutenant C.W. St. C. Lambert) was torpedoed and sunk with all hands by the German U-Boat U-123, 120 miles south of Freetown. The other, P-614, returned to Britain in 1943 to continue as an ASW training submarine and, in 1945, was finally transferred to the Turkish Navy and reverted to her original Turkish name BURAK REIS. All were taken out of service and scrapped in 1957.

HMS 611 DATA (TYPICAL OF THE CLASS)

Builder:	Vickers-Armstrong's Ltd, Barrow-in-Furness Yard Number: 751
Significant Dates:	Laid Down: 24th May 1939; Launched: 19th Jul 1940; Completed: 1st Dec 1941
Dimensions:	Length: 201ft 6ins; Beam: 22 feet 3 ins; Draught: 10 feet 6 ins
Displacement:	Surfaced: 683 tons; Dived: 856 tons
Machinery:	Surfaced: Twin diesels (1,550 bhp); Dived: Twin electric motors (1,300 bhp); Twin shafts
Speed:	Surfaced: 13¾ knots; Dived: 10 knots
Endurance:	Surfaced: 6,500 nautical miles at 10 knots; Fuel: 40 tons
Armaments:	5 x 21-inch torpedo tubes (4 bow 1 stern); 1 x 3-inch gun; 1 machine gun
Complement:	41 (Officers and Ratings)

The VINCE ESTATE is both pleased and proud to sponsor this painting in memory and celebration of JIMMY VINCE, a much loved Husband, Father and Grandfather. He came to Barrow-in-Furness in WW2 to take a Barrow built submarine to war. After the hostilities he settled in this, our Town.

HM SUBMARINES "S" CLASS
HMS SERAPH

The Painting and the HMS SERAPH Story

The main picture (a pencil drawing) shows HMS SERAPH at sea with the WW1 destroyer HMS SERAPH in the background. The lower mount depicts the submarine in the 1950's as a 'Training and Target' boat.

After working up, commanded by Lieutenant Norman L.A. Jewell, DSO, MBE, DSC, Legion of Merit, Legion d'Honneur, Croix de Guerre, HMS SERAPH joined the 8th Submarine Flotilla in Gibraltar in August 1942 and was selected to carry out special operations, in which she was involved for the next seventeen months. Three stand out:

Operation Flagpole (20th to 25th October 1942): This was to carry American General Mark Clarke and his staff to and from Vichy controlled Algiers to meet Vichy General Charles Maret to negotiate an unopposed Allied landing in North Africa.

Operation Kingpin (27th October to 10th November 1942): This was to smuggle anti-Vichy General Henri Harove Giraud from Vichy occupied France to Gibraltar to rally French North African Forces to the Allied cause. He refused to co-operate with the British and would only travel in an American submarine. In consequence, HMS SERAPH became the American USS SERAPH in all respects under the command of Captain Jerauld Wright USN, becoming known as "the ship with two Captains".

Operation Mincemeat (16th October 1942 to 21st April 1943): This was to mislead the Germans over the invasion of Sicily. HMS SERAPH took the body of an unidentified man in the uniform of a Royal Marine Major to the coast of Spain and dropped him close inshore so that he would wash up on the beach. It was hoped that the false papers in his briefcase would be found by the neutral Spaniards, who would pass the contents to Germany. The outcome was a complete success. The "Man Who Never Was" completely fooled the Germans. The episode was later made into a film of that name.

Between special operations HMS SERAPH contributed to savaging Italian and German shipping in the Mediterranean. In December 1943 she sailed for Chatham to undergo for refit, after which she carried out her final patrol in the English Channel during D-Day operations before moving to Rothesay, Scotland as a training boat. In the early 1950's she was armour plated and used as a torpedo target boat. Scrapped in December 1965 her periscopes, fore hatch and other items were placed in the Citadel Campus at the Military College of South Carolina at Charleston (which General Mark Clarke had attended) as a Memorial to the "The Ship with two Captains".

Class Information

The "S" class was intended as a replacement for the "H" class which had been in service from WW1. There were sixty four of the class built over thirteen years (1932-1945) in 4 Groups. The first group, completed 1932-33, was the "Swordfish" variant (4 built). These were followed by the larger and internally-rearranged "Shark" variants, completed 1934-38 (8 built). By 1941 33 "War Programme" variants had been ordered being slightly bigger than "Shark" and fitted with an extra, external, torpedo tube. War Programmes of 1942/43 ordered seventeen repeats of these but mostly without the external tube. The submarines were all intended for short operations in enclosed waters; four variants were ordered from Barrow by Turkey (see P-611 Class). Three of the "S" class were built at Barrow-in-Furness - HMS SERAPH (P69), HMS SHAKESPEARE (P71) and HMS P72 (completed as P222). This last submarine was never given a name because it was sunk before Winston Churchill's naming edict (see "U" class).

Of the other two Vickers-built "S" class submarines, HMS P71/SHAKESPEARE was sent first to the Mediterranean and then to the Indian Ocean to be based at Trincomalee. With a new Commanding Officer (Lieutenant D A Swanston) she was sent on her first Far East patrol in the Andaman Sea on 20th December 1944. After attacking a convoy on 2nd January 1945 the submarine underwent gun and air attacks over 2 days during which she was unable to dive owing to damage. Two Ratings were killed and seventeen injured. She made it back to base but was declared a total constructive loss and was sold for scrap in July 1946. HMS P72, later P222 (Lieutenant Commander A.J. Mackenzie) was launched 20th September 1941 and was sent to the Mediterranean. She left Gibraltar to patrol off Naples on 30th November 1942 and was expected to return to Algiers on 21st December. She is believed lost with all hands after depth charge attack by the Italian destroyer escort FORTUNALE off Naples on 12th December 1942.

HMS Seraph Data

Builder:	Vickers Armstrong Ltd, Barrow-in-Furness	Yard Number: 790
Significant Dates:	Ordered: 23rd June 1940; Laid down: 16th August 1940; Launched: 25th October 1941; Completed: 10th June 1942	
Dimensions:	Length: 217 feet; Beam: 24 feet; Draught: 13 feet 3 inches	
Displacement:	Surfaced: 814 tons; Dived: 990 tons	
Machinery:	Surfaced: Twin 8 cylinder diesel engines (1,550 bhp); Dived: Twin electric motors (1,330 bhp); Twin shafts	
Speed:	Surfaced: 14¾ knots; Dived: 9 knots	Endurance: Surfaced: 6,000 nautical miles at 10 knots
Armament:	7 x 21-inch torpedo tubes (6 forward, 1 aft); 1 x 3-inch deck gun; 3 machine guns.	
Complement:	48 (Officers and Ratings)	

The artist for the Barrow Submarine Heritage Collection, Tom Murphy, donated this painting free. Tom stated *"When I was a lad at school at Walney Juniors and then the Seniors, Seraph was my School House name. It was also the submarine that the Barrow-in-Furness Branch of the Submariners Association asked me to paint for the front cover of the S.A. brochure that was used for the Centenary Celebrations in Barrow in May 2001. This submarine has, therefore, always been part of my life in one way or another. I decided to do this as a pencil drawing."*

HM SUBMARINES "X" CRAFT
SUBMARINES X-5 to X-10

The Painting and the "X" Craft Story

This painting shows, from top left clockwise HMS VARBEL 1 (the ex-Isle of Bute Hydro Hotel and 12th Flotilla HQ at Port Bannatyne), TIRPITZ (within its fjord and safety nets), HMS VARBEL 2 (ex-country house and Flotilla HQ at the head of Loch Striven - today it is called Ardtaraig), the attack to cut telephone lines between Singapore, Saigon and Hong Kong, HMS TITANIA (depot ship for the 12th Flotilla), escape of Bill Morrison and Leslie Swatton from XE-11, HMS BONAVENTURE (depot ship for the 12th Flotilla), a two man torpedo carrying out an attack. The centre picture shows XE-20 carrying the Delta flag. Along the lower border is the 12th Flotilla badge and a photograph of four of the 'X' Craft men in BAE Systems yard (ex Vickers Shipyard) in September 2001.

The best known exploit of the Royal Navy's midget submarines ("X" Craft), immortalised by the film *"Above Us the Waves,"* was the raid to sink or at least disable the German battleships TIRPITZ, LÜTZOW and SCHARNHORST in their lairs in Altenfjord and Kaafjord, Norway, in 1943. The operation was designated "Operation Source". All six of the Barrow-built "X" Craft (X-5 to X-10) took part. The only way to get them there was by tow from larger submarines, a perilous process. Conditions were so arduous that those on the "X" craft would be exhausted on arrival near the Norwegian coast, so they used a passage crew who were replaced by a fresh, operational crew. The "X" craft then proceeded independently to their targets.

X-5 sank whilst attempting its attack on TIRPITZ in Altenfjord on 22nd September. The Operational Crew, who were all lost, was: Lieutenant D. Henty-Creer, RNVR, Commanding Officer, Sub Lieutenant T.J. Nelson, RNVR, Midshipman D.J. Malcolm, RNVR and ERA4 J.J. Mortiboys.

X-6's attack on TIRPITZ on the same day was successful. The submarine was then scuttled and the crew were all taken prisoner. The Operational Crew was: Lieutenant. D. Cameron, RNR. Commanding Officer, Sub Lieutenant J.J. Lorimer, RNVR., Sub Lieutenant R.H. Kendall, RNVR and ERA4 F. Goddard RN.

X-7's attack on TIRPITZ, also the same day, was also successful. The vessel was scuttled following the attack but unfortunately two crew members did not escape from the submarine. They were Sub Lieutenant L.B. Whittam, RNVR and ERA4 M. Whitley, RN. The other two crew members - Lieutenant B.C.G. Place DSC, RN - Commanding Officer and Sub Lieutenant R. Aitken, RNVR were taken prisoner.

X-8's intended target was SCHARNHORST, also in Altenfjord but she had to be scuttled on passage on 17th September 1943 because of damage after her leaking side cargoes exploded soon after being jettisoned. The passage ccrew on board at the time were all recovered.

X-9's intended target was LÜTZOW in Kaafjord but she foundered on 16th September after her tow parted during passage. The passage crew were all lost.

X-10's intended target was also SCHARNHORST. However her attack had to be abandoned due to a variety of defects in the submarine's equipment. The operational crew headed back out to sea where they met HMS STUBBORN to which they transferred safely. X-10 was then scuttled. The operational crew was: Lieutenant K. Hudspeth, RANVR, -Commanding Officer, Sub Lieutenant B. Enzer, RNVR, Sub Lieutenant G. Harding, RNVR and ERA4 L. Tilley RN.

As a result of Operation Source, TIRPITZ was badly damaged and did not put to sea again until April 1944. Lieutenant D. Cameron, RNR and Lieutenant B.C.G. Place, DSC, RN were both awarded a Victoria Cross. Lorimer, Kendall and Aitken were awarded the DSO and Goddard, the CGM.

Class Information

The letters HMS do not generally prefix "X" class and similar midget submarines but it is noted that the citation for the VCs that were awarded for Operation Source quotes HMS X-6 and HMS X-7. X-1 was a submarine cruiser which was not developed. X-2 was allocated to a captured Italian submarine. X-3 and X-4 were the prototypes for the final "X" craft design.

X-20 – X-24 were built to replace the lost "X" craft and were used in operations in Norway and prior to the D-Day landings.

X-5 TO X-10 DATA

Builder:	Vickers Armstrong Ltd, Barrow-in-Furness.	Yard Number: 883	Six in class (X-5 to X-10)
Significant Dates:	Ordered: 12th May 1942; Laid Down: 5 in September 1942; Completed: X-10 in January 1943		
Dimensions:	Length: 51 feet 3 inches; Beam: 5 feet 9 inches; Draught: 5 feet 9 inches		Displacement: Surfaced: 27 tons ; Dived: 30 tons
Machinery:	Surfaced: 42 bhp Gardner diesel (as per London buses); Dived: One Keith Gardner electric motor (30 bhp); Single shaft		
Speed:	Surfaced: 6½ knots; Dived: 5½ knots		
Endurance:	Surfaced: 1,860 nautical miles at 4½ knots; Dived: 80 nautical miles at 5½ knots		
Armament:	2 x time fused side cargoes of 4,480 pounds (2 tons) high explosive; Limpet mines.		Complement: 4 Officers and Ratings

Twelfth Submarine Flotilla

This painting was commissioned by Bill Butters - a member of the 12th Submarine Flotilla Association - in recognition of the men who served in the "X" and "XE" midget submarines during WW2.

HM SUBMARINES "XE" CLASS
SUBMARINE XE-3

The Painting and the XE3 Story

The main picture is a watercolour showing the midget submarine XE-3 underneath the Japanese heavy cruiser TAKAO. It depicts Leading Seaman Magennis, VC, attaching limpet mines to the hull of the cruiser. The lower mount consists of pencil drawings of a midget submarine and TAKAO together with the signature of Lieutenant Commander Ian Fraser, VC.

The aim of Operation 'Struggle' was to sink the TAKAO which was lying in the Jahore Straits. The submarine HMS STYGIAN (Commanding Officer Lieutenant. G.C. Clarabut, DSO, DSC, Royal Navy) towed XE-3 with a passage crew to the Horsburgh Light off Singapore. The operational crew then took over and navigated XE-3 through 40 miles of Japanese controlled waters, mainly on the surface but dived on sighting enemy vessels. She reached the target during the morning of 31st July 1945.

Once XE-3 had manoeuvred under TAKAO, LS Magennis exited the boat to place limpet mines. It was very difficult to get them to stick on the extremely fouled bottom of the ship. Magennis returned to XE-3 with the mines finally positioned; the side cargo was laid and XE-3 tried to manoeuvre from beneath TAKAO. It then became obvious that the limpet mine container had not released and the tide had dropped, wedging XE-3 under TAKAO with charges already set to explode. LS Magennis once again exited the boat, and with the aid of a crowbar, sledgehammer and chisel, freed the container. As a result, XE-3 escaped and withdrew back to the Horsburgh light, arriving at 0330 hrs on 1st August where HMS STYGIAN was waiting for them to take XE-3 back under tow to their base.

It was an epic operation in which the crew were without sleep for 52 hours, and the Coxswain - ERA Reed had been at the wheel without relief for over 30 hours. TAKAO, in fact, did not sink due to the shallowness of the water but was so badly damaged as to be of no further operational use.

For their endeavours the crew were awarded the following decorations:-

Lieutenant Ian Fraser, RNVR:	Victoria Cross
Engine Room Artificer C Reed, RN:	Conspicuous Gallantry Medal
Leading Seaman James Magennis, RN:	Victoria Cross
Sub Lieutenant J L Smith, RNZNVR:	Distinguished Service Order

Class Information

Six "XE" craft were ordered from Barrow in 1943 and all were completed by December 1944. The "E" is generally taken to stand for "East", to where the Admiralty's eyes were increasingly focussed. They were similar to "X" craft 5-10 built 1942-43. All six of the "XE" boats served in the Far East and carried out various operations there. They were all scrapped in Sydney, Australia in October 1945.

XE-1 TO XE-6 DATA

Builder:	Vickers Armstrong, Barrow-in-Furness
Cost:	£93,783 for all six XE Craft
Significant Dates:	Ordered: 17th January 1944; Completed: 15th December 1944 (XE-3)
Dimensions:	Length: 53 feet; Beam: 5¾ feet; Draught: 5¾ feet
Displacement:	Surfaced: 30 tons; Dived: 34 tons
Machinery:	Surfaced: Gardner diesel engine (42 bhp); Dived: Single Blackman-Metro Vickers electric motor; One shaft
Speed:	Surfaced: 6½ knots; Dived: 6 knots
Endurance:	Surfaced: 1,350 nautical miles; Dived: 80 nautical miles
Armaments:	2 x 2 ton explosive side cargoes (port and starboard) and/or Limpet mines in containers (port and starboard)
Complement:	4 Officers and Ratings

Yard Number: 939 (6 x 'XE' craft plus one spare Tail Unit)

This painting was the second painting to be commissioned for the Barrow Submarine Heritage Collection. The Chairman of the Barrow-in-Furness Branch of the Submariners Association Ken Collins stated *"It is only fitting that the second painting in the collection should honour the men that accomplished so much during Operation Struggle in July 1945. We were also fortunate and honoured to have the Submarine Service's last remaining VC, Lieutenant Commander Ian Fraser, RNR (Retired), VC, DSO, to sign the painting."*

HM SUBMARINES "XT" CLASS
"XT" TRAINING SUBMARINES

The Painting and "XT" Submarines

The main picture is a watercolour depicting an "XT" class midget submarine off the south end of Walney Island, Barrow-in-Furness. The vessel on the surface is a small coaster owned by James Fisher's of Barrow-in-Furness passing Walney Lighthouse and Piel Island. The Vickers Armstrong shipyard can be seen in the distance. The lower mount shows an XT craft at sea and a sketch entitled *Up Periscope*.

As these were training vessels there are no stand out stories recorded for the class. Their purpose was to assist in training Royal Navy anti-submarine units against the threat of German Navy (Kreigsmarine) Biber class midget submarines that were developed by Germany following the 1944 Normandy landings.

Class Information

Admiral Max Horton, Flag Officer Submarines, proposed that a non-operational class of X-craft should be built to be used for training purposes, freeing up the submarines, until then being used for anti-submarine targets, for operational duties. They were originally to be called Z craft but were subsequently reclassified as "XT" class. The XT's were simplified versions of X craft, without side cargo release gear, night periscope or automatic pilot. The day periscope, projector compass and air induction system were all fixed in the raised position. The XT craft were based at Loch Fyne and Campbeltown in Scotland, Portsmouth and Harwich in the south of England. The six XT craft were scrapped in October 1945.

XT Data

Builder:	Vickers Armstrong Ltd, Barrow-in-Furness	Yard Number: 927	Six in class	XT1 – XT6
Significant Dates:	Ordered: 1943 (all six); Completed: Between 18th January 1944 (XT-1) and 15th March 1944 (XT-6)			
Dimensions:	Length: 51 feet 4 inches; Beam: 5 feet 9 inches; Draught: 5 feet 11 inches			
Displacement:	Surfaced: 26.5 tons; Dived: 29.5 tons			
Machinery:	Surfaced: One Gardner diesel (42 bhp); Dived: One Keith Blackman electric motor (30 bhp); Single shaft			
Speed:	Surfaced: 6 knots; Dived: 5 knots			
Endurance:	Surfaced: 500 nautical miles at 6 knots; Dived: 80 nautical miles at 5½ knots			
Armament:	None			
Complement:	3 Officers and Men (No diver carried)			

This painting was commissioned by members of the social team of the Submariners Association, Barrow-in-Furness Branch. The funds for the painting were raised by raffles which were conducted at the Branch Monthly Meetings. At the time the painting was commissioned in December 2003 the social team consisted of John Houlding (Social Secretary) and Jeff Thomas (Assistant Social Secretary).

This painting is dedicated to all men who trained in "X" and "XT" craft and later served in the 12th and 14th Submarine Flotillas.

HM SUBMARINES "V" CLASS
HMS VENTURER

The Painting and the HMS VENTURER Story

The main picture is a watercolour showing HMS VENTURER sailing out on patrol accompanied by two other "V" class vessels and by a Sunderland flying boat as used by Coastal Command. The vessel in the background is the submarine depot ship HMS MAIDSTONE. The lower mount shows the HMS VENTURER badge and also a pencil sketch of a "V" Class submarine.

HMS VENTURER is believed to be not just the only RN submarine during WW2 to sink an enemy submarine whilst both boats were dived but the only submarine ever to have done so.

The first of the "V" class submarines built at Barrow-in-Furness between 1943 and 1944, HMS VENTURER distinguished herself by sinking two German U-Boats. The first, U-771, was sunk on the 11th November 1944 - by periscope observation.

The second, U-864, was sunk on the 9th February 1945 in a unique action as both boats were dived at the time. The U-boat was detected by HMS VENTURER's ASDIC used in 'passive' mode so that there would be no telltale 'ping'. HMS VENTURER's Commanding Officer, Lieutenant J.S. Launders, was at first able to obtain sightings on the U-boat's periscopes due to what he described as "most shameful periscope drill" on the U-boat's part. From the information provided by the ASDIC and his sightings, Launders concluded that he was broad on to U-864's starboard bow. For the next hour, with both boats dived he used the ASDIC to plot U-864's course and, when finally certain of direction and speed, he fired a salvo of four Mk VIII** tor-

pedoes. The range was 3,000 yards. U-864 was hit by one torpedo of the salvo and sank with the loss of all hands.

Class Information

The "V" class was a modified version of the "U" class, having similar characteristics but even easier to build. The hull was stronger and partly welded. This practice was still regarded with misgivings by the Admiralty but well-established in German submarines. It was a lot cheaper and quicker than riveting. They were almost eight feet longer than the "U" class and a little faster. Twenty two were built - fourteen at Barrow-in-Furness.

There were no war losses except for the Barrow Built HMS VANDAL which had the shortest career of any submarine in the Royal Navy. She had sailed from Holy Loch on the 22nd February 1943 for the exercise area between the Mull of Kintyre and the Isle of Arran as part of her working-up period. She was last seen leaving Lochranza on the afternoon of the 24th February. At nightfall she had failed to make her 'surfacing signal'. On daybreak a search of the area was made but no trace was found. In 1995, her wreck was positively identified in three hundred feet of water about one and a half miles North West of Lochranza. The cause of her loss remains unknown.

Several "V" class Submarines were transferred to Allies during and after the war. HMS VENTURER went to the Royal Norwegian Navy in 1946 and was renamed HNoMS UTSTEIN, extensively modernised in 1956 and scrapped in 1965.

HMS Venturer Data (Typical of the class)

Builder:	Vickers Armstrong Ltd, Barrow-in-Furness Yard Number: 860
Significant Dates:	Ordered: 15th July 1941; Laid down: 24 August 1942; Launched: 4th May 1943; Completed: 19 August 1943
Dimensions:	Length: 204 feet 6 inches; Beam: 16 feet; Draught: 12 feet 9 inches
Displacement:	Surfaced: 545 tons; Dived: 740 tons
Machinery:	Surfaced: Twin diesels (1,600 bhp); Dived: Twin electric motors (1,520 bhp); Twin shafts
Speed:	Surfaced: 13 knots; Dived: 9 knots
Endurance:	Surfaced: 4,100 nautical miles at 10 knots; Dived: 30 nautical miles at 9 knots
Armament:	4 x 21-inch torpedo tubes; 8 torpedoes carried; 1 x 3-inch gun; 3 x 0.303 machine guns
Complement:	31 (Officers and ratings.)

This painting is sponsored by the Scottish Branch of the Submariners Association. They have chosen this particular class of submarine as they are directly involved with the memorial which is held each year in Scotland regarding the loss of HMS VANDAL in Scottish waters.

HM SUBMARINES "IMPROVED T" CLASS
HMS TIPTOE

The Painting and the HMS TIPTOE Story

The main picture is a watercolour showing HMS TIPTOE leaving Barrow after a courtesy visit in the 1950s. The lower mount has two pencil drawings of HMS TIPTOE as built during WW2, the ship's badge and a painting of red ballet shoes presented to HMS TIPTOE by the actress Moira Shearer who wore these ballet shoes in the film *"Red Shoes"*. These ballet shoes are now on display in the Royal Naval Submarine Museum at Gosport.

After the war, HMS TIPTOE was converted along with the other newer "T" class vessels. HMS TIPTOE was the submarine featured in the film *"We Dive at Dawn"* which starred Sir John Mills. Her anchor was mounted on a stone plinth at Blyth in 1969 and, on 29th August 1969, HMS TIPTOE became the last "T" class submarine to be paid off.

Class Information

HMS TIPTOE along with seven other submarines was built as a standard "T" class vessel (see page 52) but, by the time hostilities ended in 1945, submarine development, particularly by the Germans, had made the majority of existing submarines obsolete.

The whole concept of the submarine was changing dramatically, particularly regarding underwater speed and endurance. Captured Type XXI and Type XXIII battery powered submarines achieved underwater speeds of seventeen knots in trials, if only for short periods.

As a consequence, eight of the most modern, all welded "T" class boats, were lengthened by inserting a 20 foot parallel section of pressure hull aft of the engine room bulkhead, with two additional motors and a fourth battery, to increase underwater power and endurance. Also all external projections were removed and the hull and bridge structure streamlined.

HMS TIPTOE DATA (AFTER CONVERSION)

Builder:	Vickers Armstrong Ltd, Barrow-in-Furness Yard Number: 868
Significant Dates:	Ordered: December 1941; Laid Down: 10th November 1942; Launched: 25th February 1944; Completed: 8th March 1944
Converted:	HM Dockyard, Chatham July 1952 to September 1954
Dimensions:	Length: 285 feet 4 inches; Beam: 26 feet 6 inches; Draught: 15 feet 8 inches
Displacement:	Surfaced: 1,260 tons; Dived: 1,680 tons
Machinery:	Surfaced: 2 x Vickers 6 cylinder diesel engines (2,500 bhp); Dived: Four electric motors total (6,000 bhp); Twin shafts
Speed:	Surfaced: 15 knots; Dived: 14½ knots for 1 hour; 5 knots for 11 hours
Endurance:	Surfaced: 11,500 nautical miles at 12 knots
Armament:	11 x 21-inch torpedo tubes; 8 Bow (2 external), 2 Midships (external) 1 Stern; 17 torpedoes carried; 1 x 4-inch gun; 3 x machine guns; 1x 20mm AA gun
Complement:	60 (Officers and Ratings)

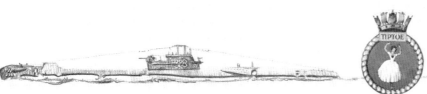

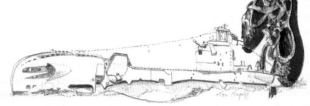

This painting was commissioned by Mr. Hughie Short, a member of the Submariners Association, Barrow-in-Furness Branch.

HM SUBMARINES "A" CLASS
HMS AMBUSH

The Painting and the HMS Ambush Story

The main picture is a watercolour of a modified HMS AMBUSH passing under the Angus L. Macdonald Bridge in Halifax, Nova Scotia. The lower mount is a view of the ship's badge and a pencil drawing of HMS AMBUSH as built. The captured German Type XXI submarine gave the Royal Navy the design for submarine snorkels (snort masts). However, the effects of prolonged snorting on the crew were not fully understood at that time, nor was the most effective / tactical use of the snort capability. To research these, HMS AMBUSH left the Clyde on 12th February 1948 to carry out a prolonged snort cruise between Jan Mayen Island and Bear Island in the Barents Sea, returning on 18th March 1948.

HMS AMBUSH was one of several "A" class submarines to be part of the Royal Navy's Sixth Submarine Squadron, based in Halifax. The others were ALCIDE, ALDERNEY, AMBUSH, ASTUTE, AURIGA and AUROCHS; the last one being Barrow built. They are remembered as a familiar part of the Halifax waterfront under the Angus L. Macdonald Bridge. In 1954, the first draft of Canadian naval personnel was sent to Britain for submarine training. On completion they went to sea in Royal Navy submarines, many of them in the Sixth Submarine Squadron. The Royal Navy remained in Canada until HMCS OJIBWA, the first of the Canadian ""O class submarines, arrived in Halifax to form the First Canadian Submarine Squadron. She was later joined by HMCS ONONDAGA and HMCS OKANAGAN.

In 1957 HMS AMBUSH was streamlined and 'guppified' (Greater Underwater Propulsive Power) at HM Dockyard, Chatham. In 1977 she was scrapped at Inverkeithing, Scotland.

Class Information

British submarine production during WW2 was almost entirely limited to pre war designs, repeated or modified. The only exceptions were the X craft and the "A" class, a modified and larger "T" class. The "A" class was intended for the Far East, which drove the need for long range, powerful armament with many reloads and good crew comfort in tropical climates. Efforts were made to reduce underwater noise. They were among the first RN submarines to be fitted with a mast mounted radar antenna but not, initially, a snorkel. The "A" class was a projected class of 46, but only 16 were built as 30 were cancelled at the end of WWII.

The first of class, HMS ANCHORITE (later renamed HMS AMPHION) was laid down on 14th November 1943. Only this boat and HMS ASTUTE were completed before hostilities ended in August 1945 and no A class boat fired a shot in anger in WW2. The Royal Navy thus had by the late 1940's, 16 new submarines of an outdated design and poor performance levels when compared to the innovations introduced by the German Type XXI U-boats. Snorkels were progressively fitted but it was only after the "T" class conversions were complete that the "A" class was modernised, between 1955 and 1960. Unlike the "T" class conversions, no changes were made to the "A" class hull, diesels, electric motors or battery arrangements. Work was limited to external streamlining, providing a new fin and removal of the external torpedo tubes. The gun was retained, to good effect when the class became involved in confrontations in South East Asia where there was need to challenge, usually unarmed, surface vessels. The only "A" boats not modernised were AFFRAY (sunk with the loss of the entire crew in 1951, probably due to a failure in the snort system) and AUROCHS which was in poor condition and not assessed to be worth the cost. The last submarine gun action surface was conducted in December 1974 by the Barrow built HMS ANDREW. A signal sent by the CO, Lieutenant Commander A.P. Hoddinott, to Flag Officer Submarines read *"The reek of cordite has passed from the Royal Navy's Submarine Service. Last gun action surface conducted at 031330 zulu. Time to first round, 36 seconds. May the art of submarine gunnery rest in peace but never be forgotten."*

Barrow-in-Furness built ten "A" class submarines one of which, HMS ALLIANCE, has recently been extensively refurbished and is on display at the Royal Navy Submarine Museum, Gosport.

HMS AMBUSH DATA (AS BUILT)

Builder:	Vickers Armstrong's Limited, Barrow-in-Furness Yard Number: 910
Significant Dates:	Laid Down: 17th May 1945; Launched: 14th September 1945; Completed: 22nd July 1947
Dimensions:	Length: 281½ feet; Beam: 22¼ feet; Draught: 17 feet
Displacement:	Surfaced: 1,385 tons; Dived: 1,620 tons
Machinery:	Surfaced: 2 x 8 cylinder supercharged Vickers diesels (4,300 bhp); Dived: 2 x electric motors (1,250 bhp); Twin shafts
Speed:	Surfaced: 18 knots; Dived: 8 knots
Endurance:	Surfaced: 10,500 nautical miles at 11 knots; Dived: 114 nm at 3knots
Fuel:	300 tons
Armament:	10 x 21-inch torpedo tubes (Bow – 4 internal 2 external) (Stern – 2 internal 2 external) or 26 mines instead of torpedoes; 1 x 4-inch gun; 1 x 20 mm Oerlikon AA gun; 3 x machine guns
Complement:	60 Officers and Ratings

The Submarines Association of Canada are pleased to sponsor the "A" class submarine painting as these were the submarines in the mid-1950s to form the Sixth Submarine Squadron in Halifax, Nova Scotia.

HM SUBMARINES "EX" CLASS
HMS EXPLORER and HMS EXCALIBUR

The Painting and the HMS Explorer & HMS Excalibur Story

The main picture, a pencil drawing, shows HMS EXPLORER at full speed, passing HMS METEORITE (ex U-1407) in the Kyle of Lochalsh, with the Isle of Skye and the new bridge (artistic licence here!) in the background. Also shown is the sister submarine HMS EXCALIBUR together with support vessels HMS KINGFISHER and RFA SPABECK. The lower mount shows the ships' badges of HMS EXPLORER and HMS EXCALIBUR.

The class of two vessels was unarmed and experimental. Based upon the captured HTP powered U-boat, U-1407 (which had been salvaged and re-named HMS METEORITE), they were used to assess the air independent HTP (High Test Peroxide) system developed by the German engineer, Dr Helmuth Walther. The engine was essentially a steam turbine, with the steam being generated by the interaction of HTP with diesel oil and a catalyst. HMS EXPLORER and HMS EXCAL-IBUR were a long time in building and, by the time they were launched in 1954 and 1955, the development of nuclear powered submarines, and technical problems, had rendered them effectively obsolete. The two boats formed part of the 3rd Submarine Squadron in Faslane for almost 10 years. They tended to work separately from the other boats in the Squadron having their own depot ship, HMS KING-FISHER, and a fuel carrier, the converted water carrier RFA (Royal Fleet Auxiliary) SPABECK. They were scrapped at T. W. Ward's, Barrow-in-Furness between 1968 and 1970.

Class Information

From 1933 the German engineer, Dr Walther, had worked on a revolutionary fast U-boat design that would operate with the battle-fleet and engage fast ships, much as the earlier, unsuccessful, British "K" class (page 32). However, there were two key differences - first high speed would be achieved underwater and secondly the boats would use the decomposition of hydrogen peroxide to provide oxygen to run diesel engines underwater. It became clear quickly that the heat generated by the decomposition could be better used by turbines, just as "K" class had attempt-ed. In 1940 a trial, turbine powered, submarine achieved over 28 knots, three times then typical submarine underwater speeds. By 1944 he had developed a 1750 ton design capable of twenty five knots. It was not built, but its hull was the basis of the U-Boat Type XXI which was to revolutionise post-war submarine thinking (see "T" class conversion page 68). A smaller, 800 ton turbine-powered, peroxide-fuelled design, the Type XXVI, was built and six fell into Allied hands. One, U-1407, was scuttled in Cuxhaven in May 1945, raised by the British in June and brought back to Barrow-in-Furness to be refitted with a complete set of machinery that was also captured in Germany. U-1407 was re-commissioned as HMS METEORITE and carried out a lengthy series of trials under the guidance of Dr Walther and his original team from Germania-Werft, Kiel who lived with their families, mostly on Walney Island, Barrow-in-Furness. The USSR was pursuing the same line of submarine development and this, together with the need for high speed submarines to train ASW forces and the apparent success of the METEORITE trials, encouraged the Admiralty to place an order for the two experimental boats EXPLORER (known to her ship's company as EXPLODER due to the frequency of major and minor explosions on board), and EXCALIBUR (known to her ship's company as EXCRUCIA-TOR). At this time the Admiralty saw Walther propulsion as the best way to achieve the step-change in submarine performance that the emerging Cold War necessitated, viewing nuclear propulsion as an expensive and distant, aspiration.

In 1955, EXCALIBUR began her trials and the Americans put the nuclear-powered NAUTILUS to sea. It was quickly evident that, although Walther submarines were fast they were not truly independent; unlike NAUTILUS which was not only independent of the surface but could sustain high speeds for much longer. It was also becoming evident just how difficult and dangerous peroxide was in submarines (in 1955, a peroxide-fuelled torpedo exploded in HMS SIDON, killing twelve people). British work with peroxide and Walther turbines was stopped and the task became how best to develop British nuclear-powered submarines.

HMS Explorer & HMS Excalibur Data

Builder:	Vickers Armstrong Ltd, Barrow-in-Furness.	Yard Number: 979 & 980	Cost: £2,000,000 each
Significant Dates:	EXPLORER Ordered: 26th August 1947; Launched: 5th March 1954; Completed: 25th November 1956		
	EXCALIBUR Ordered: 26th August 1947; Launched: 25th February 1955; Completed: 22nd February 1958		
Dimensions:	Length: 225½ feet; Beam: 15¾ feet; Draught: 16 feet		
Displacement:	Surfaced: 780 tons; Dived: 1,000 tons		
Machinery:	High Test Peroxide (H.T.P.) steam raising plant driving steam turbines (15,000 bhp) and electric motors; Diesel engines (surface only); Twin shafts		
Speed:	Surfaced: 27+ knots on steam turbines; Dived: 18 knots on electric drive		
Complement:	EXPLORER: 49 Officers and Ratings	EXCALIBUR: 41 Officers and Ratings	

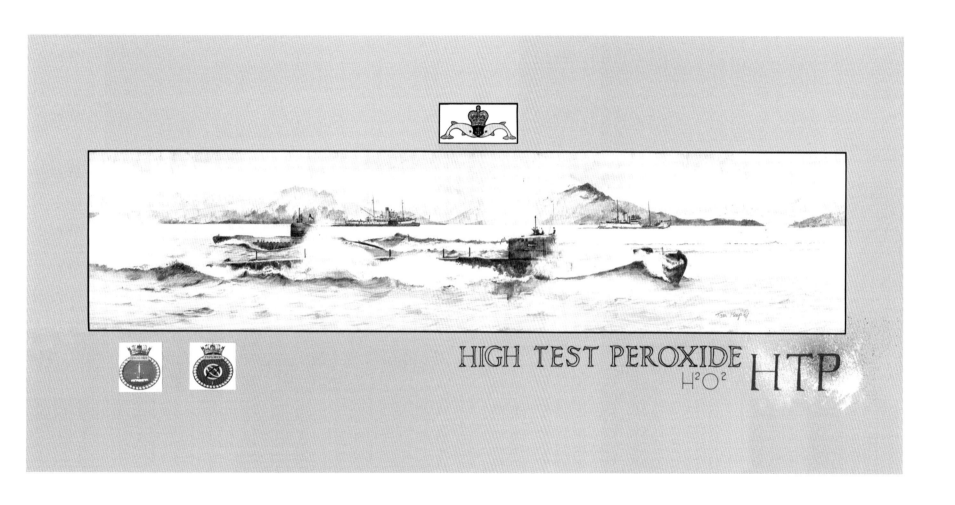

HIGH TEST PEROXIDE H^2O^2 HTP

This painting was commissioned by the Submariners Association, West of Scotland Branch. "The Explorer/Excalibur" class submarines are often the forgotten post-war submarines, but they were a part of the 3rd Submarine Squadron based in Faslane, Scotland, for more than a decade. As the local Submarine Association Branch, we are proud to remember and honour them."

HM SUBMARINES "PORPOISE" CLASS
HMS PORPOISE

The Painting and the HMS PORPOISE Story

The main picture was created in inks on glazed card and shows HMS PORPOISE (1954 – 1985) with HMS PORPOISE (1930s) in the background together with a school of porpoises. The lower mount is a painting of a Greek coin with the god Perseus riding a porpoise.

Although HMS PORPOISE was ordered in 1951 it was not until 1958 that she joined the Fleet. She was the first of class of eight submarines, three of which were built at Barrow. The other two were HMS RORQUAL and HMS NARWHAL. After 25 years of service, during which she was a key component of the Royal Navy's Submarine Flotilla, HMS PORPOISE was placed on the disposal list in 1983 and on the 20th October 1985 was sunk as a target for the British Underwater Test and Evaluation Centre (BUTEC) range in the Western Isles of Scotland.

Class Information

This was the first operational class of Royal Navy submarines to be designed after WW2. It drew upon wartime experience, the "T" class conversions, the similar American 'Guppy' (Greater Underwater Propulsive Power) conversions and the ubiquitous German Type XXI. Work began in 1949 on the design, after the Admiralty decided that a Walther-powered operational design could not be produced sufficiently soon. One view was to take and modify the US "Tang" design, but an all British "Porpoise" class was developed instead. Many regard the "Porpoise" class (and the follow on "Oberon" class) as the best of the post WW2 submarine designs in the world. Attention was paid to a streamlined form, albeit still optimised for surface running and also on suppressing internal noise from machinery. Combined with a large battery capacity and powerful motors the result was a high submerged speed of 17 knots and a very low noise signature, making them very difficult to detect. Designated Patrol Submarines they could, with their improved Snorkel (or Snort) systems, avoid surfacing fully for a much longer than previous boats, further helping to reduce detection opportunities. Sonar equipment was improved to produce the most modern submarine listening platform in the world. Good crew accommodation, including effective air conditioning, allowed the boats to operate efficiently world wide.

HMS PORPOISE DATA

Builder:	Vickers Armstrong Ltd, Barrow-in-Furness. Yard Number: 1029 Cost: £2,000.000 (approx)
Significant Dates:	Ordered: 1951; Laid Down: 15th June 1954; Launched: 25th April 1956; Completed: 17th April 1958
Dimensions:	Length: 295 feet 3 inches; Beam: 29 feet 9 inches; Draught: 16 feet
Displacement:	Surfaced: 1,768 tons; Dived: 2,053 tons
Machinery:	Surfaced: 2 x Admiralty Standard Range (ASR) 16 cylinder diesel engines (3,680 bhp); Dived: 2 x electric motors total (6,000 bhp); Twin shaft
Speed:	Surfaced: 12 knots; Dived: 17 knots
Endurance:	Surfaced: 10,350 nautical miles
Armament:	6 x 21-inch bow torpedo tubes; 2 x 21-inch stern torpedo tubes; 30 torpedoes carried
Complement:	6 Officers and 65 Ratings

This painting has been sponsored by Mr. Russ Taylor of Barrow Island, Barrow-in-Furness, who served on HMS PORPOISE from 1971 to 1974. Russ joined as a Marine Engineering Mechanic (MEM) and left as a Petty Officer Marine Engineering Mechanic (POMEM) or Stoker Petty Officer (SPO) in submarine parlance.

HM SUBMARINES "X-51" CLASS
X-51 (STICKLEBACK)

The Painting and the X-51 Class Story

The main picture is a watercolour showing the four "X-51" class midget submarines at sea off HMS DOLPHIN (Gosport). The lower mount shows a stickleback, a shrimp, a minnow and a sprat on the left hand side. On the right, the "X-51" class submarines are shown being transported by two Vickers steam trains on a low loader to be lowered by the 20 ton hammerhead crane into Devonshire Dock. In the early days of the Cold War Britain had limited means of delivering a nuclear weapon into the USSR and its Warsaw Pact Allies. It was decided that the strategic deterrent was to be the V bomber force, supplemented later by the Blue Steel stand-off missile. However, the use of nuclear weapons in tactical (battle) situations was still being explored. One line of thought was that midget submarines like the WW2 X-craft could be used to lay nuclear mines in Warsaw Pact dockyards and harbours. To this end the "X-51" class was built, an improvement on the earlier X-craft. Four were built - STICKLEBACK (X-51), SHRIMP (X-52), SPRAT (X-53), and MINNOW (X-54).

By the time they entered service, the V bomber force was operational and thinking had moved on over tactical use of nuclear weapons. In consequence, they spent their lives in reserve or training roles. The four X-51 boats were scrapped when Flag Officer, Submarines was required to reduce the number of hulls under his Command.

Class Information

All were launched between July 1954 and May 1955. There was an approximate six month delay in the build of the X-51 boats owing to difficulties with the welding of the UXW hull steel causing cracking leading to a change to S type steel. The boats completed initial trials in Devonshire and Buccleuch Docks before being transported by rail to Faslane where sea trials were carried out before each was handed over to the Royal Navy.

In 1958 STICKLEBACK was sold to the Royal Swedish Navy for use in harbour defence exercises. She was renamed SPIGGEN (Swedish for STICKLEBACK). In 1976 she was returned to the United Kingdom and was stored at the Imperial War Museum, Duxford. In 2016 STICKLEBACK was loaned to the Submarine Heritage Museum in Helensburgh to become the centrepiece of their displays.

On completion of sea trials, SHRIMP was immediately placed in Reserve in Portsmouth. She was broken up by Metal Industries at Faslane, Scotland in 1966. SPRAT was also immediately placed in Reserve at Portsmouth on completion of sea trials. She was employed on occasion to test harbour defence systems of various ports in the United States of America and was also broken up at Faslane in 1966. On completion of sea trials MINNOW returned to Barrow to have the class spare tail unit fitted for proving trials before acceptance. The submarine also carried out trials on an early version of the pump-jet propulsion system (shrouded propeller). MINNOW was then placed in Reserve and broken up at Faslane in 1966.

The Main Motors for the "X-51" class submarines were re-conditioned Metropolitan Vickers motors from the "XE" class boats (page 62) refurbished by Fife, Wilson and Co. of Bishops Stortford.

STICKLEBACK DATA (TYPICAL OF THE CLASS)

Builder:	Vickers Armstrong Ltd, Barrow-in-Furness	Yard Number:	037 4 in class (SSX01 to SSX04 plus 1 x 'Spare' Tail Unit)
Cost:	£310,542 for 4 x 'X-51' class, the Spare Tail Unit, spares and drawings		
Significant Dates:	Ordered: 6th September 1951; Launched: 1st Oct 1954; Completed: 4th Nov 1954		
Dimensions:	Length: 53 feet 9 inches; Beam: 6 feet 3 inches; Draught: 7 feet 6 inches		
Displacement:	Surfaced: 36 tons; Dived: 41 tons		
Machinery:	Surfaced: Single six cylinder Perkins diesel engine; Dived: Single electric motor; Single shaft		
Speed:	Surfaced: 7 knots; Dived: 6 knots		
Endurance:	Not known		
Armaments:	Two 2 ton side cargoes; Limpet mines		
Complement:	5		

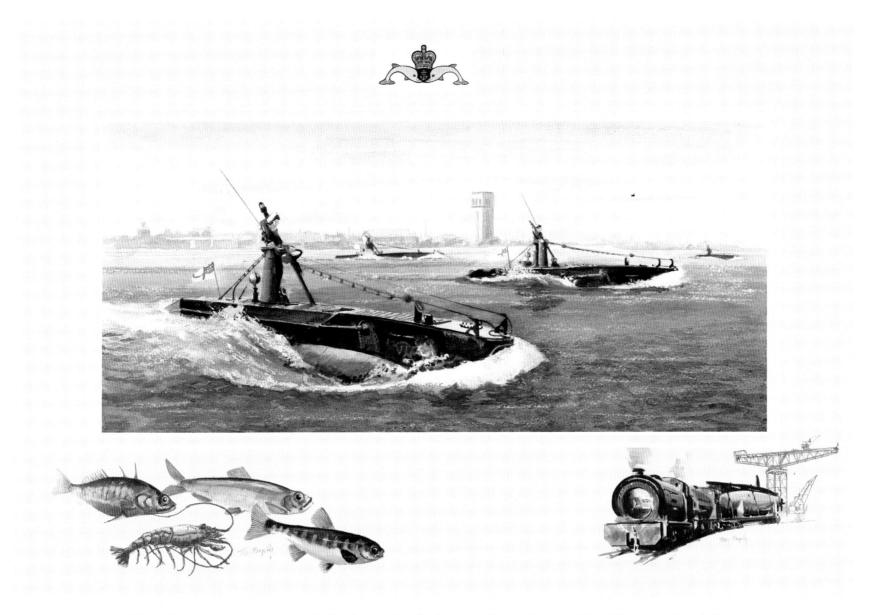

This painting was commissioned with funds raised by the Barrow-in-Furness Branch of the Submariners Association.

HM SUBMARINES "OBERON" CLASS
HMS OLYMPUS

The Painting and the HMS OLYMPUS Story

This painting is an ink and wash picture showing HMS OLYMPUS at sea. The lower mount shows a pencil drawing of HMS OLYMPUS passing Walney Lighthouse, Piel Castle and Barrow.

HMS OLYMPUS was built at Barrow in the early 1960s. Two other "Oberon" class submarines were also built there for the Royal Navy. These vessels served around the world and, in 1989, HMS OLYMPUS was sold to the Canadian Navy as a training vessel. Plans were being made early this century to bring her back home to Barrow to go on permanent exhibition. Money was being raised but it became obvious that the cost of a tow or other means of transport from Halifax to Barrow would be prohibitive.

Around 2005 an offer was made by a Barrow born business man to present to Barrow another vessel of this class. She was HMS ONYX. The offer was accepted and the submarine was brought to Barrow-in-Furness from Merseyside where the submarine had been on public display since 1991. Regrettably, with the demise of the Barrow Submarine Heritage Centre project it proved impossible to retain HMS ONYX and she left Barrow in April 2014 for eventual scrap.

Class Information

The "Oberon" class was a follow up to the successful "Porpoise" class. It had the same propulsion machinery, displacement and dimensions. The pressure hull was made from higher-strength steel than the "Porpoise" class so it could dive deeper. The sonar equipment was more advanced than that of "Porpoise" class. The first

of class, HMS OBERON, had steel superstructure, the second, HMS ORPHEUS, had aluminium but all the rest used Glass Reinforced Plastic, the first wide use of GRP by the Admiralty. Three of the class were built at Barrow-in-Furness - HM Submarines OLYMPUS, ORPHEUS and OSIRIS.

In addition to the three "Oberon" class submarines built at Barrow-in-Furness another ten were built for the Royal Navy in other British Ship Yards. This was a very successful design and there were many overseas orders. Six were built for the Royal Australian Navy by Scott's of Greenock. Three more were built for the Royal Canadian Navy by Cammell Lairds. However, the Canadians refused to accept OJIB-WA when completed and an arrangement was reached whereby HMS ONYX (building at Chatham) was taken instead. HMCS OJIBWA became HMS ONYX. Later, after some of the "Oberon" class were paid off by the Royal Navy, ex-HMS OLYMPUS was bought by the Canadian Navy to cannibalise to keep their three boats operational. Three more of the class were built at Barrow for the Brazilian Navy and two were built at Scott's for the Chilean Navy.

Along with the "Porpoise" class, the "Oberon's" were rightly recognised as being probably the quietest and most effective conventional submarines in the world and, together, they became the work horses of the Royal Navy Submarine Service in the years of the Cold War. In the Royal Navy and four other Navy's the "Oberon" class gave long service in all parts of the world. HMS ONYX was the only conventional Royal Navy submarine involved in the Falklands war. She picked up Special Forces mid-Atlantic and carried them to a quiet beach where they were landed and carried out their required duties. By the early years of the 21st Century "Oberon" class submarines had been retired from service.

HMS OLYMPUS DATA

Builder:	Vickers Armstrong Ltd, Barrow-in-Furness Yard Number: 1060 Cost: £2,305,000
Significant Dates:	Ordered: 28th August 1956; Laid Down: March 1960; Launched: 14th July 1961; Completed: 7th July 1962
Dimensions:	Length: 295 feet 3 inches; Beam: 26 feet 6 inches; Draught: 18 feet 3 inches
Displacement:	Surfaced: 2,030 tons; Dived: 2,410 tons
Machinery:	Surfaced: 2 x 16 cylinder Admiralty Standard Range (ASR) diesel engines (3,680 bhp); Dived: 2 x electric motors (6,000 bhp)
Speed:	Surfaced: 12 knots; Dived: 17 knots
Endurance:	9,000 nautical miles at 12 knots
Armament:	6 x 21-inch forward torpedo tubes; 2 x 21-inch stern torpedo tubes; Thirty torpedoes carried
Complement:	69 Officers and Ratings.

This painting was a donation, as opposed to a commission, by Mrs Joan Cole of Barrow-in-Furness. Joan said *"Whilst having a coffee in the Forum 28 in Barrow during August 2001 I spotted a painting of the submarine HMS OLYMPUS by Tom Murphy. It was only the previous week that I had read an article in the local newspaper that a Submarine Heritage Centre was to be opened here in Barrow and that HMS OLYMPUS would possibly be the centre piece. I decided to purchase the painting and present it to the Submarine Heritage Centre when it is opened."*

HM SUBMARINES "DREADNOUGHT" CLASS
HMS DREADNOUGHT

The Painting and the HMS Dreadnought Story

The main picture is a montage of watercolours depicting, clockwise from top left, the keel laying ceremony performed by HRH the Duke of Edinburgh, the launch ceremony performed by Her Majesty the Queen, HMS DREADNOUGHT at the North Pole, the sinking of the disabled chemical tanker ESSENBERGER CHEMIST and various snapshot drawings, including the symbol of nuclear energy. The upper mount has two pencil drawings of HMS DREADNOUGHT. The lower mount shows previous warships named DREAD-NOUGHT. The most recent in a long line of firsts for HMS DREADNOUGHT is that this original painting was signed by HRH the Duke of Edinburgh at Buckingham Palace on 3rd December 2002. His signature is also on the lower mount.

HMS DREADNOUGHT (Pennant No. S101) spent much of her first commission trialling her new equipment and exercising with the Royal and United States Navies. In the five years of that commission, in which she travelled over 144,000 nautical miles, there were visits to Norfolk (USA), Bermuda, Southampton, Rotterdam and Kiel. In August 1965 she was visited by Her Majesty the Queen, HRH the Duke of Edinburgh, HRH Prince Charles, Princess Anne and six Admirals at the Home Fleet Review. Notable events in that commission included the sinking, in June 1967, of the disabled and drifting German chemical tanker ESSENBERGER CHEMIST using a salvo of four Mk. VIII Mod 4 torpedoes; between 10th September and 17th October 1967 she made a high speed transit dived from Faslane Submarine Base to Langkawi, Malaysia via the Cape of Good Hope carrying out exercises with Royal Navy and Royal Australian Navy units and returning from Singapore to Faslane between 18th November and 15th December 1967. This was a round trip of 31,185 nautical miles of which 25,545 miles were dived at an average speed of around 23 knots. She paid off at Rosyth Dockyard on 1 April 1968 for the first refit and refuelling of a nuclear submarine in the United Kingdom She re-commissioned' on 10th September 1970 and on 3rd March 1971, DREADNOUGHT was the first Royal Navy submarine to surface at the North Pole. In December 1980 cracks were discovered in the secondary cooling system requiring a complete reactor shutdown, the anticipated high costs of effecting a full repair to the unique design led to the decision to take her out of active service. She was laid-up afloat in 1983, awaiting a means of disposal.

Class Information

Recognising that notionally air independent submarines powered by the Walther cycle and peroxide (see EXPOLORER/EXCALIBUR page 72) would not keep the Royal Navy in

the front rank led to early British design work on nuclear propulsion. The first step was to expand work begun at Harwell in 1953; by 1956 a contract was placed to construct prototype nuclear propulsion machinery, with American cooperation and based on their reactor. The British consortium charged with this was Rolls-Royce, Foster-Wheeler and Vickers. The US Navy had begun nuclear propulsion studies in 1946 following the development of nuclear weapons and the Manhattan Project. The first US Navy nuclear submarine (NAUTILUS) was ordered in 1951 and became operational in January 1955. It became clear that it would be many years before a complete British nuclear propulsion package could put to sea. There were different views on how to proceed, the Royal Navy could either rely on the new Porpoise/Oberon diesel-electric submarines and live with the nuclear development timescales for the sake of national independence and prestige or continue the all British programme but also buy a complete American nuclear plant and put it in a British designed submarine, thus getting build and sea-going experience much sooner. The latter view won the day and led to HMS DREADNOUGHT.

However, initially the Americans insisted that this contract be solely with Rolls-Royce, whom they knew and trusted. This would have put Rolls-Royce in overall charge of Britain's future nuclear submarines as well being the single supplier of reactors. They found this an attractive prospect and for a time contemplated becoming submarine builders but it was not acceptable to the Admiralty or to Vickers, with the redoubtable Leonard Redshaw (later Sir Leonard) well to the fore, and the Americans were persuaded that this contract would best be handled by Vickers. Within Vickers there were disputes over whether the Shipbuilding Division or Engineering Division should hold the contract. Vickers Engineering had traditionally been responsible for ship and submarine machinery design and installation, and often its manufacture. Engineering's case was that, since building hulls was relatively simple, it was they who should hold the overall contract to provide the complex design and and engineering to build HMS DREADNOUGHT. Vickers Shipbuilding took a robustly different view and Leonard Redshaw led the Shipbuilding Division to deliver the DREADNOUGHT programme.

HMS DREADNOUGHT DATA

Builder:	Vickers Armstrong Ltd, Barrow-in-Furness	Yard Number: 1062 Cost: £18,500,000
Significant Dates:	Ordered: 1958; Laid Down: 12th June 1958; Launched: 21st October 1960; Completed: 17th April 1963	
Dimensions:	Length: 265 feet 9 inches; Beam: 32 feet 3 inches; Draught: 26 feet Displacement: Surfaced: 3,500 tons; Dived: 4,000 tons	
Machinery:	1 Westinghouse S5W pressurised water nuclear reactor; 2 Westinghouse steam turbines geared to a single shaft (15,000 shp) Diesel-electric auxiliary propulsion	
Speed:	Surfaced: 15 knots; Dived: 28 knots; Endurance: Limited only by stores carried.	
Armament:	4 x 21-inch torpedo tubes; 30 x Mk VIII Mod 4** and later, Mk 23 Wire Guided torpedoes	Complement: 11 Officers and 77 Ratings

This painting was commissioned by the Members of the Dreadnought Association. A spokesman for the Association commented as follows, *"This excellent painting is a fine tribute to both HMS DREADNOUGHT herself and to the Vickers Armstrong workforce that took up the challenge of a new era of submarine building so successfully."*

HM SUBMARINES "VALIANT" CLASS
HMS VALIANT

The Painting and the HMS VALIANT Story

The main picture is a watercolour showing HMS VALIANT leaving HMS NEPTUNE, the Faslane Naval Base, in the Gareloch, Western Scotland, with a helicopter in attendance. Also showing is the Faslane Floating Dock (AFD60) in the background. The lower mount shows from the left, HMS VALIANT (1864) which was renamed VALIANT III in 1897 and became an oil hulk in 1924 being sold in 1956 at almost a century old; next the HMS VALIANT badge; then the WW2 HMS VALIANT which was scrapped at Cairn Ryan in 1948 and on the right, HMS VALIANT (1914) firing a salvo.

HMS VALIANT, adopted by Barrow-in-Furness, was the first all British nuclear submarine, the American reactor and propulsion machinery of HMS DREADNOUGHT being replaced by British designed and manufactured equivalents. She was followed by the second of class HMS WARSPITE. Overall, the two boats were similar to HMS DREADNOUGHT but about 19 feet longer, in part to accommodate the British propulsion plant. In April 1967, HMS VALIANT set a new dived record for a British submarine when she completed the 12,000 mile dived passage from Singapore to the UK in 28 days. In 1982 she participated in the Falklands Campaign, when she transmitted more than 300 early air-warning alerts and spent 101 days on patrol off Argentina's coast. VALIANT suffered minor damage while submerged when an Argentine aircraft coming back from a mission jettisoned its bombs near the submarine. After 30 years of service HMS VALIANT was laid up at Devonport Dockyard in 1994 awaiting disposal.

Class Information

HMS VALIANT brought the Royal Navy into a new era, providing it with a submarine class that could keep up with, in fact outpace, the battle fleet. Fleet submarines became the striking power of the fleet in which they served, the new capital ships. They were also the most effective anti-submarine platform of the fleet. Their nuclear propulsion capability meant that they could remain at sea for extended periods, the only limitations being the amount of food that could be carried and the psychological effects on the ship's company of long submerged periods. From 1988, concerns arose over the class reactors and in consequence the submarines were not modernised as had been intended. They were gradually decommissioned and their nuclear fuel removed

---

HMS VALIANT DATA

Builder:	Vickers Armstrong (Shipbuilders) Ltd Barrow-in-Furness　　　Yard Number: 1066　　　Cost: £24,900,000
Significant Dates:	Ordered: August 1960; Laid Down: 22nd Jan 1962; Launched: 3rd Dec 1963; Completed: June 1966
Dimensions:	Length: 285 feet; Beam: 33 feet 3 inches; Draught: 27 feet
Displacement:	Surfaced: 3,500 tons; Dived: 4,500 tons
Machinery:	1 RR Pressurised Water Reactor supplying steam to 2 turbines (15,000 shp); 1 electric motor for emergency drive; 1 auxiliary retractable motor and propeller
Speed:	Surfaced: 20 knots; Dived: 28+ knots
Endurance:	Limited only by stores carried
Armaments:	6 - 21-inch bow torpedo tubes Mk 24 (Tigerfish) dual role Wire Guided torpedoes or up to 64 x Mk. 5 Stonefish mines or Mk. 6 Sea Urchin mines
Complement:	103 officers and ratings.

1863-1956 (RE-NAMED VALIANT III IN 1897)   VALIANT   WW2   1914-1948   WW1

This painting was sponsored by Mr. Tom Homewood.

HM SUBMARINES "RESOLUTION" (POLARIS) CLASS
HMS RESOLUTION

The Painting and the HMS Resolution Story

The main picture is a watercolour showing HMS RESOLUTION at sea. On the horizon are the four capital ships that had the same names as the "Polaris" class submarines, namely, from left to right, HMS RENOWN, HMS REPULSE, HMS RESOLUTION, and HMS REVENGE. The lower mount has two pencil drawings of POLARIS submarines whilst the upper mount has the four Polaris boats' badges. HMS RESOLUTION was commissioned in October 1967, four years from order, and went on her first operational patrol on schedule in June 1968. This despite Barrow's heavy workload in building two other nuclear submarines, HMS VALIANT and HMS WARSPITE whilst meeting the Polaris deadline. The second Vickers' "Polaris" submarine – HMS REPULSE was also commissioned on time in September 1968. HMS RESOLUTION was fitted in 1984 with the Chevaline upgrade to the Polaris missile system, which enabled it to fire missiles with multiple warheads able to be independently targeted. In 1991 HMS RESOLUTION carried out the longest ever Polaris patrol of 15 weeks and 3 days. HMS RESOLUTION was decommissioned with the introduction of the "Vanguard" class ballistic missile submarines in 1996.

Class Information

During the 1950s and early 1960s, Britain's nuclear deterrent was based around the Royal Air Force's V Bombers. However, by the early 1960s developments detection and defence meant that bombers were vulnerable, and unlikely to penetrate successfully Soviet airspace; free-fall nuclear weapons would no longer be a credible deterrent. In May 1960 Britain agreed with the US to equip the V-bombers with a US designed 1,000-mile range ballistic missile, Skybolt, allowing launching bombers to remain well clear of Soviet defences. By 1962 there were serious reservation in the US over the Skybolt programme. The US broached the idea of cancelling Skybolt with Britain in November 1962.

When this was reported a storm of protest broke out and the Prime Minister, Harold Macmillan, insisted that the UK would retain an independent nuclear deterrent capability. After intense discussions the US and Britain concluded the Nassau Agreement which allowed Britain to purchase the Polaris Submarine Launched Ballistic Missile (SLBM) system, and fit the missiles with British warheads. The Polaris submarine launched ballistic missile system would enter service with the Royal Navy in 1968 and the V-bombers withdrawn from the nuclear role in 1969. The submarine design was to be based on the "Valiant" class, with a section added to accommodate sixteen vertical missile tubes, but there was much new design and engineering work involved, most obviously integration with the US missile system. The missiles, their fittings and their control and firing system were brought from America and integrated into the submarine by Vickers at Barrow. The massive achievement of the shipyard, the MoD and British industry in delivering the Polaris programme on time and budget was not as widely recognised as it deserved. Design began in early 1963 and by May 1963 Vickers were appointed as lead yard and builder of two of the four submarines; the other two to be built by Cammell Laird in Birkenhead. The contract required that the first, HMS RESOLUTION, be operational within 5 years by 1968. The original plan was for a class of five submarines (the 5th would have been RAMILLIES) to ensure that two "Polaris" class submarines were always at sea on deterrent patrol. In the event only four were built as a cost saving move by the then new Labour Government. That decision placed enormous pressure on the Polaris submarine force because it was required to maintain a boat on patrol at all times. By using two crews (Port and Starboard), tight refit and maintenance schedules the "Resolution" class or 'Bombers' met the requirement and carried out deterrent patrols for thirty years without a break, until the introduction of the "Vanguard" class Trident missile submarines. When the final Polaris patrol was completed in 1996, the four "Resolution" class submarines had carried out a total of 229 patrols between them.

HMS RESOLUTION DATA

Builder:	Vickers Ltd. (Shipbuilding Group), Barrow-in-Furness Yard Number: 1074 Cost: £40,200,000
Significant Dates:	Ordered: 8th May 1963; Laid Down: 26th Feb 1964; Launched: 15th Sep 1966; Commissioned: 3rd Oct 1967
Dimensions:	Length: 425 feet; Beam: 33 feet; Draught: 30 feet
Displacement:	Surfaced: 7,500 tons; Dived: 8,400 tons
Machinery:	1 RR Pressurised Water Reactor supplying steam to 2 turbines (15,000 shp); 1 electric motor for emergency drive; 1 auxiliary retractable motor and propeller
Speed:	25+ knot
Endurance:	100,000 nautical miles (approx) and patrols limited only by stores carried
Armament:	Sixteen x A3 Polaris missiles with a range of 2,500 miles; Six x 21-inch bow torpedo tubes
Complement:	140 Officers and Ratings

This painting was commissioned by the Officers and Men of the 1st Submarine Squadron based at HM Naval Base, Clyde (Faslane) May 2002.

HM SUBMARINES "IMPROVED VALIANT" CLASS
HMS CHURCHILL

The Painting and the HMS CHURCHILL Story

The main picture is a watercolour showing HMS CHURCHILL at sea. Astern is HMS CHURCHILL from WW2, a 'lease-lend' destroyer, ex USS HERADON. Abeam is the Arleigh Burke Class destroyer USS WINSTON S CHURCHILL, the only ship in the United States Navy to be named after a foreign statesman, although Churchill's mother was an American. The lower mount shows, from left to right, Winston Churchill, a stern view of HMS CHURCHILL, the ship's crest and a trawler called CHURCHILL owned by Consolidated Fisheries Ltd., Grimsby.

HMS CHURCHILL was launched by Mary Soames, Winston Churchill's youngest daughter, and commissioned into the Royal Navy in 1971 where she spent the next twenty years carrying out routine Cold War patrols and other submarine tasks. Churchill was chosen to trial the first full-size submarine pump jet shrouded propeller (propulsor) system. Trials of a high-speed unit were followed by further trials with a low-speed unit, and these were successful enough for the same propulsion to be fitted in the rest of the class. Later Royal Navy submarine classes also featured the pump jet. The submarine was decommissioned in 1991 and laid up at Rosyth Dockyard in Scotland.

Class Information

This was a class of three fleet submarines, more commonly known as 'Hunter-Killers' (NATO designation - Ship Submersible Nuclear [SSN]), HMS CHURCHILL and

HMS COURAGEOUS built at Barrow, and HMS CONQUEROR built by Cammell Laird at Birkenhead. Although identified here as a separate class, they were "Valiant" class Submarines but their build was delayed to some years after VALIANT and WARSPITE in order to allow the more build of the strategic deterrent Polaris submarines. The three boats therefore incorporated the build and operational experience of the previous six nuclear submarines and also upgraded electronic surveillance equipment. HMS CONQUEROR (Commander Christopher Wreford-Brown, Royal Navy) deployed to the Falkland Islands in 1982 and sank the Argentine Cruiser GENERAL BELGRANO (ex USS PHOENIX) with a salvo of three Mark VIII Mod 4** torpedoes. He was awarded the DSO for the attack.

HMS CONQUEROR was decommissioned in 1992 and laid up at Devonport as was HMS COURAGEOUS in 1992. COURAGEOUS was selected for the museum ship to represent the SSN fleet of the Royal Navy during the Cold War and is on display at the Devonport Naval Heritage Centre, Plymouth. Organised groups and coach groups are welcome, subject to the visit being pre-arranged and accompanied by authorised guides and escorts.

HMS CHURCHILL DATA

Builder:	Vickers Ltd. Shipbuilding Group, Barrow-in-Furness.　　　　　Yard Number:　1076
Significant Dates:	Ordered: 21st October 1965; Laid Down: 30th June 1967; Launched: 20th December 1968; Commissioned: 15th July 1970
Dimensions:	Length: 285 feet; Beam: 33 feet 3 inches; Draught: 27 feet
Displacement:	Surfaced: 3,500 tons; Dived: 4,500 tons
Machinery:	1 RR Pressurised Water Reactor supplying steam to 2 turbines (15,000 shp); 1 electric motor for emergency drive; 1 auxiliary retractable motor and propeller
Speed:	25+ knots surfaced, 28+ knots dived
Endurance:	Limited only by amount of stores carried.
Armament:	Six x 21-inch bow torpedo tubes; Twenty six reloads Mk 24 Tigerfish Mod II and/or Sub-Harpoon missiles
Complement:	13 officers 90 ratings

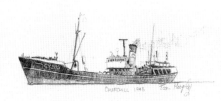

This painting was sponsored by Mike (Ginge) Cundell who was a member of the Submariners Association, Barrow-in-Furness Branch. Mike served aboard HMS CHURCHILL's two sister submarines (HMS COURAGEOUS – Vickers Ltd. and HMS CONQUEROR – Cammell Laird), from 1970 to 1976. Mike commented as follows: *"These fine submarines gave outstanding service to our country, and were considered the work horses of the fleet at that time."*

HM SUBMARINES "SWIFTSURE" CLASS
HMS SOVEREIGN

The Painting and the HMS Sovereign Story

The main picture is a watercolour depicting HMS SOVEREIGN (1970s) passing the previous HMS ROYAL SOVEREIGN, a Battleship (1915-1949). The lower mount shows two sketches of "Swiftsure" class submarines at sea. HMS SOVEREIGN was the second of class of six "Swiftsure" nuclear powered submarines all of which were built at Barrow-in-Furness. Termed Fleet Submarines, but more usually known as 'Hunter Killers', their role was to protect Britain's Strategic Deterrent Polaris ballistic missile submarines; to undertake surveillance and monitoring of hostile nations; to track the submarines and surface shipping of the Soviet Union; to participate in Anti Submarine Warfare (ASW) and to attack ships and land targets.

HMS SOVEREIGN carried out operational Cold War patrols and other submarine tasks throughout her commissions. She also sailed under the Arctic ice cap and surfaced at the geographical North Pole in 1976 as part of Operation Brisk. SOVEREIGN was decommissioned in September 2006.

Class Information

This was the third class of British nuclear submarines. The first of class, HMS SWIFT-SURE, became operational in 1973. Their hulls are about 13 feet shorter than the preceding "Valiant" class and their flat upper casing gives them a very different appearance. Unlike the "Valiant" class, the fore planes were retractable, were set much lower and were not visible shen the boat was on the surface. They were the first British submarines to be fitted as standard with anechoic tiles, designed to reduce significantly their acoustic signature and make them more difficult to detect. They were also the first to substitute the conventional propeller for a pump-jet propulsor (shrouded propeller), again in interests of signature reduction.

The submarines of the Class were: HMS SWIFTSURE, HMS SOVEREIGN, HMS SUPERB, HMS SCEPTRE, HMS SPARTAN and HMS SPLENDID.

HMS SWIFTSURE was the first of the class to be de-commissioned in 1992 after the discovery of a reactor problem and was laid up at Rosyth. Despite similar problems, which significantly reduced their operational availability, the remaining five submarines were kept in service and modified to launch Tomahawk land attack cruise missiles (TLAM). The remaining five boats of the class were progressively retired from service and, on 10th December 2010, the last of the class, HMS SCEPTRE, was de-commissioned. They are laid up in the Dockyards at Devonport and Rosyth awaiting a decision on disposal.

HMS SOVEREIGN DATA

Builder:	Vickers Ltd. Shipbuilding Group, Barrow-in-Furness Yard Number: 1086
Significant Dates:	Ordered: 1969; Laid Down: 17th Sep 1970; Launched: 17th Feb 1973; Commissioned: 9th Jul 1974
Dimensions:	Length: 272 feet; Beam: 32¼ feet; Draught: 27 feet
Displacement:	Surfaced: 4,400 tons; Dived: 4,900 tons
Machinery:	1 Rolls-Royce Pressurised Water Reactor (PWR-1) supplying steam to 2 turbines (15,000 shp); 1 electric motor for emergency drive and 1 pump-jet propulsor; 1 auxiliary retractable motor and propeller
Speed:	30+ knots dived
Endurance:	Limited only by amount of stores carried
Armaments:	Five x 21-inch bow torpedo tubes; Twenty reload Mk 24 Mod 2 Tigerfish torpedoes and/or Sub-Harpoon missiles.
Complement:	97 Officers and Ratings

This painting was commissioned by Captain Richard E. Crawford, Royal Navy. Captain Crawford (at the time a Lieutenant) stood by HMS SOVEREIGN during her build at Barrow-in-Furness and served on board for the first commission.

HM SUBMARINES "TRAFALGAR" CLASS
HMS TRAFALGAR

The Painting and the HMS TRAFALGAR Story

The main picture is a watercolour showing HMS TRAFALGAR at sea with the WW2 "Battle" class destroyer of the same name. The lower mount shows a stern view of the submarine and HMS TRAFALGAR being launched. Like the other SSNs of the flotilla HMS TRAFALGAR carried out Cold War patrols and other submarine tasks. In a recent history of the Royal Navy's Submarine Service 'The Silent Deep' TRAFALGAR is credited with trailing a Soviet Victor III class submarine, commanded by a particularly experienced Soviet submariner nicknamed 'The Prince of Darkness', for several days from ranges as close as 600 yards. In 2001 she fired a missile strike against the Taliban in Afghanistan. On the 4th December 2009, HMS TRAFALGAR was the first of the class to be decommissioned.

Class Information

All seven submarines of this class were built at Barrow-in-Furness, making it to date the largest class of nuclear submarines built for the Royal Navy. HMS TRAFALGAR, HMS TURBULENT, HMS TIRELESS, HMS TORBAY, HMS TRENCHANT, HMS TALENT and HMS TRIUMPH. They were intended to replace the DREADNOUGHT and the "Valiant" class, joining the "Swiftsure" class to bring SSN numbers to 13. The design was effectively SWIFTSURE with improvements to make them faster, quieter and improve endurance. Like the "Swiftsure" class, they were covered in anechoic tiles, but with better adhesive (the "Swiftsure" class had a tendency to lose tiles, making them more detectable and giving them a somewhat bedraggled appearance after time at sea). "Trafalgars" are about eight feet longer than the "Swiftsure" class, and have a larger displacement. All have been upgraded to fire Tomahawk cruise missiles, giving them the ability to hit targets far from the sea. In 2017 three of the class, TRENCHANT, TALENT and TRIUMPH, remain in service as the workhorses of the Submarine Flotilla but are being successively replaced as the "Astute" class are commissioned.

HMS Trafalgar Data

Builder:	British Shipbuilders-Vickers Shipbuilding Group, Barrow-in-Furness	Yard Number:	1100
Significant Dates:	Ordered: 7th Sep 1977; Laid Down: 1977; Launched: 1st July 1981; Commissioned: 27th May 1983		
Dimensions:	Length: 85.4 metres; Beam: 9.83 metres; Draught: 9.5 metres		
Displacement:	Surfaced: 4,700 tonnes; Dived: 5,208 tonnes		
Machinery:	1 RR Pressurised Water Reactor supplying steam to 2 turbines (15,000 shp); 1 electric motor for emergency drive;1 auxiliary retractable motor and propeller		
Speed:	25+ knots		
Endurance:	Limited only by amount of stores carried.		
Armament:	5 x 21-inch bow torpedo tubes; Spearfish or Mk 24 Mod 2 Tigerfish torpedoes and/or Sub Harpoon/Tomahawk missiles		
Complement:	130 Officers and Ratings.		

The Morecambe Bay Branch of the Submariners Association has always had a very close relationship with the Ship's Company of HMS TRAFALGAR. Branch Secretary Craig Farebrother comments as follows: "When we as a Branch were approached by a presentation team from the Barrow Submarine Heritage Collection, and we saw the quality of the paintings that had been completed at that time, the Branch voted unanimously to sponsor a painting for this collection. When advised that a commission had not yet been placed for the nuclear submarine HMS TRAFALGAR, and due to our close relationship with this particular submarine, this is the painting our Branch chose to commission. Now that we have had sight of the completed painting we are more than pleased with the result."

HM SUBMARINES "UPHOLDER" CLASS
HMS UPHOLDER/HMCS CHICOUTIMI

The Painting and the HMS Upholder Story

The main picture shows the four submarines of this class in their new life as the Canadian Navy's "Victoria" class, entering an inlet on the Canadian coastline, escorted by killer whales and pintado petrels. The lower mount has the ship's badges of each of the four boats from left to right HMS UNSEEN HMCS VICTORIA (HMS UNSEEN); HMCS WINDSOR (HMS UNICORN); HMCS CORNER BROOK (HMS URSULA); and HMCS CHICOUTIMI (HMS UPHOLDER), a profile of one of the class and the Canadian national flag.

HMS UPHOLDER was the only vessel of this class of four to be built at Barrow-in-Furness. She was commissioned into the Royal Navy in June 1990 but by this time the Cold War was drawing to a close. She was de-commissioned in the mid 1990's and laid up in Barrow docks together with the other three vessels of the class. In 1998 it was agreed that the four boats would be leased to the Canadians following a refit to convert them to Canadian Navy standards. HMS UPHOLDER was renamed HMCS CHICOUTIMI. Following refit and refurbishment HMCS CHICOUTIMI sailed for Canada in 2004 but, while on passage from Faslane to Halifax, Nova Scotia she was damaged by an electrical fire when water entered the submarine and shorted out electrical circuits. Three crew members were overcome by smoke and one died. The submarine returned to the UK and was later taken to Canada by transport ship in 2005. Repairs in Canada were much delayed but by 2014 CHICOUTIMI was repaired and the boat was officially re-commissioned into the Royal Canadian Navy in September 2015. All four submarines are currently (2017) in service.

Class Information

The introduction of a new conventionally powered class of submarines was decided upon in the 70s in order to replace the "Porpoise" and "Oberon" class boats and maintain submarine hull numbers without incurring the time and costs of building additional nuclear submarines. The final design was known as the Vickers Type 2400 (2,400 tons, 24,000 patrol range and 28 days on station) becoming the "Upholder" class in 1980. Although the Royal Navy, unusually, agreed to vary its requirements to improve export prospects, the performance levels and standards required by the Navy resulted in the class being almost nuclear submarines without nuclear power, with high-tech sensor, control and weapon systems. The outcome was that the class was both too expensive and too sophisticated for potential export customers.

Commissioned as the Cold War was ending, it was first decided that the class would be limited to four submarines and then that the RN would not operate both diesel-electric and nuclear submarines. The boats were withdrawn from service in 1994 as a cost saving measure and put up for sale. That decision not only killed the export potential for the class but it also meant that Barrow's export market in the submarine field would be limited to the sale of technology, services and material (nuclear submarines cannot be exported). MoD(N) was persuaded to lay up the class at Barrow-in-Furness under Vickers' care and to make the company their preferred supplier for their post-sale refit and support. On 2nd July 1998 an agreement was reached between the Governments of Great Britain and Canada for the lease and support of the four boats for a period of eight years at a cost of over £250 million, with an option to purchase them at a later date. VSEL refitted the boats for MoD(N) and provided ongoing support services to Canada. The four boats were re-commissioned into the Canadian Navy as:

HMS UNSEEN:	HMCS VICTORIA	December 2000
HMS URSULA:	HMCS CORNER BROOK	March 2003
HMS UNICORN:	HMCS WINDSOR	June 2003
HMS UPHOLDER:	HMCS CHICOUTIMI	September 2004

HMS UPHOLDER DATA

Builder:	Vickers Shipbuilding and Engineering Ltd, Barrow-in-Furness	Yard Number:	1106

Significant Dates:	Ordered: 2nd November 1983; Laid down: November 1986; Launched: 2nd December 1986
Dimensions:	Length: 230 feet 6 inches; Beam: 25 feet; Draught: 17 feet 9 inches
Displacement:	Surfaced: 2,200 tons; Dived: 2,455 tons
Machinery:	Two x Paxman Valenta 1600 RPA-200SZ diesels powering two x 1.4 Mw GEC Alternators; One x GEC electric motor 5,400 bhp; Single shaft
Speed:	Surfaced: 12 knots; Snorting: 12 knots; Dived: 20 knots
Endurance:	8,000 nautical miles at 8 knots snorting
Armament:	Six x 21-inch bow torpedo tubes; Twelve reloads of GEC Marconi Tigerfish Mk 24 Mod 2 Torpedoes and/or Sub Harpoon missiles and/or Stonefish mines
Complement:	46 Officers and Ratings

GEMC Ltd. are pleased to sponsor the painting in recognition of the unique relationship between Canada and the United Kingdom.

HM SUBMARINES "VANGUARD" CLASS
HMS VANGUARD

The Painting and the HMS VANGUARD Story

The main picture is a watercolour showing HMS VANGUARD leading the other "Vanguard" class submarines, escorted by Merlin helicopters. The lower mount has previous ships with the same names as the submarines of this class, along with their crests. These are the battleship HMS VANGUARD, the aircraft carrier HMS VICTORIOUS as-built and as-rebuilt, the destroyer HMS VIGILANT as-built and as-rebuilt and the aircraft carrier HMS VENGEANCE, which was sold to Brazil and renamed MINAS GERAIS.

All four of the class were built by Vickers Shipbuilding and Engineering PLC at Barrow-in-Furness. HMS VANGUARD was the first nuclear submarine to have the new Pressurised Water Reactor (PWR2) installed. In June 1994 HMS VANGUARD launched her first Trident missile off Cape Canaveral, Florida. In 2004 she completed a major refit and in October 2005, VANGUARD concluded her return to service trials DASO (Demonstration and Shakedown Operations) with the firing of an unarmed Trident missile. In February 2009 VANGUARD collided with the French submarine TRIOMPHANT in the Atlantic, she returned to base 10 days later under her own power. She remains in service and undertaking routine deterrent patrols.

Class Information

The decision to replace the Polaris missile system with the Trident system required new submarines, by far the biggest ever built for the Royal Navy. Unlike Polaris, where Britain bought its own stock of missiles, Britain leased 65 Trident II D-5 missiles from a larger pool of weapons based in the United States. The US would maintain and support the missiles and the UK would manufacture its own warheads to go on the missiles. When a "Vanguard" class submarine needs to change its missiles, it travels to the USA, exchanges the missiles (less their warheads) for new and then returns to Britain, where British warheads are fitted. The class came into service as the Cold War was ending and, in consequence, their continued operation had to be reconsidered.

The Government has defined the Strategic Deterrent's purpose as being 'to deter the most extreme threats to [British] national security and way of life, which cannot be done by other means'. The aim being to halt a would-be aggressor, first by a limited and selective nuclear strike capability (through equipping some missiles with only a single nuclear warhead of relatively low explosive power), whilst also carrying some missiles with a full, multiple warhead nuclear capability, should the need arise. Like their Polaris predecessors, the "Vanguard" class submarines operate with two crews (Port and Starboard) to maximise hull utilisation. All four "Vanguard" class remain in service in 2017 but will be replaced in service by the successor "Dreadnought" class from 2028.

HMS VANGUARD DATA

Builder:	Vickers Shipbuilding and Engineering PLC, Barrow-in-Furness. Yard Number: 1109
Significant Dates:	Ordered: 1980; Laid down: 3rd September 1986; Rolled out: 4th March 1992; Commissioned: 14th August 1993
Dimensions:	Length: 492 feet; Beam: 42 feet; Draught: 39¼ feet
Displacement:	Submerged: 15,000 tonnes.
Machinery:	New design of pressurised water nuclear reactor; 2 steam turbines geared to single shaft (27,500 shp); Diesel electric emergency propulsion (2,700 bhp)
Endurance:	Limited only by amount of stores carried.
Armament:	Sixteen Trident II Submarine Launched Ballistic Missiles, range 7,500 miles; Four x 21-inch bow torpedo tubes firing Spearfish torpedoes
Complement:	135 Officers and Ratings (2 crews per boat)

Furness Plastics Ltd. are most pleased to sponsor this painting in celebration of the involvement of the people in the Furness area in the development and build of this class of vessel and the direct involvement of Furness Plastics with the Shipyard, in facets of the build programme.

HM SUBMARINES "ASTUTE" CLASS
HMS ASTUTE

The Painting

The painting, a watercolour, shows on the left HMS ASTUTE leaving for Sea Trials with Devonshire Dock Hall in the background. To the left of HMS ASTUTE is a Merlin helicopter which flew over the Naming Ceremony. On the right of the picture is a view of the WW2 HMS ASTUTE sailing into Barrow Docks with the shipyard skyline as it would have appeared then.

At the top centre are the Submarine Service's Dolphins surmounted by a crown. The lower mount shows, at bottom left the keel laying ceremony for HMS ASTUTE and at bottom right the submarine's Sponsor, HRH Camilla, Duchess of Cornwall at the launching ceremony accompanied by Mr Murray Easton, Shipyard Managing Director. Between these two pictures are the crests of the first four of the class - HMS ASTUTE, HMS AMBUSH, HMS ARTFUL and HMS AUDACIOUS, with the signatures of HRH Camilla, Duchess of Cornwall, Commodore Steve Lloyd, Royal Navy, Mr Murray Easton and Commander Mike Walliker, Royal Navy, the first Commanding Officer of HMS ASTUTE.

Class Information

In the late 1980's, looking to a "Trafalgar" class successor, MoD(N) involved Barrow shipyard in studies for an entirely new design, termed SSN-20 or the "W" class. By 1990 it was evident that its cost would be too high for post Cold War budgets to bear and work was stopped. It was decided to proceed instead in a less ambitious way, using as a basis the current "Trafalgar" class fitted with the new reactor then just going to sea in the "Vanguard" class. From this developed the much larger "Astute" class. Three "Astute" class submarines, ASTUTE, ARTFUL and AMBUSH, from a projected class of seven, were ordered on 17th March 1997. HMS ASTUTE was named by her Sponsor, Camilla, Duchess of Cornwall, at roll-out on 8th June

2007 and was commissioned into service at Faslane on 27th August 2010. AMBUSH was commissioned in March 2013 and ARTFUL in March 1916. Two more of the class, AUDACIOUS & ANSON, were ordered in August 2007 and AGAMEMNON was ordered in March 2010. AUDACIOUS was launched in 2017 and is expected to become operational in 2018 with ANSON expected to launch in 2019 and commission in 2020. The seventh of the class is expected to be named AJAX, for which steel has been cut, with commissioning planned for 2024. The largest attack submarines ever built for the Royal Navy at 7,400 tonnes, the "Astute" class will be based at Faslane on the Clyde and each will be operated by the Royal Navy for twenty-five years without needing to be refuelled.

In a move that ended almost 40 years of what had been effectively a monopoly, MoD(N) decided in 1992 that rather than simply award the build contract to Barrow it should compete against other bidders. In 1994 two consortia bid, GEC-Marconi with BMT and Barrow (VSEL) with Rolls-Royce. The contract was won by the GEC-Marconi consortium. Barrow had no place in GEC's submarine plans their winning bid had assumed that technical and support work would be done by a labour force in the south of England and that, with their partners, the submarines would be built on a new, greenfield site. However, in 1995 GEC bought out VSEL to become owner of Barrow's modern submarine construction facility and employer of an experienced labour force; GEC changed its plans to include Barrow. As design work progressed the quoted timescales and costs that had been influential in GEC winning the contract became steadily apparent to both GEC and MOD (N). Before matters came to a head, GEC was taken over in 1999 by BAE Systems. The contract was re-negotiated amidst much publicity to reflect realistic timescales and costs and, in an echo of HOLLAND a century earlier, the Barrow in Furness labour force was bolstered by personnel seconded from Electric Boat in America.

HMS ASTUTE DATA

Builder:	GEC Marconi (now BAE Submarine Solutions Ltd) Yard Number: 1122
Significant Dates:	Ordered: 17th March 1997; Laid Down: 31st Jan 2001; Rolled Out: 8th June 2007; Launched: 14th Jun 2007
Dimensions:	Length: 97 metres; Beam: 10.4 metres; Draught: 11 metres
Displacement:	Surfaced: 7,000 tonnes; Dived: 7400 tonnes
Machinery:	1 Rolls-Royce pressurised water nuclear reactor; 2 GEC steam turbines geared to single shaft (27,500 shp) Diesel electric emergency propulsion (2,700 bhp)
Endurance:	Limited only by amount of stores carried.
Armament:	Six x 533-mm (21-inch) Torpedo Tubes; Thirty two reloads Spearfish torpedoes and TLAM (Tomahawk land attack cruise missiles).
Complement:	98 Officers and Ratings

This painting of HMS ASTUTE was commissioned by the ASTUTE Submarine IPT (Implementation Project Team) based both at Barrow-in-Furness and at MoD Abbeywood using funds raised by Members of the IPT at both Sites.

Yard No.	Name	Laid Down	Launched	Comments
143	NORDENFELT	Not known	14 Apr 1886	Served in Turkish Navy. Sold to Danish owners in 1890. Scrapped 1921
149	NORDENFELT	Not known	25 Mar 1887	Wrecked off Jutland on passage to Russia. Sold to Danish Owner and Scrapped
280	Holland No. 1	Not known	02 Oct 1901	Lost off Eddystone Light on tow in 1913. Salvaged in 1983. On display at Royal Navy Submarine Museum, Gosport
281	Holland No. 2	Not known	21 Jan 1902	Sold for scrap Oct 1913
282	Holland No. 3	Not known	10 Jun 1902	Lost on tow to breakers 08 Aug 1912
283	Holland No. 4	Not known	09 May 1902	Sunk as gunnery target 17 Oct 1912
284	Holland No. 5	Not known	23 May 1902	Sold for scrap Oct 1913
285	A1	19 Feb 1902	09 Jul 1902	Lost in Solent 18 Mar 1904. Raised Apr 1904 and refitted. Sunk in trials in Aug 1911
294	A2	06 Nov 1902	16 Apr 1903	Foundered Bomb Ketch Lake, Portsmouth Harbour Jan 1919. Raised & Sold 22 Oct 1925, scrapped at Pounds of Portsmouth
295	A3	06 Nov 1902	09 May 1903	Lost 02 Feb 1912 in Solent collision with HMS HAZARD. Raised but later sunk in gunnery trials
296	A4	06 Nov 1902	09 Jun 1903	Sold 16 Jan 1920 and scrapped by J H Lee of Bembridge, Isle of Wight
303	A5	01 Sep 1903	03 Mar 1904	Broken up at Portsmouth Dockyard 1920
304	A6	01 Sep 1903	03 Mar 1904	Sold 16 Jan 1920 and scrapped by J H Lee of Bembridge, Isle of Wight
305	A7	01 Sep 1903	23 Jan 1905	Sunk in accident off Plymouth 16 Jan 1914
306	A8	01 Sep 1903	23 Jan 1905	Sold 08 Oct 1920 and scrapped by Phillips of Dartmouth
307	A9	01 Sep 1903	08 Feb 1905	Broken up 1920
308	A10	01 Sep 1903	08 Feb 1905	Sold 01 Apr 1919 to the Ardrossan Dockyard Company and scrapped
309	A11	01 Sep 1903	08 Mar 1905	Broken up Portsmouth Dockyard in May 1920
310	A12	01 Sep 1903	08 Mar 1905	Sold 16 Jan 1920 and scrapped by J H Lee of Bembridge, Isle of Wight
311	A13	01 Sep 1903	18 Apr 1905	First diesel powered British submarine. Broken up at Portsmouth 1920
312	B1 (ex A14)	Not known	25 Oct 1904	Sold 25 Aug 1921 to J Smiths of Poole and scrapped
320	B2	Not known	19 Aug 1905	Lost on 14 Oct 1912 in collision with SS AMERIKA in Dover Straits
321	B3	Not known	31 Oct 1905	Sold 20 Dec 1919 to J Jackson and scrapped
322	B4	Not known	14 Nov 1905	Sold 01 Apr 1919 to the Ardrossan Dockyard Company and scrapped
323	B5	Not known	14 Nov 1905	Sold 25 Aug 1921 to A J Anderson, transferred to J Smiths of Poole and scrapped
324	B6	Not known	30 Nov 1905	Converted to Surface Patrol Vessel late in WW1. Sold at Malta 1919 and scrapped
325	B7	Not known	30 Nov 1905	Converted to Surface Patrol Vessel late in WW1. Sold at Malta 31 Oct 1919 and scrapped
326	B8	Not known	30 Nov 1905	Converted to Surface Patrol Vessel late in WW1. Sold at Malta 1919 and scrapped
327	B9	Not known	24 Jan 1906	Converted to Surface Patrol Vessel late in WW1. Sold at Malta 1919 and scrapped

Yard No.	Name	Laid Down	Launched	Comments
328	B10	Not known	23 Mar 1906	Sunk by bombing at Venice 9 Aug 1916. Raised, burnt out accidentally and scrapped
329	B11	Not known	21 Feb 1906	Converted to Surface Patrol Vessel late in WW1. Sold at Malta 1919 and scrapped
334	C1	13 Nov 1905	10 Jul 1906	Sold 22 Oct 1920 to Stanlee, resold to Young of Sunderland and scrapped
335	C2	13 Nov 1905	10 Jul 1906	Sold 08 Oct 1920 to Maden and Mckee and scrapped
336	C3	25 Nov 1905	03 Oct 1906	Expended as block ship at Zeebrugge 23 Apr 1918
337	C4	25 Nov 1905	18 Oct 1906	Sold 28 Feb 1922 to the Hallamshire Metal Company and scrapped
338	C5	24 Nov 1905	20 Aug 1906	Sold 31 Oct 1919 at Malta and scrapped
339	C6	24 Nov 1905	20 Aug 1906	Sold 20 Nov 1919 to J A Walker and scrapped
340	C7	09 Dec 1905	15 Feb 1907	Sold 20 Dec 1919 to J Jackson and scrapped
341	C8	09 Dec 1905	15 Feb 1907	Sold 22 Oct 1920 to Stanlee, resold to Young of Sunderland and scrapped
342	C9	30 Jan 1906	03 Apr 1907	Sold Jul 1922 to Stanlee and scrapped
343	C10	30 Jan 1906	15 Apr 1907	Sold Jul 1922 to Stanlee and scrapped
346	C11	04 Apr 1906	17 May 1907	Lost 14 Jul 1909 in collision with SS EDDYSTONE off Cromer
350	D1	14 May 1907	16 May 1908	First of class of Submarines with Diesel Engines as standard fit. Sunk as gunnery target 23 Oct 1918
351	C12	27 Nov 1906	09 Sep 1907	Sold 02 Feb 1920 to J H Lee and scrapped
352	C13	29 Nov 1906	09 Nov 1907	Sold 02 Feb 1920 J H Lee and scrapped
353	C14	04 Dec 1906	07 Dec 1907	Sold 05 Dec 1921 to C A Beard of Upnor and scrapped
354	C15	07 Dec 1906	21 Jan 1908	Sold 28 Feb 1922 to the Hallamshire Metal Company and scrapped
355	C16	14 Dec 1906	19 Mar 1908	Sold 12 Aug 1922 to C A Beard of Upnor and scrapped
366	No.8	Not known	19 May 1908	'C' Class submarine for Japan – renamed Ha. 1 in 1920s. Paid Off Dec 1929 and scrapped.
367	No.9	Not known	19 May 1908	'C' Class submarine for Japan – renamed Ha. 2 in 1920s. Paid Off Dec 1929 and scrapped.
375	C21	04 Feb 1908	26 Sep 1908	Sold to C A Beard of Upnor on 15 Dec 1921 and scrapped
376	C22	04 Feb 1908	10 Oct 1908	Sold 02 Feb 1920 to J H Lee and scrapped
377	C23	07 Feb 1908	26 Nov 1908	Sold 05 Dec 1921 to C A Beard of Upnor and scrapped
378	C24	12 Feb 1908	26 Nov 1908	Sold to B Fryer of Sunderland on 26 May 1921 and scrapped
379	C25	27 Feb 1908	10 Mar 1909	Sold 05 Dec 1921 to C A Beard of Upnor and scrapped
380	C26	14 Feb 1908	20 Mar 1909	Scuttled in Baltic 04 Apr 1918
381	C27	04 Jun 1908	22 Apr 1909	Scuttled in Baltic 05 Apr 1918
382	C28	06 Mar 1908	22 Apr 1909	Sold to B Fryer of Sunderland on 25 Aug 1921 and scrapped
383	C29	04 Jun 1908	19 Jun 1909	Mined in North Sea 29 Aug 1915
384	C30	10 Jun 1908	19 Jul 1909	Sold to B Fryer of Sunderland on 25 Aug 1921 and scrapped
387	C31	07 Jan 1909	02 Sep 1909	Lost off Belgian Coast 04 Jan 1915
388	C32	12 Jan 1909	29 Sep 1909	Blown up by own crew after running aground in the Baltic on 17 Oct 1917

Yard No.	Name	Laid Down	Launched	Comments
390	D2	14 May 1907	25 May 1910	Sunk by gunfire in the Ems Estuary 25 Nov 1914
391	C35	03 Mar 1909	02 Nov 1909	Scuttled in Baltic 05 Apr 1918
392	C36	03 Mar 1909	30 Nov 1909	Sold 25 Jun 1919 and scrapped at Hong Kong
393	C37	07 Apr 1909	01 Jan 1910	Sold 25 Jun 1919 and scrapped at Hong Kong
394	C38	05 Apr 1910	10 Feb 1910	Sold 25 Jun 1919 and scrapped at Hong Kong
397/8/9				Engines for Japanese 'C' class Submarines - built under licence in Japan
403	D3	10 Jul 1909	17 Oct 1910	Lost in English Channel on 15 Mar 1918. Bombed in error by French Airship
404	D4	15 Mar 1910	27 May 1910	Sold to H Pound of Portsmouth on 19 Dec 1921 and scrapped
405	D5	03 Feb 1910	28 Aug 1911	Mined off Great Yarmouth 03 Nov 1914
406	D6	24 Feb 1910	23 Oct 1911	Torpedoed off Ulster by UB-73 26 Jun 1918
415	E3	27 Apr 1911	29 Oct 1912	Torpedoed in North Sea by U-27 18 Oct 1914
416	E4	16 May 1911	05 Feb 1912	Sold to the Upnor Shipbreaking Company on 21 Feb 1922 and scrapped
417	E5	09 Jun 1911	17 Feb 1912	Lost in North Sea on 07 Mar 1916
418	E6	12 Sep 1911	12 Nov 1912	Mined in North Sea on 26 Dec 1915
419	AE1	03 Nov 1911	22 May 1913	Lost off New Britain in the Pacific on 14 Sep 1914
420	AE2	10 Feb 1912	18 Jun 1913	Scuttled in Sea of Marmora on 27 Apr 1915
430	E9	01 Jun 1912	29 Nov 1913	Scuttled in Baltic on 08 Apr 1918
431	E10	10 Jun 1912	29 Dec 1913	Lost in North Sea on 18 Jan 1915
432	E11	13 Jul 1912	25 Apr 1914	Sold at Malta on 07 Mar 1921 and scrapped
436	NAUTILUS	13 Mar 1913	31 Dec 1914	Sold at 09 Jun 1922 and scrapped
437	V1	12 Nov 1912	23 Jul 1914	Sold to J Kelly on 29 Nov 1921 and scrapped
438	E14	14 Dec 1912	07 Jul 1914	Sunk by mining in the Dardanelles on 27 Jan 1918
439	E15	31 Jan 1913	23 Apr 1914	Grounded & destroyed in Dardanelles on 16 Apr 1915
440	E16	09 May 1913	23 Sep 1914	Mined off Heligoland on 22 Aug 1916
449	V2	15 Oct 1913	17 Feb 1915	Sold to J Kelly on 29 Nov 1921 and scrapped
450	V3	17 Jan 1914	01 Apr 1915	Sold to J W Towers on 08 Oct 1920 and scrapped
451	V4	25 Feb 1914	25 Nov 1915	Sold to J W Towers on 08 Oct 1920 and scrapped
452	E17	29 Jul 1913	16 Jan 1915	Wrecked off the Texel on 06 Jan 1916
453	E18	15 Jan 1914	04 Mar 1915	Mined in Baltic around 25 May 1916
458	E25	Not known	23 Aug 1915	Launched at Beardmore, Clyde – completed at Barrow. Sold to Pedersen and Albrecht and scrapped
459	E26	Not known	11 Nov 1915	Launched at Beardmore, Clyde – completed at Barrow. Sunk in North Sea on 06 Jul 1916
463	G8	18 Dec 1914	01 May 1916	Lost in North Sea on 14 Jan 1918

Yard No.	Name	Laid Down	Launched	Comments
464	G9	08 Dec 1914	05 Jun 1916	Sunk in error by HMS PETARD on 16 Sep 1917
465	G10	12 Mar 1915	11 Jan 1916	Sold to J Smith of Poole on 20 Jan 1923 and scrapped
466	G11	28 Mar 1915	22 Feb 1916	Wrecked off Howich on 22 Nov 1918
467	G12	07 Apr 1915	24 Mar 1916	Sold to J G Petts on 14 Feb 1920 and scrapped
468	G13	09 Apr 1915	18 Jul 1916	Sold to J Smith of Poole on 20 Jan 1923 and scrapped
469				Engines for Submarine F3 –built at Thorneycroft, Southampton
470	E19	27 Nov 1914	13 May 1915	Scuttled in Baltic on 08 Apr 1918
471	E20	25 Nov 1914	12 Jun 1915	Torpedoed by UB-15 in Sea of Marmora on 30 Oct 1915
472	E21	29 Nov 1914	24 Jul 1915	Sold to Pedersen and Albrecht on 14 Dec 1921 and scrapped
473	E22	25 Nov 1914	27 Aug 1915	Torpedoed by UB-18 in North Sea on 25 Apr 1916
474	E23	01 Dec 1914	28 Sep 1915	Sold to Young of Sunderland on 06 Jul 1922 and scrapped
475	E24 (Minelayer)	18 Jan 1915	09 Dec 1915	Mined in the North Sea 24 Mar 1916
478				Submarine Machinery for the Admiralty
480	K3	26 May 1915	20 May 1916	Sold 26 Oct 1918 and scrapped
481	K4	28 Jun 1915	15 Jul 1916	Sunk in collision with HMS INFLEXIBLE in Firth of Forth on 31 Jan 1918
482	K8	28 Jun 1915	10 Oct 1916	Sold 11 Oct 1923 and scrapped
483	K9	28 Jun 1915	08 Nov 1916	Sold 23 Jul 1926 and scrapped
484	K10	28 Jun 1915	27 Dec 1916	Sold 04 Nov 1921 and scrapped
489	L1 (ex E57)	18 May 1916	10 May 1917	Sold to Cashmores in 1930 and scrapped
490	L2 (ex E58)	18 May 1916	06 Jul 1917	Sold to Wards of Grays in Mar 3190 and scrapped
491	K18 (M1)	13 Jul 1916	09 Jul 1917	Fitted with 12-inch gun. Sunk in collision with SS VIDAR off Start Point on 12 Nov 1925
492	K17	16 May 1916	10 May 1917	Sunk in collision in Firth of Forth with HMS FEARLESS on 31 Jan 1918
494	K19 (M2)	13 Jul 1916	19 Oct 1918	Originally completed with 12 inch gun. Converted to carry aircraft. Lost by accident off West Bay, Dorset on 26 Jan 1932
495	L3	21 Jun 1916	01 Sep 1917	Sold to Metal Industries at Charlestown in 1931 and scrapped
496	L4	21 Jun 1916	17 Nov 1917	Sold to Wards of Grays in Feb 1934 and scrapped
499	H21	02 Mar 1917	20 Oct 1917	Sold to Cashmores on 13 Jul 1926 and scrapped
500	H22	06 Mar 1917	14 Nov 1917	Sold to Alloa on 19 Feb 1929 and scrapped
501	H23	03 Mar 1917	29 Jan 1918	Sold to Youngs of Sunderland on 04 May 1934 and scrapped
502	H24	03 Mar 1917	14 Nov 1917	Sold to Youngs of Sunderland on 04 May 1934 and scrapped
503	H25	03 Mar 1917	27 Apr 1918	Sold to Alloa on 19 Feb 1929 and scrapped
504	H26	02 Mar 1917	15 Nov 1917	Sold to Wards on 21 Apr 1928 and scrapped

Yard No.	Name	Laid Down	Launched	Comments
510	L11 (Minelayer)	17 Jan 1917	26 Feb 1918	Sold to Cashmores on 16 Feb 1932 and scrapped
511	L12 (Minelayer)	22 Jan 1917	16 Mar 1918	Sold to Wards of Grays on 16 Feb 1932 and scrapped
512	L17 (Minelayer)	22 Jan 1917	13 May 1918	Sold to Wards of Pembroke Dock in Feb 1934 and scrapped
513	L14 (Minelayer)	18 Jul 1917	10 Jun 1918	Sold to Cashmores on May 1934 and scrapped
514 to 526				13 sets of Submarine machinery for Russia – later sold to Anglo Saxon Petroleum Ltd
527	H27	20 Mar 1917	25 Sep 1918	Sold to Cashmores on 30 Aug 1935 and scrapped
528	H28	18 Mar 1917	08 Jun 1918	Sold 18 Aug 1944 and scrapped at Troon
529	H29	19 Mar 1917	12 Mar 1918	Sunk in accident alongside at Devonport on 09 Aug 1926. Sold 07 Oct 1927 to Wards and scrapped
530	H30	18 Mar 1917	09 May 1918	Sold to Cashmores on 30 Aug 1935 and scrapped
531	H31	19 Apr 1917	16 Nov 1918	Mined in Bay of Biscay on 24 Dec 1941
532	H32	20 Apr 1917	18 Jan 1918	Sold 18 Oct 1944 and scrapped at Troon
534	L18	22 Jun 1917	21 Nov 1918	Sold to Wards of Pembroke Dock in Oct 1936 and scrapped
534	L19	18 Jul 1917	04 Feb 1919	Sold to Wards of Pembroke Dock in 1937 and scrapped
545	L20	26 Jul 1917	23 Sep 1918	Sold to Cashmores on 07 Jan 1935 and scrapped
536	L21	15 Sep 1917	11 Oct 1919	Sold to Arnott Young of Dalmuir in Feb 1939 and scrapped
537	L22	28 Nov 1917	25 Oct 1919	Sold to Cashmores on 30 Aug 1935 and scrapped
538	L23	29 Aug 1917	01 Jul 1919	Launched at Barrow. Completed at Chatham. Sold 1946. Lost on tow in May 1946
539	L24	24 Feb 1918	19 Feb 1919	Launched at Barrow. Completed at Chatham. Sunk in collision with HMS RESOLUTION off Portland 14 Jan 1924
540	L25 (Minelayer)	23 Feb 1918	13 Feb 1919	Launched at Barrow. Completed at Sheerness. Sold to Cashmores in 1935 and scrapped
541	L26	31 Jan 1918	29 May 1919	Launched at Barrow. Completed at Portsmouth. Sunk as A/S target 25 Sep 1945
542	L27	30 Jan 1918	14 Jun 1919	Launched at Barrow. Completed at Sheerness. Scrapped 1947
543 to 547	L28 to L32			All Cancelled (L32 was launched on 23rd Aug 1919 but was sold incomplete)
549	R7	14 Nov 1917	14 May 1918	Sold to E Suren on 21 Feb 1923 and scrapped
550	R8	14 Nov 1917	28 Jun 1918	Sold to E Suren on 21 Feb 1923 and scrapped
564	K26	14 Jun 1918	26 Aug 1919	Launched at Barrow. Completed at Chatham. Sold at Malta in 1931 and scrapped
565 & 566	K27 & K28			Construction cancelled
593				Drawings for Dutch submarines
597				Oil engines for Mitsubishi, Japan – possibly for 'L' Class Submarines built under license
609				Diesel engine for Spanish submarine.
621	OA1 (OXLEY)	24 Aug 1925	07 Sep 1926	Built for RAN - transferred back to RN in 1932. Torpedoed in error by HMS TRITON 10 Sep 1939
622	OA2 (OTWAY)	24 Aug 1925	07 Sep 1926	Built for RAN but transferred back to RN in 1932. Sold 1945 and scrapped at Inverkeithing

Yard No.	Name	Laid Down	Launched	Comments
633	OSIRIS	12 May 1927	19 May 1928	Sold 1945 and scrapped at Durban
634	OSWALD	30 May 1927	19 Jun 1928	Sunk by ramming by Italian VIVALDI off Calabria on 01 Aug 1940
635	OTUS	31 May 1927	31 Aug 1928	Scuttled of Durban in 1946
638	PERSEUS	02 Jul 1928	22 May 1929	Torpedoed by Italian S/M ENRICO TOTI off Zante on 01 Dec 1941
639	POSEIDON	05 Sep 1928	21 Jun 1929	Sunk in collision SS YUTA off Wei-Hai-Wei on 09 Jun 1931
640	PROTEUS	18 Jul 1926	23 Jul 1929	Scrapped at Troon after blast trials in 1946
641	PANDORA	09 Jul 1928	22 Aug 1929	Sunk by bombing at Malta on 01 Apr 1942. Broken up 1955
645	CAPITAN O'BRIEN	15 Nov 1927	02 Oct 1928	'O' Class Submarine for Chile - Scrapped 1958/59
646	CAPITAN THOMPSON	15 Nov 1927	15 Jan 1929	'O' Class Submarine for Chile - Scrapped 1958/59
647	ALMIRANTE SIMPSON	15 Nov 1927	15 Jan 1929	'O' Class Submarine for Chile - Scrapped 1958/59
652	ARAUCANO	01 Mar 1929	22 Oct 1929	Submarine Depot Ship for Chile
653	REGENT	19 Jun 1929	11 Jun 1930	Mined in Straits of Otranto on 16 Apr 1943
654	REGULUS	17 Jul 1929	11 Jun 1930	Lost in Straits of Otranto on 07 Dec 1940
655	ROVER	24 Jul 1929	14 May 1930	Broken up in Durban in 1946
672	THAMES	06 Jan 1931	26 Jan 1932	Mined off Norway on 23 Jul 1940
673				Engines for 'S' Class submarine built at Chatham
678	PORPOISE	22 Sep 1931	30 Aug 1932	Bombed and sunk by Japanese A/C in Malacca Straits on 19 Jan 1945
679	SEVERN	27 Mar 1933	16 Jan 1934	Broken up in Ceylon (Sri Lanka) in 1946
683	CLYDE	15 May 1933	15 Mar 1934	Sold 30 Jul 1946 and scrapped at Durban
684	DELPHIN	Not known	01 May 1934	Submarine for Portuguese Navy - Scrapped in 1950's
685	ESPARDARTE	Not known	30 May 1934	Submarine for Portuguese Navy - Scrapped in 1950's
686	GOLFINO	Not known	30 May 1934	Submarine for Portuguese Navy - Scrapped in 1950's
687				Generating sets for SEVERN
689				Generating sets for CLYDE
701	NARWHAL	29 May 1934	29 Aug 1935	(ML) Lost off Norway possibly on 01 Aug 1940
705	KALEV	Not known	07 Jun 1936	Submarine for Estonian Navy – sunk by mine in Baltic in 1941
706	LEMBIT	Not known	07 Jun 1936	Submarine for Estonian Navy – on display as Museum Boat in Tallinn
708	RORQUAL	01 May 1935	21 Jul 1936	(ML) Sold 17th Mar 1946 and scrapped at Newport
716	TRITON	28 Aug 1936	05 Oct 1937	Sunk by Italian T/B CLIO in Adriatic on 18 Dec 1940
728	UNDINE	19 Feb 1937	05 Oct 1937	Sunk by depth charge attack by German mine sweeping trawlers off Heligoland on 06 Jan 1940
729	UNITY	19 Feb 1937	16 Feb 1938	Sunk in collision with SS ATLE JARL off River Tyne on 29 Apr 1940
730	URSULA	19 Feb 1937	16 Feb 1938	Sold 1950 and scrapped at Grangemouth

Yard No.	Name	Laid Down	Launched	Comments
731	TRIUMPH	19 Mar 1937	16 Feb 1938	Commissioned on 2nd May 1939. Lost in the Aegean Sea on 9 Jan 1942
736	THISTLE	07 Dec 1937	25 Oct 1938	Torpedoed by German U-4 off Skudeneshaven, Norway on 10 Apr 1940
739	TRIAD	24 Mar 1938	05 May 1939	Lost off coast of Libya on 20 Oct 1940
740	TRUANT	24 Mar 1938	05 May 1939	Sold 19 Dec 1945 - Lost on tow
745	TETRARCH	24 Aug 1938	14 Nov 1939	Lost in western Mediterranean on 02 Nov 1941
751	P611	24 May 1939	19th Jul 1940	Built for Turkey as ORUC REIS. Briefly operated by Royal Navy before delivery to Turkey by RN Crews during WW2
752	P612	24 May 1939	20th Jul 1940	Built for Turkey as MURAT REIS. Briefly operated by Royal Navy before delivery to Turkey by RN Crews during WW2
753	P614	24 May 1939	19th Oct 1940	Built for Turkey as BURAK REIS. Operated by Royal Navy WW2. Returned to Turkey in 1945
754	P615	30 Oct 1939	1st Nov 1940	Built for Turkey as ULUC ALI REIS. Transferred to Royal Navy. Torpedoed by U-123 off West Africa 15 Apr 1943
757	UTMOST (P42)	02 Nov 1939	20 Apr 1940	Sunk by Italian MTB GROPPO off Cape Marittimo on 24 Nov 1942
758	UPRIGHT (P38)	06 Nov 1939	21 Apr 1940	Scrapped at Troon in Mar 1946
759	UNIQUE (P36)	30 Oct 1939	06 Jun 1940	Lost off Gibraltar on 24 Oct 1942
760	USK (P41)	06 Nov 1939	07 Jun 1940	Mined off Cape Bon on 03 May 1941
761	UPHOLDER (P37)	30 Oct 1939	08 Jul 1940	Sunk off Tripoli on 14 Apr 1942
762	UNBEATEN (P33)	22 Nov 1939	09 Jul 1940	Sunk in error by RAF in Bay of Biscay on 11 Nov 1940
763	URGE P40 (i)	30 Oct 1939	19 Aug 1940	Mined in Eastern Mediterranean on 28 Apr 1940
764	UNDAUNTED P34 (i)	02 Dec 1939	20 Aug 1940	Sunk by depth charge attack by Italian T/B off Tripoli on 13 May 1941
765	URCHIN (P39)	09 Dec 1939	30 Sep 1940	P39(i) Polish SOKÓŁ broken up 1949
766	UNION (P35)	09 Dec 1939	01 Oct 1940	P35(i) Sunk by Italian patrol craft off Tunisia on 22 Jul 1941
770	TRUSTY	15 Mar 1940	14 Mar 1941	Sold in 1947 – Scrapped at Milford Haven in Jul 1947
771	TURBULENT	15 Mar 1940	12 May 1941	Sunk off Sardinia on 23 Mar 1943
775	ULLSWATER P31 (ii)	30 Apr 1930	27 Nov 1940	Later renamed UPROAR Sold in 1946 and broken up at Inverkeithing
776	P32 (ii)	30 Apr 1940	15 Dec 1940	Not named. Mined off Tripoli on 18 Aug 1941
777	P33 (ii)	18 Jun 1940	28 Jan 1941	Not named. Sunk by mining off Tripoli on 23 Aug 1941
778	ULTIMATUM P34 (ii)	19 Jun 1940	11 Feb 1941	Sold in 1950 and scrapped at Port Glasgow
779	UMBRA P35 (ii)	19 Jul 1940	15 Mar 1941	Sold in 1947 and scrapped at Blyth
780	P36 (ii)	26 Jul 1940	28 Apr 1941	Not named. Sunk by bombing at Malta on 1st Apr 1942
781	UNBENDING P37 (ii)	30 Aug 1940	12 May 1941	Sold in 1950 and scrapped at Gateshead
782	P38 (ii)	02 Sep 1940	09 Jul 1941	Not named. Sunk depth charge attack Italian T/Bs CIRCE & USODIMARE off Tunisia 25 Feb 1942

Yard No.	Name	Laid Down	Launched	Comments
783	P39 (ii)	14 Oct 1940	23 Aug 1941	Not named. Sunk by bombing at Malta on 26 Mar 1942
784	UREDD P41 (ii)	15 Oct 1940	24 Aug 1941	Completed for Norway Sunk off Bodo, Norway on 24 Feb 1943
789	P72 P222	10 Oct 1940	20 Sep 1941	Not named. Sunk by Italian T/B FORTUNALE off Naples on 12 Dec 1942
790	SERAPH P69 P219	16 Aug 1940	25 Oct 1941	Sold in 1965 and scrapped at Briton Ferry. Conning tower preserved as Memorial in USA
791	SHAKESPEARE/P71/P221	13 Nov 1940	18 Dec 1941	Sold in 1946 and scrapped at Briton Ferry
797	UNBROKEN P42 (ii)	30 Dec 1940	04 Nov 1941	To Russia as B2 1944 to 1949. Returned and sold in 1950 and broken up at Gateshead
798	UNISON P43	30 Dec 1940	05 Nov 1941	To Russia as B3 1944 to 1949. Returned and sold in 1950 and broken up at Stockton on Tees
799	UNITED P44	25 Feb 1941	18 Dec 1941	Sold in 1946 and scrapped at Troon
800	UNRUFFLED P46	25 Feb 1941	19 Dec 1941	Sold in 1946 and scrapped at Troon
801	UNRIVALLED P45	12 May 1941	16 Feb 1942	Sold in 1946 and scrapped at Briton Ferry
802	UNSHAKEN P54	12 Jun 1941	17 Feb 1942	Sold in 1946 and scrapped at Troon
803	P48	02 Aug 1941	15 Apr 1942	Not named. Sunk depth charge attack by Italian corvette ARDENTE Gulf of Tunis on 25 Dec 1942
804	UNSEEN P51	30 Jul 1941	16 Apr 1942	Sold in 1949 and scrapped at Hayle
805	DOLFIJN P47	19 Nov 1941	27 Feb 1942	Completed for Holland. Sold 1947 and scrapped
806	UNRULY P49	19 Nov 1941	28 Jul 1942	Sold in 1946 and scrapped at Inverkeithing
807	DZIK P52	30 Dec 1941	11 Oct 1942	Completed for Poland. Sold 1958 and scrapped
808	ULTOR P53	30 Dec 1941	12 Oct 1942	Sold in 1946 and scrapped at Briton Ferry
811	P311 P91	25 Apr 1941	05 Mar 1944	TUTANKAMUN Lost by mining north of Corsica on 8 Jan 1913
812	TRESPASSER P312 (P92)	08 Sep 1941	29 May 1942	Sold in 1961 and scrapped at Gateshead
813	TAURUS P313 (P93)	30 Sep 1941	27 Jun 1942	To Holland in 1948 as DOLFIJN. Returned 1953. Broken up at Dunston in 1960
814	TACTICIAN P314 (P94)	13 Nov 1941	29 Jul 1942	Sold in 1964 and scrapped at Newport
815	TRUCULENT P315 (P95)	04 Dec 1941	12 Sep 1942	Sunk in collision with M/V DVINA in River Thames on 12 Jan 1950
816	TEMPLAR P316 (P96)	28 Dec 1941	26 Oct 1942	Sold in 1959 and scrapped at Troon
817	TALLY HO P317 (P97)	25 Mar 1942	23 Dec 1942	Sold in 1967 and scrapped Briton Ferry
818	TANTALUS P318 (P98)	06 Jun 1942	24 Dec 1942	Sold in 1950 and scrapped at Milford Haven
819	TANTIVY P319 (P99)	04 Jul 1942	06 Apr 1942	Sunk as target in Cromarty Firth in 1951. Raised and sold in 1951 and scrapped
820 to 826				'S' Class Contracts – 3 transferred to Scott's at Greenock & 4 transferred to Cammell Laird at Birkenhead
837	VANDAL P64	17 Mar 1942	23 Nov 1942	Lost by accident in Firth of Clyde on 24 Feb 1943
838	UPSTART P65	17 Mar 1942	24 Nov 1942	To Greece as XIPHIAS. Sunk as target in Jul 1957
839	VARNE (1) P66	29 Apr 1942	22 Jan 1943	To Norway as ULA. Sold in 1965 and scrapped at Hamburg
840	VOX (1) P67	29 Apr 1942	23 Jan 1943	To France as CURIE. Returned 1946. Sold in 1949 and scrapped at Milford Haven

Yard No.	Name	Laid Down	Launched	Comments
842	TELEMACHUS P321	25 Aug 1942	19 Jul 1943	Sold in 1961 and scrapped at Charlestown
843	TALENT (1) P322	13 Oct 1942	17 Jul 1943	To Holland as ZWAARDVIS. Sold in 1961 to Antwerp Ship Breakers
844	TERRAPIN P323	19 Oct 1942	31 Aug 1943	Declared constructive total loss in 1945. Sold in 1946 and scrapped at Troon
845	THOROUGH P324	26 Oct 1942	30 Oct 1943	Sold in 1961 and scrapped at Dunston
860	VENTURER P68	25 Oct 1942	04 May 1943	To Norway as UTSTEIN in 1946. Broken up at Sarpsborg Ship Breakers in 1965
861	VIKING P69	03 Sep 1942	05 May 1943	To Norway as UTVAER in 1946. Broken up at Sarpsborg Ship Breakers in 1965
862	VELDT P71	02 Nov 1942	19 Jul 1943	Completed as PIPINOS for Greece Nov 1943. Returned 1957. Sold in 1958 and broken up at Dunston
863	VAMPIRE P72	09 Nov 1942	20 Jul 1943	Sold in 1950 and scrapped at Gateshead
864	VOX (2) P73	19 Nov 1942	28 Sep 1943	Sold in 1946 and scrapped at Cochin
865	VIGOROUS P74	14 Dec 1942	15 Oct 1943	Sold in 1949 and scrapped at Thornaby on Tees
866	VIRTUE P75	17 Feb 1943	29 Nov 1943	Sold in 1946 and scrapped at Cochin
867	VISIGOTH P76	15 Feb 1943	30 Nov 1943	Sold in 1950 and scrapped at Charlestown
868	TIPTOE P332	10 Nov 1942	25 Feb 1943	Completed 13 Jun 1944. Sold 1972 to Pounds of Portsmouth
869	TRUMP P333	31 Dec 1942	25 Mar 1943	Completed 09 Jul 1944. Sold and scrapped at Newport in 1971
870	TACITURN P334	09 Nov 1942	07 Jun 1944	Completed 07 Oct 1944. Sold and scrapped at Briton Ferry in Aug 1971
871	TAPIR P335	29 Mar 1943	21 Aug 1944	To Holland as ZEEHOND 1948 to 1953. Returned in 1953. Broken up at Metal Industries at Faslane in 1967
872	TARN P336	12 Jun 1943	29 Nov 1944	To Holland as TIJGERHAAI. Scrapped by Amsterdam Ship Breakers in 1966
873	TASMAN P337	21 Mar 1944	13 Feb 1945	Completed as TALENT. Sold and scrapped at Troon in 1970
874	TEREDO P338	17 Apr 1944	27 Apr 1945	Completed on the Clyde on 13 Apr 1946. Scrapped Jun 1965
875	THEBAN			Cancelled 'T' class Submarine
876	TABARD			Contract transferred to Scott's, Greenock
877 to 822				6 x cancelled 'T' Class Submarines (TALENT, THREAT, P345, P346, P347 & P348)
--				Two 'Mid Sections' for Prototype X-Craft (X-3 and X-4)
883	X-5	Dec 1942		Commissioned 29 Dec 1942. Lost during TIRPITZ attack on 22 Sep 1943
883	X-6	11 Jan 1943		Commissioned 21 Jan 1943. Lost during TIRPITZ attack on 22 Sep 1943
883	X-7	Jan 1943		Commissioned 14 Jan 1943. Lost during TIRPITZ attack on 22 Sep 1943
883	X-8	Jan 1943		Commissioned 19 Jan 1943. Scuttled off Norway 17 Sep 1943
883	X-9	Jan 1943		Commissioned 29 Jan 1943. Lost on tow in North Sea on 15 Oct 1943
883	X-10	Feb 1943		Commissioned 08 Feb 1943. Scuttled off Norway on 27th Sep 1943
886	UPSHOT P82	03 May 1943	24 Feb 1944	Completed 15 May 1944. Sold 1949 and scrapped at Preston in Nov 1949
887	URTICA P83	27 Apr 1943	23 Mar 1944	Completed 20 Jun 1944. Sold 1950 and scrapped at Milford Haven
888	VINEYARD P84	21 May 1943	08 May 1944	Completed as DORIS for France. Returned in 1947. Sold in 1950 and scrapped at Inverkeithing

Yard No.	Name	Laid Down	Launched	Comments
889	VARIANCE P85	21 May 1943	22 May 1944	Completed 24 Aug 1944 as UTSIRA for Norway. Scrapped in Hamburg in Dec 1965
890	VENGEFUL P86	30 Jul 1943	20 Jul 1944	Completed 16 Oct 1944 as DELPHIN for Greece. Sold 1958 and scrapped at Gateshead
891	VORTEX P87	13 Aug 1943	19 Aug 1944	Completed 01 Dec 1944 as MORSE for France & to Denmark as SAELEN 1947. Returned Jan 1958
892 to 897				6 x cancelled 'V' Class Submarines (VETO, VIRILE, VISITANT, UPAS, ULEX & UTOPIA)
899 & 900				4 Pairs of 'T' Class Submarine Engines
901 & 902	SEA ROVER & SIRDAR			Outfitting of 2 x 'S' Class Submarine launched at Scott's, Greenock
903	AMPHION P439	14 Nov 1943	31 Aug 1944	Ex HMS ANCHORITE. Scrapped at Inverkeithing in 1971
904	ASTUTE P447	04 Apr 1944	30 Jan 1945	Completed on 30th Jun 1945. Scrapped at Dunston on Tyne in Sep 1970
905	AURIGA P419	07 Jun 1944	29 Mar 1945	Completed on 12 Jan 1946. Scrapped at Newport in 1970
906	AUROCHS	21 Jun 1944	28 Jul 1945	Completed on 07 Feb 1947. Scrapped at Troon from Feb 1967
907	ALCIDE P415	02 Jan 1945	12 Apr 1945	Completed on 18 Oct 1946. Scrapped at Hull in 1974
908	ALDERNEY P416	06 Feb 1945	25 Jun 1945	Completed on 10 Dec 1945. Scrapped at Cairnryan in 1972
909	ALLIANCE P417	13 Mar 1945	28 Jul 1945	On permanent display at Royal Navy Submarine Museum, Gosport
910	AMBUSH P418	17 May 1945	24 Sep 1945	Commissioned on 20 May 1947 and completed 20 Jul 1947. Scrapped at Inverkeithing in 1971
911	ANCHORITE	19 Jul 1945	22 Jan 1946	Completed on 18 Nov 1947. Scrapped at Troon in 1970
912	ANDREW	13 Aug 1945	06 Apr 1946	Completed on 16 Mar 1948. Scrapped in 1977
913 to 923				11 x cancelled 'A' Class Submarines (ANDROMACHE, ANSWER, ANTAGONIST, ANTAEUS, ANZAC, APHRODITE, APPROACH, ARCADIAN, ARDENT, ARGOSY & ATLANTIS)
924 & 925				17 pairs of Submarine Engines
927				6 x 'XT' Class Submarines – all completed Jan to Mar 1944 – all scrapped 1945
939				6 x 'XE' Class Submarines (XE-1 to XE-6). Scrapped in Sydney, Australia, late 1945/46
979	EXPLORER	20 Jul 1951	05 Mar 1954	Previously E-14. Sold 08 Feb 1965 and scrapped by T W Ward at Barrow
980	EXCALIBUR	13 Feb 1952	25 Feb 1955	Previously E-15. Sold 05 Feb 1970 and scrapped at T W Ward at Barrow
1029	PORPOISE	25 Apr 1956	25 Apr 1956	Sunk in STINGRAY torpedo trials off Gibraltar in Nov 1985
1030	RORQUAL	05 Dec 1956	05 Dec 1956	Completed 24 Apr 1958. Explosion in Engine Room in Indian Ocean in 1966 killed two crew members. Scrapped from 1976.
1031	NARWHAL	25 Oct 1957	25 Oct 1957	Completed 04 May 1959. Sunk as target off Fowey on 3rd Aug 1983
1035				Generating sets for Submarines
1037	X-51 MINNOW	01 Oct 1954	09 Nov 1954	Also SSX-01. Loaned to Sweden. Returned 1977. On display at Imperial War Museum at Duxford.
1037	X-53 SHRIMP	01 Mar 1955	02 Apr 1954	Also SSX-03. Disposal List 1961. Broken up at Rosyth 1965
1037	X-54 SPRAT	05 May 1955	25 Jun 1954	Also SSX-04. Disposal List 1961. Broken up at Rosyth 1965
1037	X-52 STICKLEBACK	20 Dec 1954	21 Feb 1954	Also SSX-01. Loaned to Sweden. Returned 1977. On display at Submarine Heritage Museum, Helensburgh

Yard No.	Name	Laid Down	Launched	Comments
1051				Submarine engines for Scott's, Greenock
1059	ORPHEUS	16 Apr 1959	17 Nov 1959	Completed 25 Nov 1960. Scrapped in 1994
1060	OLYMPUS	** Mar 1960	14 Jun 1961	Completed 07 Jul 1960. CACHALOT's fin fitted to OLYMPUS in 1970s to replace fin damaged in collision. Transferred to Canada. Awaiting Disposal in Halifax, Nova Scotia in 2010
1062	DREADNOUGHT	12 Jun 1959	21 Oct 1960	SSN01 Completed 17 Apr 1963. First British Nuclear Submarine. Laid up at Rosyth in 1982 awaiting disposal.
1064	OSIRIS	26 Jan 1962	29 Nov 1962	Completed 11 Jan 1964. Sold to Canada for spares.
1066	VALIANT	22 Jan 1962	03 Dec 1963	SSN02 Completed 1965. Commissioned Jun 1966. First 'All British' Nuclear Submarine. Deployed to South Atlantic as part of the Falklands Task Force in Apr 1982. laid up in 1992 awaiting disposal
1072	WARSPITE	10 Dec 1952	25 Sep 1965	SSN03 Commissioned 18 Apr 1967. Laid up at 1990 awaiting disposal
1074	RESOLUTION	26 Dec 1964	15 Sep 1966	SSBN01 Commissioned 03 Oct 1967. Laid up at Rosyth in 1994 awaiting disposal
1075	REPULSE	26 Feb 1964	04 Nov 1967	SSBN03 Commissioned 28 Sep 1968. Laid up at Rosyth in 1996 awaiting disposal
--	STV			The 'Shock Test Vessel' was completed for the Royal Navy in 1969. The STV Barge, fitted with submarine propulsion machinery, was delivered to Rosyth for use in 'Shock Trials' conducted by the Research Establishment at Dunfermline.
1076	CHURCHILL	30 Jun 1967	20 Dec 1968	SSN04 Commissioned 15 Jul 1970. Laid up in 1991 awaiting disposal
1077	COURAGEOUS	15 May 1968	07 Mar 1970	SSN06 Commissioned 16 Oct 1971. Deployed to South Atlantic as part of the Falklands Task Force in Apr 1982. Laid up at Devonport awaiting disposal but currently used as a Museum Boat
1078	SWIFTSURE	03 Nov 1967	07 Sep 1971	SSN07 Commissioned 17 Oct 1972. Laid up in 1992 awaiting disposal
1081 - 1083	PV01 to PV03			3 x Private venture 'O' Class Submarines – cancelled
1087	HUMAITA	03 Nov 1970	15 Oct 1971	'O' Class Submarine for Brazil. Paid off in 1966
1088	TONELERO	18 Nov 1971	22 Nov 1972	'O' Class Submarine for Brazil. Sank in harbour in 2001- raised and paid off.
1086	SOVEREIGN	17 Sep 1970	17 Feb 1973	SSN08 Commissioned 09 Jul 1974. Laid up at Devonport awaiting disposal in 2010
1090	SUPERB	20 May 1970	30 Nov 1974	SSN09 Commissioned 13 Nov 1976. Paid off in 2010 and to be laid up awaiting disposal
1092	SCEPTRE	25 Oct 1973	20 Nov 1976	SSN10 Commissioned 14 Feb 1978. Paid off on 16th May 2010. Laid up at Devonport awaiting disposal in 2010
1093	GAL	04 Dec 1972	02 Dec 1975	Completed for Israel 1976 - Paid off 2001 - Museum Ship at Haifa
1094	TANIN	28 Nov 1972	25 Oct 1976	Completed for Israel Feb 1977 - Paid off 2001
1095	RAHAV	06 Dec 1972	08 May 1977	Completed for Israel 21 Jun 1977 - Paid off 2001
1096	RIACHUELO	06 Dec 1972	06 Dec 1972	'O' class Submarine for Brazil. Museum Ship at Rio de Janeiro
1097	SPARTAN	24 Apr 1976	07 Apr 1978	SSN11 Commissioned 22 Sep 1979. Deployed to South Atlantic as part of the Falklands Task Force in Apr 1982. Laid up awaiting disposal

Yard No.	Name	Laid Down	Launched	Comments
1099	SPLENDID	** Nov 1977	05 Oct 1979	SSN12 Commissioned Deployed to South Atlantic as part of the Falklands Task Force in Apr 1982. Sank hulk of HMS DEVONSHIRE in Tigerfish torpedo proving firings in 1984. Laid up in 2004 awaiting disposal
1100	TRAFALGAR	15 Apr 1979	01 Jul 1981	SSN13 Commissioned 27 May 1983. Paid off and laid up. Awaiting disposal
1101	TURBULENT	08 May 1980	01 Dec 1982	SN14 Commissioned 28 Apr 1984. Paid off and laid up. Awaiting disposal
1103	TIRELESS	06 Jun 1981	17 Mar 1984	SSN15 Commissioned 05 Oct 1985. Paid off and laid up. Awaiting disposal
1104	TORBAY	03 Dec 1982	08 Mar 1985	SSN16 Commissioned 07 Feb 1987. Paid off and laid up. Awaiting disposal
1105	TRENCHANT	28 Oct 1985	03 Nov 1986	SSN17 Commissioned 14 Jan 1989. Still in Service in 2017
1106	UPHOLDER	** Nov 1983	02 Dec 1985	S40 Commissioned 09 Jun 1990. Transferred to Canada in 2004 (see below)
1107	TALENT	13 May 1986	15 Apr 1988	SSN18 Commissioned 12 May 1990. Still in Service in 2017
1108	TRIUMPH	02 Feb 1987	16 Feb 1991	SSN19 Commissioned 12 Oct 1991. Still in Service in 2017
1109	VANGUARD	03 Sep 1986	04 Mar 1992	SSBN05 Commissioned 21 Aug 1994. Still in Service in 2017
1110	VICTORIOUS	04 Dec 1987	29 Sep 1993	SSBN06 Commissioned 07 Jan 1995. Still in Service in 2017
1111	VIGILANT	16 Feb 1991	14 Oct 1995	SSBN07 Commissioned 02 Nov 1996. Still in Service in 2017
1112	VENGEANCE	01 Feb 1993	19 Sep 1998	SSBN08 Commissioned 27th Jan 1999. Still in Service in 2017
--	UNSEEN			Re-activated for RCN as HMCS VICTORIA. Commissioned Halifax, N.S. Dec 2000
--	UNICORN			Re-activated for RCN as HMCS WINDSOR. Commissioned Halifax N.S. Jun 2003
--	URSULA			Re-activated for RCN as HMCS CORNER BROOK. 'Commissioned' Halifax N.S. Mar 2003
--	UPHOLDER			Re-activated for RCN as CHICOUTIMI. Handed over at Barrow 02 Oct 2004
1122	ASTUTE	31 Jan 2001	14 Jun 2007	SSN20 Ordered 17th Mar 1997 - Commissioned at Faslane 27th Aug 2010
1123	AMBUSH	22 Oct 2003	05 Jan 2011	SSN21 Ordered 17th Mar 1997 - Commissioned at Faslane 1st Mar 2013
1124	ARTFUL	11 Mar 2005	19 May 2014	SSN22 Ordered 17th Mar 1997 - Commissioned at Faslane 18th Mar 2016
1127	AUDACIOUS	24 Mar 2009		SSN23 Ordered 21st May 2007. Under construction in 2017. Projected in service date 2018
1128	ANSON			SSN24 Ordered 21st May 2007. Under construction in 2017. Projected service date date 2020
1129	AGAMEMNON			SSN25 Ordered 25th Mar 2010. Under construction in 2017. Projected service date date 2022
--				Bow & Stern Domes for four Spanish Submarines. 1st pair delivered Aug 2009, 2nd pair delivered Apr 2010
1130	AJAX			SSN26 7th Astute Class Submarine. Under construction in 2017. Projected service date date 2024
1131	DREADNOUGHT			SSBN09. Ordered 21st October 2016. Steel cut 21st October 2016. Projected service date date 2028
1132	Not yet named			SSBN10
1133	Not yet named			SSBN11
1134	Not yet named			SSBN12

Section Two
Miscellaneous Paintings

"GAL" CLASS SUBMARINES
INS GAL

The Painting and the "Gal" class

The main picture is a watercolour showing the three Israeli submarines of the "Gal" class at sea. The upper and lower mounts show the Ships' Badges, the Israeli Navy Ensign, and various pencil sketches of the submarines.

The "Gal" class was built for the Israeli Navy to meet the then current demands of their 'Maritime Battle Plan'. The three boats of the class were known in Barrow-in-Furness as the "540 Project" (after their surfaced displacement of 540 cubic metres) and were named INS GAL (meaning 'Wave' in Hebrew), INS TANIN (meaning 'Crocodile'), and INS RAHAV (meaning 'Sea Monster'). Gal is popular in Israel as both a boy's and a girl's name. They were replacements for the ageing WW2 "S" and "T" class boats that formed the Israeli Submarine Service at that time.

They had a mixed start to their service. INS GAL ran aground off Haifa soon after arrival and, whilst INS TANIN was on trials three crew members were killed in a road accident in Scotland, creating unwelcome publicity and regenerating an Arab boycott. Subsequently, for more than twenty five years, all these submarines gave outstanding service to their Country. All three were paid off in 2001. The GAL is preserved in Israel at Haifa as a Submarine Memorial. Another is in the Kiel Science Park and is open to the public – a Barrow-built submarine at the capital of German submarines! The third "Gal" class submarine has been scrapped.

Class Information

The "Gal" class were a modified version of the Type 206, of which eighteen were built for the German Navy. For political reasons it was not possible for them to be built in Germany so they were built by Vickers at Barrow-in-Furness under a collaboration agreement with the German designers (IKL) and the Type 206 builders, HDW of Kiel. There were a number of differences from the 206 - slightly increased length, changed weapons and anti-magnetic measures being perhaps the most significant but the most evident was the much larger fin. This was primarily to accommodate the large, pressure-proof chamber of a Vickers-designed anti-helicopter missile system called Blowpipe which, in the event, was never installed.

The Sub-Harpoon anti-ship missile system was installed in the early 1980's, making them the smallest submarines to operate the system They were significantly updated in 1994/5 but were all taken out of service from 2001. The "Gal" class have been replaced by the "Dolfin" class, German-built and derived from the German Navy's Type 212 class.

INS GAL DATA

Builder:	Vickers Shipbuilding Group Ltd, Barrow-in-Furness Yard Number: 1093
Significant Dates:	Ordered: April 1972; Laid Down: 4th Dec 1972; Launched: 2nd Dec 1975; Completed: 1976
Dimensions:	Length: 48.9 metres; Beam: 4.90 metres; Draught: 3.66 metres
Displacement:	Surfaced: 540 tonnes (approx); Dived: 660 tonnes (approx)
Speed:	Surfaced: 11 knots; Dived: 17 knots
Armament:	Six x 21-inch bow torpedo tubes; Ten torpedoes and/or Sub-Harpoon Missiles
Complement:	23 Officers and Ratings

This painting was commissioned by Mr. Tony Peak. Mr. Peak was a part of the Senior Management team that worked on the "Gal" class submarines for the Israeli Navy - or the 540 Project as they were known during their build for security reasons.

BRAZILIAN "OBERON" CLASS SUBMARINES
S HUMAITA

The main picture is a watercolour depicting the three Brazilian Navy "Oberon" class submarines S HUMAITA*, S TONELERO and S RIACHUELO entering Rio de Janeiro. The small craft on the left is a modern version of an ancient native craft called a Jangada. The lower mount shows, from left to right, the three submarine badges, the Brazilian Naval Ensign and a view of Corcovado Peak, Rio de Janeiro. The upper mount has the Submarine Service badge of the Brazilian Navy.

These were three of the fourteen "Oberon" class submarines exported by Britain. S HUMAITA and S TONELERO were ordered in 1969 with a further order for S RIACHUELO following in 1972. The names commemorate battles in the River War with Paraguay (The War of the Triple Alliance). They brought to a total of eleven the number of Brazilian naval vessels built at Barrow-in-Furness.

To confirm that a submarine can properly adjust its attitude and buoyancy on patrol it is necessary to carry out a trial in harbour by changing the attitude of the vessel through moving water between tanks and adding it if necessary. There is the potential that a hatch that is open (because of shore supply pipes and cables) may inadvertently drop below the water level, flooding the submarine and, unless quick action is taken, causing it to sink gently but inexorably to the bottom of the dock. The result is a costly embarrassment for the Navy concerned, rather than a danger to life. It should be simple to avoid, but it has happened in many Navies (e.g. HMS ARTEMIS and USS GUITARRO).

It also happened to S TONELERO, the likelihood perhaps increased by conducting the trial with an inexperienced team, at night, on Christmas Eve 2000. The nine on board escaped via the conning tower. This was the first loss of a Brazilian submarine for eighty two years. The submarine was re-floated on 3rd January 2001 but the result of the sinking was that the cost of refitting was in the order of 25 million Brazilian dollars and would take two years to complete. As she was to be

decommissioned in 2003 a decision to bring this forward was taken and the submarine was paid off on 21st June 2001. In her career S TONELERO had sailed some 168,368 miles - 80,636 miles being underwater.

During their service the submarines underwent a major conversion programme in the 1980s and were converted to fire Mk 24 Mod 2 Tigerfish torpedo. All three were given a mid-life modernisation in 1995 by the German company HDW.

S HUMAITA was decommissioned in 1996. S RIACHUELO was decommissioned in 1997 and is now on display at the Navy Cultural Centre in Rio de Janeiro.

Class Information

In layout and construction they were the same as the "Oberon" boats built for the RN but for controlling their combat systems they adopted the Vickers TIOS (Tactical Information Operating System), the first British digital Combat System to go to sea - it may have been the first in the world.

S TONELERO was seriously damaged by fire whilst fitting out at Barrow. She was towed to HM Dockyard, Chatham to have the central section of the pressure hull cut out and replaced. As a consequence, completion of the boat was delayed until 1978, making her the last "Oberon" class submarine to be completed for any Navy.

* Brazilian warships are not prefixed by a national identity, such as Brazilian Navy Ship, but rather by ship type. As such the aircraft carrier SAO PAULO is prefixed NAe (Navio-Aerodromo) while submarines are simply prefixed S (Submarino).

HUMAITA DATA

Builder:	Vickers Ltd. Shipbuilding Group, Barrow-in-Furness	Yard Number: 1087
Significant Dates:	Laid down: 3rd November 1970; Launched: 15th October 1971	Commissioned: June 1973
Dimensions:	Length: 295 feet 3 inches; Beam: 26 feet 6 inches; Draught: 18 feet	
Displacement:	Surfaced: 2,030 tons; Dived: 2,410 tons	
Machinery:	Surfaced: 2 Admiralty Standard Range 16WS-ASR diesels (3,680 bhp) driving 2 generators (2,560 kW)	
	Dived: 2 Electric motors (6,000 bhp), Twin shafts	
Speed:	Surfaced: 12 knots; Dived: 17 knots	
Endurance:	9,000 nautical miles at 12 knots (surfaced)	
Armament:	Six x 21-inch bow torpedo tubes; Two x 21-inch stern torpedo tubes	
Complement:	6 officers and 64 ratings	

This painting was sponsored by Mr. Gordon Howell, previously Production Director of VSEL and Managing Director of Cammell Lairds Shipbuilding, who has fond memories of the build of the Brazilian "Oberon" class submarines and many other boats built in Barrow-in-Furness, Newcastle and Birkenhead.

HM SUBMARINES "A" CLASS
HMS ALLIANCE

The Painting and the HMS ALLIANCE Story

The main picture is composed of combined watercolour and pencil depicting HMS ALLIANCE coming into berth alongside at HMS DOLPHIN, Gosport, Hants. In the background is a collection of various vessels, mainly landing craft to reflect the relationship between the Royal Navy and the Army. Overhead are two Avro Anson aircraft which brings in the Royal Air Force. The RAF also manned the Air Sea Rescue vessels as shown on the left hand side of the painting. On the right hand side is an Army amphibious vehicle conversing with HMS ALLIANCE crew. As the artist was also a member of the Merchant Navy some merchant vessels are shown in the distance.

HMS ALLIANCE was laid down in March 1945 shortly before the war ended and was not completed until 1947. For thirty days (from 9th October to 8th November 1947) HMS ALLIANCE using the new snorting system carried out tropical habitability trials in an area of the Atlantic Ocean bordered by the Canary Isles, Cape Verde and Freetown. She snorted for the entire period - except for three nights when she went deep to take sea temperature and salinity readings and to cycle her battery. Over this trial she sailed for 3,193 nautical miles under snort conditions, which in its day, was a record.

HMS ALLIANCE was taken out of active service and used as a harbour training vessel at HMS DOLPHIN from 1973. She was transferred on permanent loan to the Royal Navy Submarine Museum at Gosport on 28th February 1978. She now stands as a permanent memorial to the 4,334 British submariners lost in both World Wars and the 741 British submariners lost in peacetime accidents.

After 30 years as a Memorial Submarine at the Royal Navy Submarine Museum in Gosport the Submarine had deteriorated badly; repairs were needed and a fund raising operation was launched - using funds raised and a Heritage Lottery Grant her bow and stern were repaired and extensive surface corrosion addressed. The restoration included reclaiming land beneath HMS ALLIANCE using a cofferdam and backfill. This provided easy access for future maintenance and a new viewing platform for visitors, additionally opening-up the conning tower and casing. Following the 'Refit' HMS ALLIANCE was re-dedicated by Prince William, Duke of Cambridge on 12th May 2014.

Class Information

This was a projected class of forty six submarines ordered under the 1943 programme of which Vickers Armstrong built ten. Only two, HMS AMPHION and HMS ASTUTE were completed before the sudden end of WW2. In consequence the orders for thirty of the class were cancelled.

The "A" class was the only class of submarine designed for the Royal Navy during WW2 and was specifically intended to operate in Far Eastern waters against the Japanese. Submarines of the "S" and "T" class had operated successfully there since early 1942 from bases in Australia and Ceylon. However, compared to American Fleet Submarines, they were very short ranged and also (and most importantly) provided very poor habitability. To cover the vast area of the Pacific Ocean a submarine was needed with a long range, high surface speed and vastly improved living conditions. It would also require a large weapon load to avoid having to return prematurely from a distant patrol area. The result was the "A" Class. Additional "A" Class information is given with the painting of HMS AMBUSH.

HMS ALLIANCE DATA

Builder:	Vickers-Armstrong Limited, Barrow-in-Furness		Yard Number:	909	
Significant Dates	Ordered:	1943	Laid Down:	13th Mar 1945	Launched: 28th Jul 1945
Commissioned:	14th May 1947				
Dimensions:	Length:	281feet 6 inches	Beam:	22 feet 3 inches	Draught: 17 feet
Displacement:	Surfaced:	1,385 tons	Dived:	1,620 tons	
Machinery:	Surfaced:	2 x 8 cylinder Vickers supercharged diesel engines, 4,300 bhp			
	Dived:	2 x English Electric motors, 1,250 shp, Twin Shafts			
Endurance:	Surfaced:	10,500 nautical miles at 11 knots	Dived:	16 nautical miles at 8 knots 114 nautical miles at 3 knots	
Fuel:	300 tons				
Armament:	Ten x 21 inch torpedo tubes (6 bow, 4 stern); Twenty torpedoes carried or 26 mines in lieu of torpedoes; 1 x Mk XXII 4 inch quick firing gun – 125 rounds of ammunition carried; 1 x Oerlikon Anti-Aircraft Gun; 3 x 303 Vickers machine guns				
Complement:	60 Officers and Ratings				

The artist Tom Murphy was a Sea Cadet in his younger days and, as the badge of HMS ALLIANCE is composed of all three service insignia, he selected this subject as being of special interest. Because of this connection the three Barrow Cadet Forces combined to sponsor this painting. The Commanding Officers of these units were Lieutenant D. Constable, RNR, Major D. Ingram and Flight Lieutenant P. A. Rose, MBE, RAFVR (T).

'EXILE' SUBMARINES OF WORLD WAR II

The Painting

During WW2 there were six foreign Navies – the Dutch, "Free French", Greek, Norwegian, Polish and Yugoslav – who operated submarines alongside and under the control of the RN. The main picture, a montage of these 'Navies-in-Exile' has been challenging, particularly because of the large amount of detail involved. Barrow provided fourteen submarines to five of these "Navies in Exile" (Yugoslavia was the exception as they had their own vessel). The task was to show the National Flags of these five countries, the three classes of Barrow supplied submarines, the original names or pennant numbers of the submarines had they been 'Commissioned' into the Royal Navy and their names when they were 'Commissioned' into their new Navies. As the artist, I hope that I have come close and represented fully the contribution that these submarine crews made to the Allied war effort.

The upper mount shows the Vickers Armstrong "House" flag. The lower mount shows, from left to right, the badge of HMS AMBROSE (all the submarines named served at one time as part of the 9th Submarine Flotilla based on HMS AMBROSE, at Dundee) and the flags and submarine badges of the five countries. The last illustration is the logo of the Vickers Electrical Installation Department Social Club. This department carried out the electrical installation on all the "exile" submarines Vickers built and its present-day members generously sponsored this painting.

Foreign submarines that escaped to serve with the Royal Navy in WW2

As Germany overran first Poland, then Norway and finally France and Holland submarines from these countries escaped to Britain. With the Italian-German invasion of the Balkans in 1941, Greek and Yugoslav submarines joined the 1st Submarine Flotilla at Alexandria. As a result of Japanese advances in the Dutch East Indies in 1942, Dutch submarines joined British and American submarines operating from Australia. All continued to fly their National Flags throughout the war.

Nine Dutch submarines escaped to Britain, or attempted to: O9 and O10 in May 1940; O13 escaped from Holland but was lost (possibly to a mine in the North Sea) en route to the UK. O14, O15, O21, O22, O23 and O24 also joined Allied forces.

Eight French submarines plus the depot ship JULES VERNE arrived at Harwich in March 1940. A further six French submarines arrived at Dundee, whilst RUBIS and SURCOUF arrived at Portsmouth. Others from southern French ports eventually arrived at Malta and Alexandria.

Greece had a useful submarine branch in 1939 and five escaped to serve with the Allies. These were RHS KATONIS, RHS NEREUS, RHS GLAVKOS, RHS PAPANIKOLIS and RHS TRITON.

Only one Norwegian submarine escaped to the UK – Submarine B-1 in 1940 and she was scrapped on arrival. In consequence the Norwegian Submarine Branch used from the start new-build British submarines.

Two Polish submarines WILK and ORZEŁ were on patrol in the Baltic when war broke out on 2nd September 1939. They arrived in the U.K. after many adventures, including a brief internment in Latvia from where they broke out. ORZEŁ was lost in the North Sea in December 1939.

In January 1942, outside the Far East there were 19 exile submarines operating as part of RN Submarine Flotillas:

2nd Flotilla (Malta)	5 Greek, 1 Polish, 1 Yugoslav
8th Flotilla (Gibraltar)	1 Dutch
5th Flotilla (Portsmouth)	1 Norwegian, 4 French
9th Flotilla (Dundee)	1 Dutch, 2 French
7th Flotilla (Western Approaches)	1 Dutch, 1 Norwegian, 1 Polish

By May 1944 this had become 9 exile submarines operating as follows:

1st Flotilla (Malta)	1 Dutch, 1 Yugoslav
7th Flotilla (Rothesay)	1 Dutch, 1 Norwegian
3rd Flotilla (Holy Loch)	1 Dutch, 1 Norwegian
9th Flotilla (Dundee)	1 Dutch
5th Flotilla (Portsmouth)	1 French, 1 Polish

Barrow Built Submarines For Allied Navies In Exile During World War Two

The Barrow-in-Furness Shipyard built fourteen Submarines handed 'new' to five of these 'Exile' Navies:

Dutch:	DOLFIJN, ex-P47, ("U" class); ZVAARDVISCH, ex-TALENT and TIJGERHAAI, ex- TARN (both "T" class)
Free French:	CURIE, ex-VOX, DORIS, ex-VINYARD and MORSE, ex-VORTEX (all "V" class)
Greek:	XIFIAS, ex-UPSTART, ("U" class); PIPINOS, ex-VELDT and DELFIN, ex-VENGEFUL (both "V" class)
Norwegian:	UREDD, ex-P41 ("U" class); ULA, ex-VARNE and UTSIRA, ex- VARIANCE (both "V" class)
Polish:	SOKÓŁ, ex-URCHIN and DZIK, ex-P52 (both "U" class)

In addition three Barrow-built "U" class Submarines, URSULA, UNBROKEN and UNISON, were transferred from the RN to Russia – then an Ally – in 1944 and served under Russian crews as part of their Navy. They were returned in 1949 by the Soviet Union, by then becoming our Cold War enemy. The "S" class Submarine SUNFISH (built at Chatham) was also transferred to Russia but was sunk in error by the RAF on 27th Jul 1944.

The Vickers Electrical Installation Department carried out the electrical installation work on all the "Exile" submarines that Vickers built and the present day members of the EID Social Club generously sponsored this painting.

HM SUBMARINE DEPOT SHIPS
HMS MEDWAY

The Painting

The main painting is a watercolour and shows HMS MEDWAY on the Far East Station surrounded by her submarine charges and local native craft. The upper mount shows the RN Submarine Dolphins. The lower mount displays a pencil drawing of HMS MEDWAY and in the centre is the ship's badge.

The HMS MEDWAY Story

HMS MEDWAY was the first purpose built submarine depot ship for Royal Navy submarines. All previous depot ships had been converted from their original use as either warships or merchant vessels. HMS MEDWAY was designed to accommodate eighteen boats of the pre-WW2 "P" and "O" classes and more if necessary in time of war. The ship was fitted out to cover all submarine needs with a foundry, coppersmiths, plumbers and carpenters shops, heavy and light machine shops, electrical and torpedo repair shops and generators for charging submarine batteries.

On completion in 1929 HMS MEDWAY was sent to the Far East to be the depot ship for the 4th Submarine Flotilla, China Station, based at Hong Kong. The Flotilla at that time comprised "O", "P" and "R" class submarines. Following the outbreak of WW2, HMS MEDWAY and her Flotilla were brought back to the Mediterranean to form the 1st Submarine Flotilla based at Alexandria. She also acted as the depot ship for the 1st Special Boat Squadron.

In June 1942 the German Africa Korps were advancing on Egypt and the decision was taken to redeploy HMS MEDWAY and the 1st Submarine Flotilla to a new base at Haifa in Palestine. The Commander-in-Chief, Admiral Henry Harwood, precipitately gave the order for the Fleet to evacuate Alexandria. As a result, a well-planned three-week withdrawal strategy was ignored and the withdrawal was carried out in only forty eight hours, with chaos resulting. This unnecessary and hasty withdrawal resulted in the loss of the MEDWAY, the only submarine depot ship to be lost during WW2. Whilst on passage to Beirut on 30th June 1942, escorted by eight destroyers, she was torpedoed and sunk by U-372 (Kapitan Lieutenant Heinz Joachim Neumann).

The loss of HMS MEDWAY with all her facilities, including one hundred and fourteen spare torpedoes and spare submarine equipment, almost brought submarine operations in the eastern Mediterranean to a standstill. Luckily ninety four of the torpedoes floated free and were recovered and others had been sent overland. However, and as important to those affected, crews on submarines at sea at the time lost all their kit and personal belongings.

HMS MEDWAY DATA

Builder:	Vickers Armstrong Limited – Barrow-in-Furness Yard Number: 629
Significant Dates:	Laid Down: April 1927; Launched: 19th July 1928; Completed: 6th July 1929
Dimensions:	Length: 580 feet; Beam: 85 feet; Draught: 19 feet 9 inches
Displacement:	14,650 tons
Machinery:	2 x Vickers MAN 2SC SA 8 cylinder diesel engines 8,000 bhp, Twin shafts
Fuel:	500 tons plus 1,900 tons for submarines
Speed:	15 knots
Armament:	Two x 4-inch guns; Four x 4-inch high angle anti-aircraft guns in single mountings
Complement:	400 (including workshop personnel and submarine 'Spare Crews')
Accommodation:	35 Officers and 1,500 Ratings from submarines berthed alongside

This painting was sponsored by the Northern Ireland Branch of the Submariners Association.

AUSTRALIAN SUBMARINES

The Painting

This painting (painted in sepia colours) is one of two pictures in the Submarine Heritage Collection painted by a different artist. The artist in this case is Steve Kenny. Steve is a Barrow born artist who works in the BAE Shipyard in Barrow and who paints in his spare time. The painting was 'Commissioned' in 2009 in advance of the Royal Australian Navy's Submarine Centenary which took place in 2014. Several of the Submarines (AE1, AE2, OXLEY and OTWAY) depicted here were built in Barrow-in-Furness.

The Royal Australian Navy Submarine Centenary Story

This picture shows (on a background of the Australian Continent) and clockwise from the top left:

A "Collins" class Submarine at sea – a view on starboard bow. Six of these Kockums designed submarines were ordered as replacements for the six aging "Oberon" class submarines. Those Australian built submarines, currently (2017) still in service are COLLINS, FARNCOMB, WALLER, RANKIN, SHEEAN and DECHAINEUX.

Royal Australian Navy Submarine Dolphins – 'Dolphins' were introduced into the RAN to recognise qualified Submariners in the late 1960's and a similar design was introduced for the Royal Navy in the early 1970's.

A "Collins" class submarine at sea – viewed from fine on the port bow.

Yard No. 621: HMAS OXLEY (OA1), viewed on starboard bow, was one of two "O" class cubmarines ordered from Vickers Armstrong in 1925. The other was Yard No. 622 HMAS OTWAY (OA2). Both submariness were launched in 1926 but owing to engine problems they didn't arrive in Australia until late 1928. Both were paid off in 1931 and were offered back to the Royal Navy and recommisioned with RN crews at Sydney in April 1931. OXLEY was torpedoed in error by HMS TRITON in the North Sea on 10th September 1939. OTWAY was sold for scrapping in 1945.

Lieutenant Commander H.H.G.D. Stoker, DSC, Royal Navy – first and only Commanding Officer of HMAS AE2 (1913 to 1915).

Yard No. 420: HMAS AE2 at sea – view on the starboard beam. AE2 was one of two "E" class submarines ordered from Vickers launched in Barrow in May and June 1913. The other was HMAS AE1 (Yard No. 419). AE1 (Lieutenant Commander Thomas Besant, Royal Navy) was lost without trace in unknown circumstances off New Britain in the Pacific on 14th September 1914. AE2 returned to the Mediterranean in 1915. AE2, with Lieutenant Commander Stoker in Command, was

the first submarine to make the passage through the Dardanelles into the Sea of Marmora during the Gallipoli Campaign of 1915. The submarine was scuttled after being damaged in an attack by a Turkish Gunboat on 30th April 1915. The crew became Prisoners of War in Turkey until their release in November 1918.

HMAS OTWAY at sea – view on the starboard quarter.

Submarine J7 preparing to enter harbour.

Submarine J4 at anchor.

Submarine K9 in Dry Dock at Sydney.

"Hew" Stoker – Actor – a new career after leaving the Royal Navy in 1919.

HMAS AE2 entering harbour at Portsmouth in 1914.

The picture shows in the centre (from top to bottom):

An "Oberon" class submarine being launched at Scott's Shipyard, Greenock and an "Oberon" class submarine entering harbour. In the 1960's and 1970's the RAN took delivery of six "Oberon" class submarine - all built by the Scott's Shipyard at Greenock on the Lower Clyde. The submarines were OVENS, OXLEY, OTWAY, ONSLOW, ORION and OTAMA.

The submarine depot ship HMAS PLATYPUS (built by John Brown, Clydebank) was launched in 1915 and then served with the Royal Navy in home waters until March 1919. She was returned to the Royal Australian Navy and was then the escort for, and the submarine depot ship for, the six "J" class submarines gifted to the RAN by the Royal Navy. The "J" class ssubmarines, which were built in several different British Shipyards, were J1, J2, J3, J4, J5 and J7. The submarines were transferred to the RAN on 25th March 1919 but had all been paid off and laid up by the middle of 1922.

HMAS OXLEY and HMAS OTWAY alongside at Garden Island in Australia.

HMAS K9 (formerly the Royal Netherlands Navy Submarine KIX) was taken over by the RAN in WW2 to be commissioned with a mixed Australian and Royal Navy crew. It was intended to use the submarine as a 'Clockwork Mouse' for anti-submarine training for surface forces. Following many engineering difficulties the submarine was paid off in 1944, was later lost on tow and was wrecked.

ROYAL AUSTRALIAN NAVY SUBMARINE CENTENARY 1914 - 2014

This painting was 'Commissioned' to recognise the Centenary of the Royal Australian Navy Submarine Service which took place in 2014 and to mark the valuable contribution of Australian submarines and submariners to the Royal Navy over the years.

BARROW BUILT SHIPS AND SUBMARINES AT THE FALKLANDS

The Painting

This painting was completed to commemorate the contribution made by 'Barrow Built' ships and submarines during the Falklands War of April to June of 1982. In all, eight Barrow built ships and submarines were deployed to the South Atlantic and, of these, one was sunk in action. This painting shows from left to right HMS HERMES (the flagship of the Task Force), a Type 42 destroyer (representing HMS SHEFFIELD and HMS CARDIFF), a "Valiant" class submarine (representing HMS VALIANT, HMS COURAGEOUS, HMS SPARTAN and HMS SPLENDID) and HMS INVINCIBLE.

The Story

Following the Argentine occupation of the Falkland Islands a Naval Task Force was assembled and dispatched to the South Atlantic in Operation Corporate intended to remove the invaders from the Islands and restore the Islands to British rule. The Task Force was commanded by Rear Admiral Sir John 'Sandy' Woodward who selected HMS HERMES as his flagship.

HMS HERMES (Captain L. E. Middleton, Royal Navy) first entered the operational area (Exclusion Zone) on 25th April 1982. Embarked in HMS HERMES were two squadrons of Sea Harriers – 800 Naval Air Squadron (Lieutenant Commander A.D. 'Andy' Auld) and 899 Naval Air Squadron (Lieutenant Commander N. W. Thomas). Also embarked were the Sea King HAS 5 helicopters of 826 Naval Air Squadron (Lieutenant Commander D.J.S. Squier) and Sea King HC 4 Helicopters of 846 Naval Air Squadron (Lieutenant Commander Simon Thornewill).

HMS INVINCIBLE (Captain J.J. 'Jeremy' Black, Royal Navy) first entered the operational area (Exclusion Zone) on 25th April 1982. Embarked in HMS INVINCIBLE were two squadrons of Sea Harriers – 801 Naval Air Squadron (Lieutenant Commander N.D. 'Sharkey' Ward) and 809 Naval Air Squadron (Lieutenant Commander T.J.H. 'Tim' Gedge). Also embarked were the Sea King HAS 5

Helicopters of 820 Naval Air Squadron (Lieutenant Commander Ralph J. S. Wykes-Sneyd)

HMS SPARTAN (Commander J.B. 'Jim' Taylor) first entered the operational area (Exclusion Zone) on 12th April 1982. SPARTAN (armed with a mixed war load of 25 Mk 24 Mod 0 Tigerfish and Mk 8 Mod 4** torpedoes) was the first RN vessel to arrive off the Falklands and commenced patrolling immediately after arrival.

HMS SPLENDID (Commander R.C. 'Roger' Lane-Nott) first entered the operational area (Exclusion Zone) on 19th April 1982 and immediately joined HMS SPARTAN in patrolling the Exclusion Zone. SPLENDID carried a similar war load of torpedoes to SPARTAN.

HMS VALIANT (Commander T.M. 'Tom' Le Marchand) was in the second wave of submarines to arrive in the Exclusion Zone – first entering the operational area on 16th May 1982. VALIANT was armed with a mixed war load of 32 Mk 24 Mod 0 Tigerfish and Mk 8 Mod 4** torpedoes.

HMS COURAGEOUS (Commander R.T.N. 'Rupert' Best) was also in the second wave of submarines to arrive in the Exclusion Zone - first entering the operational area on 30th May 1982. COURAGEOUS was also armed with a mixed war load of 32 Mk 24 Mod 0 'Tigerfish' and Mk 8 Mod 4** torpedoes.

HMS SHEFFIELD (Captain J.F.T.G. 'Sam' Salt, Royal Navy) first entered the operational area (Exclusion Zone) on 20th April 1982. During operations in the Exclusion Zone on 4th May 1982 SHEFFIELD was hit and badly damaged by an Exocet missile fired from an Argentine Air Force Super Etendard jet. The ship later sank south east of Lafonia (the southern part of East Falkland).

HMS CARDIFF (Captain M.G.T. 'Mike' Harris, Royal Navy) first entered the operational area (Exclusion Zone) on 23rd May 1982.

Apart from HMS SHEFFIELD the 'Barrow Built' ships and submarines returned home safely in June and July 1982 after the successful conclusion of the war.

DEVONSHIRE DOCK HALL
& "ASTUTE" CLASS SUBMARINES IN BUILD

The Painting

This painting is the second of two pictures in the Submarine Heritage Collection painted by a different artist. The artist in this case is Steve Kenny. Steve is a Barrow born artist who works in the BAE Shipyard in Barrow and who paints in his spare time.

The painting shows the interior of the Devonshire Dock Hall from the Devonshire Dock end looking from the Gantry at Level Four. To the left can be seen HMS ASTUTE under construction but almost complete and ready for 'roll out' and 'launch'. To the left hand side is HMS AMBUSH in an earlier stage of construction although it is clear that the 'butt welding' together of the hull sections and installation of the casing sections and the fin is complete. The light blue rectangular shapes either side on the forward end of HMS AMBUSH are the 'Flank Array Shelters' inside of which the Sonar Arrays can be attached to the sides of the submarine under environmentally controlled conditions.

Above can be seen the overhead 'travelling cranes' used for both general lifting and transport of construction materials and also for the process of fuelling the nuclear reactors. On the DDH floor can be seen materials awaiting installation in the submarines under construction.

Access to the exterior of the submarines is by means of scaffolding. Access to the interior of the submarine is by means of gangways from 'Level Four' of the galleries down either side of the Hall.

The DDH Story

The Devonshire Dock Hall (often abbreviated to DDH) is a large Shipbuilding Hall that forms part of the Port of Barrow at the BAE Systems Submarine Solutions Shipyard in the town of Barrow-in-Furness.

Constructed in 1986 for VSEL, the covered assembly facility was named Devonshire Dock Hall after the Devonshire Dock that lies next to it. It was completed by Alfred McAlpine plc on land that was created by infilling part of the Devonshire Dock with 2.4 million tonnes of sand pumped from nearby Roosecote Sands. The DDH is the tallest building in Cumbria at 51m. With a length of 268m (879 ft), width of 51m (167 ft) and an area of 25,000 square metres (270,000 sq ft) it is also the second largest indoor shipbuilding construction complex of its kind in Europe. Due to its size, the Devonshire Dock Hall is visible from miles around, most notably from the Blackpool Promenade which is over 20 miles away.

The DDH provides a controlled environment for ship and submarine assembly and avoids the difficulties caused by building on the slope of traditional slipways. Outside the hall, a 24,300 tonne capacity ship lift allows completed vessels to be lowered into the water independently of the tide. Vessels can also be lifted out of the water and transferred to the hall. The first use of the DDH was for the construction of the later "Trafalgar" class submarines and then the "Vanguard" class submarines. The Barrow shipyard is currently (2017) constructing the "Astute" class of seven submarines in the DDH the first of which, HMS ASTUTE, was launched on 8th June 2007. The DDH will be used for the construction of the four 'Successor' submarines - the first of which will be named HMS DREADNOUGHT and is due to enter service in 2028.

This painting, which is not part of the Submarine Heritage Collection was painted by, and is the property of, the artist – Stephen Kenny. It is included in this book by kind permission of Stephen Kenny.

ADMIRALTY DEVELOPMENT ESTABLISHMENT, BARROW (ADEB)

The Painting

The picture shows a view of the Steam Raising Plant in ADEB which was used to provide the steam for testing the propulsion systems for nuclear submarines, on their machinery raft, up to full power prior to the installation of the raft into the submarine. The painting is shown as a cutaway section viewed from above showing the outside of the building, the Steam Raising Plant and a view inside the Boiler Plant. Tom Murphy worked in the Boiler House and was familiar with the layout. Tom explains that, as no high point was available, he achieved the view from above by first completing a sketch from ground level and then transferring the sketch onto a grid to achieve the correct perspective view from above.

The ADEB Story

ADEB, or to give it it's full name, the Admiralty Development Establishment, Barrow, was set up by the Admiralty in 1946 as a civilian manned facility within the Vickers Armstrong Works at Barrow-in-Furness. The task set was to carry out research into Submarine Propulsion Systems – initially into HTP (High Test Peroxide) systems and, later into nuclear propulsion and the dockside facilities required for nuclear powered vessels. The ADEB Facility was set up on the south east side of the Buccleuch and Ramsden Docks was bounded by the Cavendish Dock to the south. ADEB was managed by Doctor Forsyth as the Head of the Vickers team.

The research was initially based on the Walther propulsion system devised in Germany by Professor Hellmuth Walther and incorporated in the Type XVII U-Boats. Luckily the scientists and civilian staff had a complete Walther U-Boat of the type to study before they started their researches. This was the experimental U-1407 which had been scuttled by the Germans at Cuxhaven at the end of WW2. The U-Boat was located by British forces (who had entered Cuxhaven) and was recovered and brought back to Barrow-in-Furness in early 1946 together with Professor Walther and his team of Scientists and Engineers and a ship load of spares and support equipment carried in a captured German ship – the ELISABETH.

Professor Walther and his team were installed in a house called 'Rocklea' in Abbey Road in Barrow, which had been requisitioned by the Admiralty for this purpose and immediately started work with Vickers and the Admiralty scientists to refit, repair and modify U-1407. From 1946 to 1948 the German Team were under the control of Commander (E) L. F. Ingram for the HTP experiments and the refitting of HMS METEORITE. The submarine was commissioned into the Royal Navy as HMS METEORITE and was commanded firstly by Lieutenant James Launders, DSO**, DSC**, Royal Navy and then by Lieutenant Oliver Lascelles, Royal Navy. Two Type XXI U-Boats - U-2502 (Lieutenant Samuel Brooks, DSC, MiD, Royal Navy) and U-3017 (Lieutenant Launders and Lieutenant Maurice Atkinson, DSC, RNR) were also briefly operated by the Royal Navy and studied by the ADEB teams. After much work and many trials with HMS METEORITE a speed of eighteen knots (less than the speed anticipated) was achieved in dived trials. By 1949 the trials had reached

their conclusion and HMS METEORITE was paid off and was broken up by T. W. Ward at Barrow.

ADEB work continued with the provision of HTP propulsion systems for two experimental submarines for the Royal Navy - HMS EXPLORER (E-14 - launched on 5th March 1954) and HMS EXCALIBUR (E-15 - launched 25th February 1955) – see Painting No 33 in Section 1.

The second task of ADEB was to research into nuclear propulsion for naval ships and submarines, and the Dockside Facilities required for nuclear powered vessels. This work had been progressing at ADEB in parallel with the HTP work but in the mid 1950s the United States Navy commissioned a Nuclear powered submarine and the future of HTP propulsion was then limited. However the work with EXPLORER and EXCALIBUR continued into the 1960s.

Work continued into developing a nuclear powered propulsion system for a British built submarine but progress on the new technology of the reactor plant was slower than anticipated although the actual steam propulsion system was based on existing technology and didn't pose too many new problems. This could have led to delays in the plans for a British nuclear submarine programme commencing with HMS DREADNOUGHT. The procurement of an American nuclear propulsion plant allowed the completion of HMS DREADNOUGHT which was launched in October 1961 and went to sea in 1963. By the time the second British nuclear submarine, HMS VALIANT, went to sea in 1965 the technology issues had been resolved and the submarine had an 'all British' propulsion plant.

With the exception of the reactor systems the propulsion plant for British nuclear submarines were assembled and tested on live steam in the ADEB facility before being transported to the Top Yard at Barrow for installation in the engine room section of the submarines on the slipways. 'Live Steam' testing of the propulsion systems required a powerful steam raising plant. This was set up using equipment from wherever it was to be found. The main boilers were taken from the cancelled order for the "Battle" class destroyer RIVER PLATE which was to have been built at Swan Hunters on the Tyne. Another boiler was found from a Foster Wheeler system and a third boiler was from a German source and this boiler could produce steam at 1,000 psi at short notice. The auxiliaries for the plant were those from cancelled orders for minesweepers.

When the time came to renew the ADEB facility a totally separate facility was built to the northern side of the Slipways in the Top Yard. This facility (which was opened in 1976) was designated as the Submarine Machinery Installation and Test Establishment (SMITE).

The lower mount shows (from left to right) – a sketch of a destroyer of the class to which RIVER PLATE belonged, a sketch of the first seaplane – an AVRO 'D' flown from Cavendish Dock, the MAYFLY Rigid Airship leaving its floating Construction Shed in Cavendish Dock on 22nd May 1911 and a view of the Airship Construction Shed.

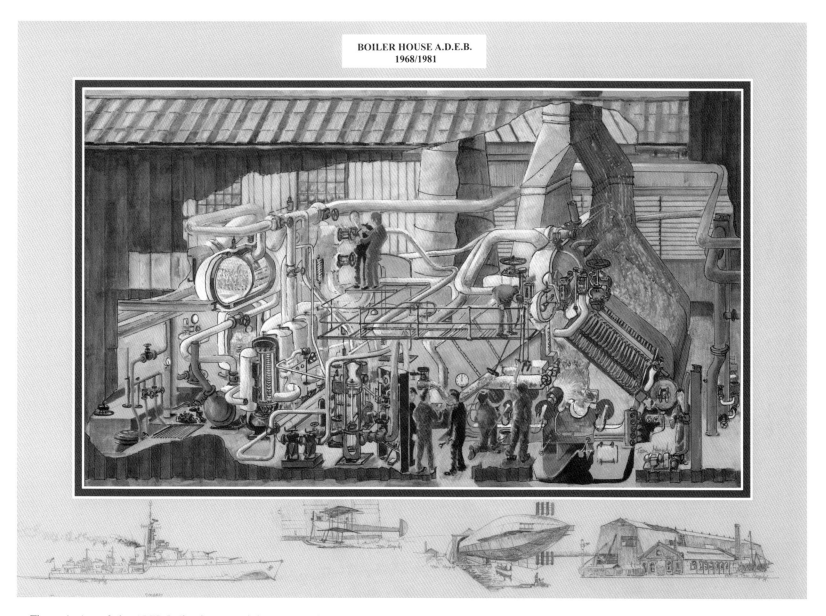

The painting of the ADEB Boiler house, whilst painted by Tom Murphy, is not part of the Submarine Heritage Collection and is the property of the Artist. It is included in this book to complete the Barrow Submarine Building story by kind permission of the Artist.

Section Three
Decade Paintings

DECADE PAINTING
1871 TO 1900

The Painting and the 1871 to 1900 Story

The Barrow Shipbuilding Company Limited was established on Barrow Island in 1871 and received its first Order in March 1871. This Order was for three 3,000 ton Passenger Ships (Yard Nos. 1, 2 & 3) and these were the DUKE OF DEVONSHIRE, the DUKE OF BUCCLEUCH and the DUKE OF LANCASTER. These ships however were not the first to be launched at the Barrow Shipyard. This honour goes to the 145 ton Steam Yacht ARIES (Yard No. 12) which was launched for Sir James Ramsden on 12th May 1873. By 1888, when the Company was renamed the Naval Construction and Armaments Company Limited, the Barrow Yard had received one hundred and sixty orders for ships, vessels and engines. This Company continued to receive orders and, by November 1897, when the Company became Vickers, Sons and Maxims Limited a further ninety eight orders had been received for a variety of naval vessels and ships for commercial and private owners – both British and Foreign. Shipbuilding orders continued to be received and, by 1900, the number of orders completed or progressed had increased to two hundred and seventy eight in the first thirty years of the Company.

The Painting (in watercolours and pencil) shows, reading from left to right:

Yard No. 1: The 3,001 ton DUKE OF DEVONSHIRE was a Steam Ship launched by Mrs Goddard on 25th June 1873 for the Eastern Steamship Company of Barrow. In 1903 the ship was renamed CONSTANZA for the journey to a scrap yard in Genoa in Italy.

Yard No. 163: The HENRY RICHARDSON – a 5 ton, tubular construction Lifeboat launched for the New Brighton Lifeboat Station in 1888. The Lifeboat was 42 feet 6 inches length overall with a beam of 12 foot and a keel depth of 3 foot 4 inches. In July 1892 the HENRY RICHARDSON rescued the 29 man crew of the fully rigged 1,800 ton ship MAXWELL which ran aground on the Mersey Bar. The Lifeboat is believed to have been in service until 1898. No other information is available on the fate of this vessel.

A sketch portrait of Sir James Ramsden.

Yard No. 25: BEN-MY-CHREE. This 1,031 ton paddle steamer for the Isle of Man Steam Packet Company was the first ship of this name built at Barrow and was launched by Lady Ramsden on 6th May 1875. She changed owners in 1877 but continued in service until December 1906 when she was scrapped at Morecambe.

Yard No. 272: ORTONA was an 8,058 ton passenger ship built for the Pacific Steam Navigation Company and launched by Miss Rankin on 10th July 1899. Transferred to the Royal Mail Steam Packet Company the ship was renamed ARCADIAN in 1910. She was torpedoed and sunk by UC-74 on 15th April 1917 whilst serving as a troopship in the Mediterranean.

Yard No. 12: The 45 ton steam yacht was launched for Sir James Ramsden by Lady Ramsden on 12th May 1873. ARIES was wrecked off Holyhead on 30th March 1880.

Yard No. 265: HMS VENGEANCE was a 12,950 ton "Canopus" class battleship launched for the Royal Navy by Mrs Albert Vickers on 25th July 1899. During WW1 the ship took part in operations in West Africa, the Dardanelles, the Eastern Mediterranean, East Africa and the East Indies. Sold to Stanlee HMS VENGEANCE was broken up at Dover from January 1922.

Yard No. 53: Steam Ferry No. 1 (shown with the Ticket Office in the background) was launched for the Furness Railway Company on 5th January 1878 and was used as the Walney Island Ferry Boat until 1902 when she was replaced by Walney Ferry No. 2.

Yard No. 248: HMS NIOBE was the 11,000 ton "Diadem" class cruiser launched for the Royal Navy by Lady Harris on 20th February 1897. After service in the Channel Squadron until December 1898 the ship was briefly deployed to the South Africa Station before returning to the Channel Fleet in October 1900 before transferring to the Reserve Fleet at Devonport. HMS NIOBE was the flagship of the Canadian Navy from October 1910 to February 1915 but then transferred to the North America and West Indies Station. From October 1915 she was the Depot Ship at Halifax, Nova Scotia and was damaged in the SS MONT BLANC explosion on 6th December 1917 – at the time possibly the largest detonation of high explosives in history. The ship was scrapped in the USA in 1922.

Yard No. 278: A 313 ton "C" class destroyer HMS VIXEN was launched for the Royal Navy on 29th May 1900. The ship served in the Home Fleet and Reserve Fleet at Devonport pre WW1 and in Home Waters during WW1. In 1916 she was in a collision with the "J" Class Submarine J5 in which both vessels were damaged. Paid off after the war the ship was sold to T.W. Ward at Grays in Essex on 19th March 1921 and was scrapped.

A view of two warships outfitting in Devonshire Dock underneath the Hammerhead Crane – from a photograph taken from the High Level Bridge.

Yard No. 155: The HAINAUT was a 1,760 ton fully rigged sailing oil tanker launched for R Speth and Co. of Antwerp on 3rd September 1887. The ship was sold to the American Petroleum Co. of Antwerp in 1899 and to the Tank Storage and Carrying Co. of London in 1911. It is believed that she was sold to Cuban owner in 1923 and was used to carry molasses from Havana to Florida. The ship was reported to be in service in 1951 but no further information is available.

A view of Floating Docks in Devonshire Dock used for the outfitting of ships in build and for ship requiring repairs.

The upper mount shows (from left to right) the Logo of the Naval Construction and Armaments Company (1888 to 1897). The decade years and the logo of Vickers, Sons and Maxim (1897 to 1911).

The lower mount shows (from Left to Right) a group of Vickers employees. The "Apollo" class cruiser HMS LATONA (Yard No. 175) launched on 22nd May 1890 under tow by the tugs LISMORE and WALNEY through the High Level Bridge for Devonshire Dock – LISMORE (Yard No. 16 was launched on 2nd September 1874). The Arms of the original Barrow Ship Building Company – founded in 1872. This piece of Barrow heritage can still be seen above the Ship Yard Gate Main Offices.

This painting was sponsored by Peter Redshaw. Peter writes *"This era may be considered as the start of a very long involvement by the Barrow Shipyard in the process of building and developing the submarine."*

DECADE PAINTING
1901-1910

The Painting and the 1901 to 1910 Story

The Orders received by, and completed by, the Vickers Sons & Maxims Shipyard in the decade 1901 to 1910 – there were one hundred and twenty eight in all – covered a variety of ship, submarine and engineering subjects. The shipyard built five battleships, eight cruisers, three destroyers and scouts and sixty five submarines for the Royal Navy and foreign customers. Seventeen commercial ship orders ranged from small steam yachts and tugs through to ferries, ice breakers, passenger ships and passenger cargo ships. The remainder were General Engineering Orders and these ranged from boilers, engines and caissons to floating docks and ship repairs.

The Painting shows:

Yard No. 289: LIBERTAD was an 11,985 ton Battleship launched on 13th March 1902 for the Chilean Navy by Madame de Gana. This ship was bought and taken over by the Royal Navy as HMS TRIUMPH in 1903. She was torpedoed and sunk by U-21 off Gaba Tepe in the Dardanelles on 25th May 1915.

Individual submarines of the "Holland", "A", "B", "C" and "D" classes - in this decade the Barrow Yard built five "Holland" class , thirteen "A" class, eleven "B" class, thirty four "C" class (two for Japan) and two "D" class 'boats'.

Submarine 'Dolphins' insignia of the Royal Navy.

Yard No. 363: The passenger steamer BEN-MY-CHREE was launched 25th March 1908 for the Isle of Man Steam Packet Company. The ship was requisitioned by the Admiralty as a Sea Plane Carrier during WW1. The ship was sunk off Castellorozo Island in the Mediterranean on 11th January 1917. She was later raised and sold for scrap at Pireaus.

Yard No. 288: SS ATHENIA is shown at sea. She was launched for Donaldson Brothers on 20th October 1903. ATHENIA was torpedoed and sunk off Instrahull on 16th August 1917.

Yard No. 319: The training ship EXMOUTH was launched for Asylums Board, London by Mrs Drage on 4th April 1905. Used as accommodation ship at Scapa Flow during WW2. Returned as training ship post war and renamed HMS WORCESTER. Discarded in 1968 and, later, broken up.

Yard No. 276: HMS EURYALUS was a "Cressey" class cruiser launched for Royal Navy by Mrs Douglas Vickers on 20th May 1901. After WW1 service the ship was sold for scrapping on 1st July 1920.

The young lady shown is typical of an 'Office Worker' of the day.

Yard No. 333: The 15,170 ton armoured cruiser IRN RURIK was launched for Imperial Russian Navy by Mrs A. T. Dawson on 17th November 1906. After WW1 service she was renamed PROFINTERN in 1921 and was scrapped about 1930.

Yard No. 318: HIJMS KATORI was a 16,400 ton battleship launched for Imperial Japanese Navy by HIH Princess Arisugawa on 19th August 1905. Discarded in 1923 the ship was broken up for scrap in 1924/25.

Yard No. 372: Although not shown two "C" class submarines (Submarines Nos. 8 – Yard No. 366 & No. 9 – Yard No. 367) were built for Imperial Japanese Navy. The transporter shown was used to deliver the submarines to Japan. The submarines were later renamed Ha. 1 and Ha. 2 and both were discarded by the Japanese Navy in December 1929.

The Boy Worker shown is typical of the many young workers of the day.

Yard No. 374: At 19,250 tons HMS VANGUARD - laid down as HMS RODNEY - was a battleship launched for the Royal Navy on 22nd February 1909. She was sunk with large loss of life after an internal explosion at Scapa Flow on 9th July 1917.

The Shipyard Worker shown is typical of the many thousands of men employed in the shipyard at the time.

Yard No. 347: BNS SÃO PAULO was a 19,281 ton battleship launched for the Brazilian Navy by Senora F. Regia de Olivieta on 20th April 1909. After being sold for scrap in 1951 the ship was lost on tow some 150 miles off the Azores

Yard No. 400: ALFONSO PENNA was a floating dock launched at Barrow for Brazilian Government in three Sections on 7th, 8th and 9th June 1910. She was designed to lift the SÃO PAULO and her sister ship MINAS GEREAS.

The upper mount shows the company logo of Vickers Sons & Maxim Limited.

The lower mount shows the Walney Ferry (Yard No. 287) at her launch on 15th March 1902 - this ferry was the only way to get from Barrow Island to Walney Island before the Jubilee Bridge was built and opened in 1910. The ferry is also shown in operation. Also shown on the lower mount are the main turbines for HMS VANGUARD and Tom Vickers and Albert Vickers who both served as the Chairman of Vickers, Sons and Maxims from October 1873 to June 1909 and June 1909 to September 1919 respectively.

1901 - 1910

This decade Painting - 1901 to 1910 - was commissioned by Mrs Mary Whetton in memory of her late husband Harry Whetton – a submariner and a former Member of the Barrow-in-Furness Branch of the Submariners Association.

DECADE PAINTING
1911-1920

The Painting and the 1911 To 1920 Story

By the beginning of this decade the company of Vickers, Sons and Maxims had firmly established itself as a submarine building yard with orders for the Royal Navy and foreign Navies – notably Japan. Another change of name came in April 1911 when the company became Vickers Limited. Orders continued to be placed with the yard and, not surprisingly, given the outbreak of WW1 in 1914 the bulk of the orders received were for naval customers – mainly the Royal Navy and, of one hundred and eighty seven orders progressed, one hundred and twenty eight were naval orders of which eighty nine were for submarines and several others were submarine related. Not all of these orders were completed as several submarines and warships were cancelled at the end of the war.

Vickers at Barrow also moved into aircraft construction in this decade with a concentration on 'lighter than air' ships the most well known of which was the MAYFLY which was so large that a special floating Airship Construction Shed or Hangar was constructed in the Cavendish Dock. Airship construction restarted during WW1 with airships being assembled in the land based shed on Walney Island. During the war Vickers built four Airships – No. 9r, Nos. R23, R26 and R80. Three 'Parseval' airships were also built – these being HM Airships Nos. 5, 6 & 7.

The Painting shows reading from left to right – as a book:

Yard No. 407: HMS PRINCESS ROYAL was a 26,350 ton "Lion" class battlecruiser which was launched for the Royal Navy by HRH the Princess Royal on 29th April 1911. At the time she was the fastest battlecruiser in the world – capable of 32.7 knots. HMS PRINCESS ROYAL took part in the Battle of the Heligoland Bight in 1914 and the Battle of Jutland in May/June 1916. The ship was sold for scrap in 1923 and broken up in 1926.

The airship MAYFLY and the Airship Construction Shed in Cavendish Dock with the MAYFLY emerging from the hangar for mooring trials on 22nd May 1911.

Yard No. 414: HIJMS KONGO was a 27,500 ton battlecruiser launched for the Imperial Japanese Navy by Madame Koike on 18th May 1912. Capable of a speed of 27.5 knots the ship was rebuilt in Japan between 1935 and 1937 which increased the displacement to 29,330 tons and speed to 30.5 knots. KONGO was torpedoed and sunk north-west of Formosa on 21st November 1944 by the American Submarine USS SEALION.

Yard No. 425: Laid down in December 1911 as the SULTAN MEHMED RESHAD V for the Turkish Navy this 25,250 ton battleship was launched on 3rd September 1913 by Naile Hanoum as the renamed REŞADIYE. On the outbreak of WW1 the ship was taken over by the Royal Navy and renamed HMS ERIN. The ship became part of the 2nd Battle Squadron and took part in the Battle of Jutland in May/June 1916. She was sold to Cox and Danks on 19th December 1922 and was scrapped at Queenborough on the Isle of Sheppey.

Yard No.493: SCYTHIA was a 19,761 ton passenger liner launched for the Cunard White Star Line by Mrs Maxwell on 23rd March 1920. The ship was fitted out at Lorient. For most of her service she carried passengers between the United Kingdom and North America and as a troop ship in the 1930s and during WW2. SCYTHIA was scrapped at Inverkeithing from 20th January 1958.

Yard No. 429: Laid down as HMS DELHI for the RN as a 25,000 ton "Iron Duke" class battleship she was launched as HMS EMPEROR OF INDIA by Lady Islington on 27th November 1913. The ship joined the Grand Fleet for work up on 1st December 1914 and then joined the 4th Battle Squadron on 10th December 1914. After WW1 service and service through the 1920s she was sunk as a target on 1st July 1931, later raised and scrapped at Rosyth from 16th February 1932.

Yard No. 506: WAR RULER. This was a 5,175 ton standard cargo ship for the British Government launched on 17th December 1918. Completed as GASCONIER for Belgian owners the ship was sold and renamed many times before being sold to Japanese owners in 1956. As shown she is completing the rescue of survivors from a wreck – there were only nine survivors out of thirty three who got off the wreck.

Yard No. 433: HMS HUMBER, a 1,250 ton River Monitor was launched sideways as JAVERY for the Brazilian Government on 17th June 1913 by Miss Lomos Basto. The ship – also shown as completed was, with its two sisters, Yard No. 434 SOLIMOES (HMS SEVERN) and Yard No. 435 MADEIRA (HMS MERSEY), bought by the Royal Navy in 1914. HUMBER saw action at the Dardanelles in WW1 and SEVERN and MERSEY sank the German Cruiser KÖNIGSBERG at the Rufiji River in West Africa in WW1. All three ships we scrapped in 1920 and 1921.

Yard No. 455: HMS REVENGE. This was a 31,250 ton "Royal Sovereign" class battleship (laid down as HMS RENOWN) which was launched for the Royal Navy by Lady Glenconnor on 29th May 1915. She took part in the Battle of Jutland as part of the 1st Battle Squadron. The ship served in the Home Fleet on Atlantic convoy duties and in the Eastern Fleet in WW2 and was later scrapped at Inverkeithing from 5th September 1948.

The Scherzer 'roll lift' bridge, opened on 12th October 1908, took Furness railway traffic over the Buccleuch Dock/Ramsden Dock to Barrow Island. Known locally as the 'Cradle' or 'Banana' Bridge it was closed to use on 31st December 1966.

Yard No. 571: CORTONA – a 7,093 ton cargo ship launched for the Donaldson Line by Mrs Donaldson on 14th September 1920 shown together with the tug LISMORE (Yard No. 16). The ship was torpedoed and sunk on 11th July 1941.

Yard No. 445: SANTA MARGHERITA (an oil tanker) was launched as the 7,496 ton OLYMPIA for the Royal Fleet Auxiliary on 23rd October 1915. After WW1 service she was sold and renamed several times. The ship was used as an oil hulk in Sierra Leone and South Africa in WW2 and in Gibraltar from 1946 before being scrapped at Rosyth in 1951.

In the bottom right hand corner of the picture is a drawing of 12-inch naval gun mounting which is representative of the output of the 'Gun Shop' in this decade.

The lower mount (l to r) shows a lathe worker, Admiral Sir David Beatty, the Vickers Ltd logo, Sir Trevor Dawson (managing director 1906 to 1931 and yard workers celebrating Armistice.

This painting was commissioned by Barrie Downer, Secretary of the Barrow-in-Furness Branch, Submariners Association. This decade was chosen as it was one of the key decades in the development of submarines and saw the transition from the small petrol engined vessels of the early years of the century through diesel power to large steam powered submarines and the emergence of the submarine as an effective weapon of sea warfare.

DECADE PAINTING
1921-1930

The Painting and the 1921 to 1930 Story

This decade became known in Barrow as the years when, at times, there was virtually no work in the shipyards and the workforce fell to very low levels. The first ship launched in the decade 1921 to 1930 was the 14,193 ton passenger liner MORETON BAY (Yard No. 573) which was the first of three ships ordered by the Australian Commonwealth Government Line and was launched on 23rd April 1921. The other two were the HOBSONS BAY (later renamed ESPERANCE BAY) and the JERVIS BAY. These were followed by a number of tanker and passenger ship orders but naval orders very nearly dried up in first half of the decade. Apart from some drawings for Dutch submarines, an order for turbines for a battlecruiser (later cancelled), turbine parts for a Japanese destroyer and a diesel engine for a Spanish submarine the first substantial naval order was for the cruiser HMS CUMBERLAND - Yard No. 618. The first submarine orders came from Australia and were two "O" class submarines – OA1 & OA2 (Yard Nos. 621 and 622) later renamed as OXLEY and OTWAY. Naval orders took off after 1926 with orders for a submarine depot ship (HMS MEDWAY), three "O" class submarines, a fleet repair ship, four "P" class submarines and a destroyer for the Royal Navy followed by a river gunboat for Siam (Thailand), three "O" class submarines and a submarine depot ship for Chile. Three "R" class submarines and another destroyer followed for the Royal Navy. Amongst the ninety orders for the shipyard in the decade only thirty four (one of which was cancelled) were for naval ships and submarines or for engines for naval ships. The other fifty six orders were for a variety of types and included passenger ships, passenger cargo ships, passenger feeder ships, tankers, colliers, coastal ships, sludge vessels, floating docks, dock gates and caissons. In December 1927 there was another change of company name when the shipyard became Vickers-Armstrong Limited.

The Painting shows from the top left reading as a book:

Yard No. 628: KEDAH, a 2,499 ton feeder passenger ship, was launched by Lady Maxwell on 16th July 1927 for the Straits Steamship Company of Singapore to act as a feeder for the Blue Funnel Line. An auxiliary patrol vessel during WW2 the ship was bought by Israeli owner in 1946, was renamed KEDMAH and was the first ship to fly the Israeli flag. The ship is shown with a painting of an Indian outrigger in the foreground. Later renamed GOLDEN ISLES she was scrapped at Newport from October 1955.

Yard No. 618: HMS CUMBERLAND was 9,750 ton "Kent" class cruiser launched for the Royal Navy by the Countess of Carlisle on 16th March 1926 and was commissioned for service on the China Station. During WW2 the ship served on the South Atlantic, Home, Eastern and East Indies Stations. After post war service as a trials ship and a farewell visit to Barrow in October 1958 the ship was scrapped at Newport. CUMBERLAND is shown whilst fitting out in Devonshire Dock and also at sea.

Yard No. 586: CARINTHIA (ex SERVIA) was a 20,277 ton passenger liner for the Cunard White Star Line launched on 24th Feb 1925 by Mrs Lister. Converted to an armed merchant cruiser in January 1940 AMC CARINTHIA was torpedoed and sunk by U-46 west of Ireland on 6th Jun 1940. Below this picture of CARINTHIA in 'cruise' colours is a view of the ship on the stocks whilst her rudder was being fitted.

Yard No. 629: HMS MEDWAY was a 14,650 ton purpose built submarine depot ship launched for the Royal Navy by Lady Chatfield on 19th July 1928. She was commissioned at Barrow on 3rd July 1929 as the depot ship for the 4th Submarine Flotilla at Hong Kong and served there until 1940 when she was transferred to Alexandria in the Mediterranean with her Flotilla and became the depot ship for the 1st Submarine Flotilla. On 30th June 1942 HMS MEDWAY was torpedoed and sunk by U-372 when on passage from Alexandria to Haifa. She is portrayed in tropical colours.

Yard No 660: LADY OF MANN. Built in only five months as a 3,140 ton passenger ship and as the 'Centenary Vessel' for the Isle of Man Steam Packet Company LADY OF MANN was launched by the Duchess of Atholl on 4th March 1930. Requisitioned by the Admiralty in WW2 she rescued over 4,200 men from the Dunkirk beaches and a further 5,000 (estimated) from Le Harve, Cherbourg and Brest. The ship later served as a troopship and as a landing ship at Normandy. She was returned to service in the Irish Sea in May 1946 and was retired from service in 1971.

Yard No. 575: JERVIS BAY. This ship was the one of three orders for 14,000 ton, 15 knot passenger liners for the Australian Government Line and was launched on 17th January 1922 by Mrs J Storey. During WW2 JERVIS BAY and her two sister ships MORETON BAY and HOBSONS BAY (later renamed ESPERANCE BAY) were converted to armed merchant cruisers. JERVIS Bay was sunk by the pocket battleship ADMIRAL SCHEER on 5th November 1940 whilst defending a North Atlantic Convoy and her Captain, Fogarty Fegen, was awarded a posthumous Victoria Cross. MORETON BAY and ESPERANCE BAY also served as troop ships and both survived the war. MORETON BAY was scrapped at Barrow from 13th April 1957.

The ships anchors shown next were previously sited on Piel Island but are no longer there.

Yard No. 598: ORAMA was launched for the Orient Steam Navigation Company on 20th May 1924 as a 19,777 ton passenger liner for the England/Australia route. The ship is shown at sea, at launch and in the 'corn' colours later used for the ORION – built at Barrow in 1934. ORAMA was sunk by gunfire from the ADMIRAL VON HIPPER whilst on passage from Tilbury to Scapa Flow on 8th June 1940.

The lower mount shows (on the left):

A pencil sketch of the passenger cargo ship MOVERIA shown under construction on the slipways - from a photograph of MOVERIA, built for the Donaldson Line, taken on 4th June 1924. In the middle is a portrait of Sir Charles Craven shown with the Vickers House Flag. Charles Craven – a former Royal Navy (pre WW1) submarine Commanding Officer was Chairman of Vickers Armstrong from January 1926 to November 1944. On the right hand side is another pencil sketch of MOVERIA - under construction - from a photograph taken on 8th January 1924 – with workmen and various ship building tools.

This painting was Commissioned by Alan Jones, Chairman of the Barrow-in-Furness Branch, Submariners Association and his wife Patricia in memory of their youngest daughter, Nicola 1970 – 2008.

DECADE PAINTING
1931-1940

The Painting and the 1931 to 1940 Story

The decade 1931 to 1940 started off with a pretty full order book with the first launch of the new decade being the 22,548 topassenger liner STRATHNAVER on 5th February 1931 followed by sister ship STRATHAIRD on 18th July 1931 with both ships built for P & O Steam Navigation Co. of London. The order book throughout the decade totalled one hundred and fourteen but the balance of naval orders to commercial orders was the opposite of the previous ten years with there being thirty six commercial orders to seventy eight naval orders. The commercial orders ranged from passenger liners through passenger cargo ships to a passenger steamer for Lake Windermere and coasters, engines and dock gates.

The naval orders included three "River" class submarines, three "Porpoise" class submarines, six "T" class submarines and thirteen "U" class submarines – all for the Royal Navy. There were also three submarines for Portugal, two for Estonia and four for Turkey. Other naval orders included "Leander", "Fiji" and "Dido" class cruiser, "C", "D", "F" & "G" class destroyers, two "Illustrious" class aircraft carriers and ships for the Brazilian, Argentinean and Turkish Navies. The reason for the preponderance of naval orders in this decade was, initially, the rearmament programme to counter the threat from Germany followed by the 'Emergency War Programme'. Two destroyers and four submarines for the Turkish Navy were taken over by the Royal Navy but three submariness and one destroyer were later delivered to their original owners.

Reading from the top left - as if reading a book - this Painting shows:

Yard No. 670: RANGATIRA - a 6,152 ton passenger cargo ship built for the Union Steamship Company of New Zealand and launched by Lady Wilford on 16th April 1931. The ship was retired from service in December 1965 and scrapped in 1968.

Yard No. 707: AWATEA was a 13,482 ton passenger cargo ship launched on 25th February 1936 for the Union Steamship Company of New Zealand. Converted to a troopship in WW2 AWATEA was bombed and sunk off Bougie in Algeria on 11th November 1942.

Yard No. 681: QUEEN OF BERMUDA. Built for Furness Withy & Co. Ltd this ship was a 22,575 ton passengerliner launched by Lady Cubitt on 2nd September 1932. During WW2 the ship was firstly an armed merchant cruiser and then a troopship. Returned to the owners post war the ship was rebuilt in the 1960s and operated between New York and Bermuda until 1966 when she was retired from service and broken up at Faslane.

Yard No. 682: HMS AJAX was a 6,985 ton "Leander" class cruiser launched on 1st March 1934 by Lady Chatfield. Most famously HMS AJAX took part in the Battle of the River Plate in 1939 following which the German pocket battleship ADMIRAL GRAF SPEE was scuttled. HMS AJAX later served as part of 'Force H' in the Mediterranean. Paid off post war she was scrapped at Newport by Cashmore in November 1949. Shown below HMS AJAX is a profile sketch of ADMIRAL GRAF SPEE.

Yard No. 688: The sail training ship ALMIRANTE SALDANHA was launched for the Brazilian Navy on 19th Dec 1933. The ship was converted to an oceanographic survey vessel in 1961. Paid off by Brazilian Navy in 1964 the ship continued to serve as a research vessel. Now registered on the Historic Ships Register ALMIRANTE SALDANHA is laid up at Niteroi in Brazil.

Yard No. 712: ORCADES was a 23,456 ton passenger ship launched on 7th December 1936 by Mrs Geddes for the Orient Steam Navigation Company. Used as a troopship during WW2 ORCADES was torpedoed and sunk by the German U-boat U-172 (Emmermann) in the south Atlantic 217 miles off Capetown on 10th October 1942.

Yard No. 717 and 718: FENELLA and TYNWALD were 2,376 ton passenger steamers built for the Isle of Man Steam Packet Company. FENELLA was launched by Miss Thin on 16th December 1936. FENELLA was sunk at Dunkirk in May 1940 when a bomb exploded between the jetty and the ship. TYNWALD, launched on 16th September 1936 was used as a troopship during WW2 TYNWALD took part in the Dunkirk evacuation rescuing some 10,000 troops. Later converted to an anti-aircraft cruiser she sank after hitting a mine off Bougie in Algeria on 12th November 1942.

Yard No. 732: HMS ILLUSTRIOUS was a 23,000 ton "Illustrious" class aircraft carrier launched by Lady Henderson on 5th April 1939. The ship served in the Mediterranean in WW2 and launched the successful Taranto attack on 11/12th November 1940. Later served in the Eastern Fleet, 'Force H' and in the British Pacific Fleet. Scrapped at Faslane in late 1956.

Yard No. 750: HMS JAMAICA was an 8,000 ton "Fiji" class cruiser launched for the Royal Navy by Mrs Fraser on 28th April 1939. She served with the Home Fleet during WW2. Post WW2 HMS JAMAICA was one of the first Royal Navy warships to arrive in the Korean War zone in July 1950 seeing action on 8th July and, in September 1950, took part in the Inchon landings. The ship was scrapped at Dalmuir and Troon between 1960 and 1962.

Yard No. 715: TEAL. There are two views of this 215 ton passenger steamer launched for the LMS Railway Company on 4th July 1936 by Miss Harris for service on Lake Windermere. After launch at Barrow TEAL was dismantled, transported to Windermere and re-assembled. TEAL was later rebuilt to extend her life and was still in service on Windermere in 2017.

Yard No. 697: ORION. This 23,371 ton passenger liner was launched by the Duke of Gloucester by radio link from Australia on 7th December 1934. Built for the Orient Steam Navigation Company ORION was used as a troopship during WW2 and took part in Operation Torch (the North Africa landing) in 1942. ORION is shown being berthed alongside the P & O passenger liner STRATHMORE (Yard No. 698 - launched on 4th April 1935) at the 'fitting out' berth in Buccleuch Dock by the tugs DONGARTH and YORKGARTH. ORION was broken up from September 1963 and STRATHMORE was scrapped in 1969.

The lower mount shows the results of a German air raid on Barrow viewed on the corner of Cornwallis Street and Hindpool Road with Devonshire Dock Hammerhead Crane and the North Shop in the background, the Vickers Armstrong house flag (backed by a sketch of the slipway cranes) and a quad 14-Inch gun mounting - as fitted in "King George V" class battleships.

Commissioned by Millard Laney – an American submariner and US Department of Defence Liaison Officer to the Astute Submarine IPT in the Barrow Shipyard.

DECADE PAINTING
1941-1950

The Painting and the 1941 to 1950 Story

This decade saw a large increase in naval orders resulting from the war and a consequent reduction in merchant orders. Some one hundred and ninety five orders were received including some single order numbers covering multiple construction of "X" craft, landing craft and engines. Naval orders were completed for three aircraft carriers, one cruiser and eight destroyers whilst seventy nine orders related to submarines and fifteen to landing craft. Merchant orders covered one oil tanker, four liners, one coaster, six passenger cargo and nine cargo ships. Thirty one orders covered engines (some multiple) and seventeen orders were for miscellaneous items such as dock gates. Twenty eight orders, mainly for submarines and engines, were cancelled and eight orders were transferred to other yards.

The 1941 to 1950 Painting shows from left to right:

Yard No. 794: The 1,087 ton "Hunt" class destroyer HMS CATTERICK which was launched for the Royal Navy by Mrs Reid Young on 22nd November 1941 was later transferred to the Greek Navy as RHNS HASTINGS.

Yard No. 831: Was the "U" class destroyer HMS URCHIN launched for the Royal Navy by Mrs Turner on 8th March 1943. In 1953 HMS URCHIN was converted to a "Type 15" anti-submarine frigate by Barclay Curle at Glasgow. She was paid off and scrapped in 1965.

Yard No. 834: The "W" class destroyer HMS WRANGLER was the second vessel of this name built at Barrow (the first was Yard No. 70 launched on 5th October 1880). The second HMS WRANGLER was launched for the Royal Navy by Mrs Glennie on 30th December 1943 and was later transferred to the South African Navy as SANS VRYSTAAT.

Yard No. 856: A 7,513 ton landing ship sarrier EMPIRE ELAINE was launched for the Ministry of War Transport (MoWT) on 30th July 1942 and is shown in a convoy escorted by Short Sunderland flying boats built by Short Bros. at Windermere in the Lake District. This ship was later converted to a cargo ship and renamed JOHN LYRAS for Marine Enterprises Ltd.

Yard No. 885: The 20,000 ton "Majestic" class aircraft carrier HMS MAJESTIC was launched for the Royal Navy by Lady Anderson on 28th February 1945. Construction was stopped in 1946 but she was completed in 1949. In 1955 MAJESTIC was sold to the Royal Australian Navy and renamed HMAS MELBOURNE. Scrapped in China from 1985.

Royal Navy White Ensign.

Yard No. 884: This 13,190 ton "Colossus" class aircraft carrier HMS PIONEER was laid down as HMS MARS on 15th April 1943 and was completed as the aircraft maintenance ship HMS PIONEER. Launched by the Lady Woolton for the Royal Navy on 20th May 1944 and saw service with the British Pacific Fleet in 1944/45. She was scrapped at Inverkeithing in September 1954.

Yard Nos. 931 to 989: The Landing Craft Tank (LCT) shown is one of eight LCTs (LCTs 7082 to 7089) launched for the Royal Navy in March & April 1944. Below is an LCT landing vehicles and troops on shore.

Yard No. 945: The 6,911 ton passenger cargo ship HINEMOA was launched by Mrs A.F. Falla for the Union Steam Ship Co. of New Zealand on 30th May 1946. HINEMOA was the first ship to be built at Barrow post WW2.

Yard No. 829: A 734 ton coaster the RIVER FISHER was launched by Mrs Poate for James Fisher Ltd. on 27th September 1941 and completed as EMPIRE JACK for the MoWT. In 1946 ownership reverted to James Fisher and she reverted to the name RIVER FISHER.

Yard Nos. 948 & 949: These two ships were the passenger cargo ships ACCRA and APAPA. They were launched for the Elder Dempster Lines on 27th February 1947 and 18th August 1947 respectively. ACCRA was broken up in Spain from 13th November 1967 and APPAPA in China from 23rd February 1975.

Yard No. 950: The 28,396 ton passenger liner ORCADES was launched for the P & O Steam Navigation Co. by the Lady Morshead on 14th Oct 1947. Broken up in Taiwan in 1973.

Yard No. 951: The passenger liner HIMALAYA (27,989 tons) was launched for the P & O Steam Navigation Co. by the Lady Currie on 5th October 1948. She was a sister ship to ORCADES.

Yard No. 964: The P & O Steam Navigation Co. passenger liner CHUSAN (24,261 tons) was launched by Viscountess Bruce on 28th June 1949. The ship was withdrawn from service in 1973.

Yard Nos. 969, 971 & 970: These ships were three 12,500 ton passenger cargo ships - PRESIDENTE PERON, 17 de OCTUBRE & EVA PERON which were launched for the Argentine Government on 3rd November 1948, 25th August 1949 & 4th April 1950 respectively. They were renamed ARGENTINA, LIBERTAD and URAGUAY in 1955 and transferred to for Empresa Linea Maratimas Argentina in November 1960.

Yard No. 976: The 27,632 ton passenger liner ORONSAY was launched for the P & O Steam Navigation Co. by Mrs Anderson on 30th June 1950. Also views of ORONSAY at sea and on fire at Barrow during fitting out on 28th October 1950.

Yard No. 994: An 8,726 ton oil tanker the BRITISH ADVENTURE was launched for the British Petroleum Tanker Co. Ltd by Mrs Fraser on 12th December 1950.

The upper mount shows Yard No. 767: "Dido" class cruiser HMS SPARTAN being launched on 27th August 1943 and the German blitz on Barrow in April and May 1943. After war service in Home Waters HMS SPARTAN was sent to the Mediterranean where she was sunk by a glider bomb at Anzio on 29th January 1944.

The lower mount shows 'hand caulking' of wooden decks, an Oil Tanker on the slips, the house hlag of Vickers Armstrong Ltd, hammerhead cranes at Buccleuch Dock fitting out berths and the launch of Yard No. 994 BRITISH ADVENTURE on 12th December 1950.

1941 - 1950

This painting was commissioned by Dez Northover. Dez is a member of the West of Scotland Branch of the Submariners Association. He served in the Royal Navy from 1970 to 1985 and as a WEM(O) and POWEM(O) in HM Submarines OPOSSUM, PORPOISE, SEALION, FINWHALE, REPULSE (Port), SOVEREIGN and OBERON. His sponsorship of this painting is a memory of his time serving at sea with his many friends in submarines.

DECADE PAINTING
1951-1960

The Painting and the 1951 to 1960 Story

Naval orders were fewer during this decade with a total of fifteen naval ships and submarines out of the total of sixty eight orders progressed. The naval orders included the aircraft carrier HMS HERMES - which had been laid down in June 1944. There were orders for five destroyers – all for overseas customers and one for the outfitting of a frigate for the Royal Navy. The eight submarine orders included two experimental High Test Peroxide submarines, four conventional diesel submarines, one order for four "X51" class submarines and the first nuclear submarine – HMS DREADNOUGHT – all for the Royal Navy. Merchant orders were predominantly for oil tankers of which eighteen were built although two passenger liners were completed - as was one ore carrier. There were thirty orders for miscellaneous items including engines, submarine machinery, generating sets and caissons.

The painting shows clockwise from the top left:

Yard No 1008: The 10,838 ton ore carrier CARL SCHEDEMAN was launched for the Tropical Steamship Co. Ltd on 12th May 1952. She was later transferred to the Caribbean Steamship Co. S.A.

Yard No 1011: The 17,540 ton tanker ESSO WESTMINSTER was launched for the Esso Petroleum Co. Ltd. on 24th September 1953.

Yard No 928: The 23,000 ton aircraft carrier HMS HERMES was laid down as HMS ELEPHANT. Launched for Royal Navy on 16th February 1953 the ship is shown with the ship's badge and White Ensign. HMS HERMES was the flagship of the Falklands Task Force (Operation Corporate) in April to June 1982. HMS HERMES was later transferred to the Indian Navy as INS VIRAAT. She was decommissioned in 2016.

Yard No 1010: The 2,600 ton destroyer ZULIA was the second of two destroyers launched for Venezuelan Navy on 29th June 1953.

Yard No 1021: The 28,790 ton passenger liner ORSOVA: Launched for Orient Steam Navigation Co. Ltd. on 14th May 1953 is also shown under construction on the slipway.

Yard No 1062: HMS DREADNOUGHT. This was the first nuclear powered submarine launched for the Royal Navy by HM The Queen on 21st October 1960 and is shown with submariners Dolphins. DREADNOUGHT was paid off in 1982 and is laid up at Rosyth awaiting disposal.

Yard No 1037: HMS STICKLEBACK was an "X51" class submarine, one of a class of four, launched for Royal Navy on 1st October 1954. STICKLEBACK, part of the Imperial War Museum collection, is now on public display at Helensburgh.

Yard No 1029: The 2,405 ton first of class submarine HMS PORPOISE. A conventional submarine launched for Royal Navy on 25th April 1956 PORPOISE was sunk as a target in Stingray torpedo trials off Gibraltar in November 1985.

Yard No 980: The 1,000 ton experimental High Test Peroxide "Ex" class submarine HMS EXCALIBUR (E15) was launched for Royal Navy on 25th February 1955. Paid off in 1970 and broken up at Barrow.

Yard No 1055: The 2,730 ton destroyer ALMIRANTE WILLIAMS was launched for Chilean Navy on 5th May 1958.

Sir Leonard Redshaw.

Vickers Armstrong workforce making their way home.

Yard No 1027: A 12,212 ton oil tanker SS HINEA was launched for Shell Bermuda (Overseas) Ltd. on 19th Aug 1955.

Yard No 1061: The 41,923 ton passenger liner SS ORIANA was launched for Orient Steam Navigation Co. Ltd. on 3rd November 1959.

Yard No 1040: The 20,889 ton oil tanker SAN GREGORIO was ordered for the Burmah Oil Co. Ltd but was launched for the Eagle Oil & Shipping Co. Ltd. on 26th July 1957. She was later transferred to Shell Oil Tankers Ltd.

Yard No 1020: A 21,153 ton oil tanker BRITISH VICTORY was launched for the British Petroleum Tanker Co. Ltd on 13th December 1954.

Yard No 1000: The 21,101 ton oil tanker WORLD CONCORD was launched for the Niarchos Group of Companies on 29th January 1952.

The upper mount shows the Vickers Armstrong Ltd. house flag.

The lower mount is a portrait of Sir Leonard 'Len' Redshaw with an original of his signature. The signature is from a letter which is enclosed in the mount, decade Years 1951 - 1960 and a view of Barrow Island slipways showing a ship on the slips and the slipway crane.

1951 - 1960

Sponsored by Joyce Murphy, wife of the artist and Peter Redshaw, son of Sir Len Redshaw - former Managing Director of the Barrow Shipyard. Peter writes *"This painting was sponsored to recognise my father, Sir Leonard Redshaw's, deep involvement in the Shipyard and decisions to build nuclear powered submarines."*

DECADE PAINTING
1961-1970

The Painting and the 1961 to 1970 Story

This picture has been completed in a variety of media including pencil, water colour and ink and wash. The painting has been laid out to be read in the form of a book – from left to right and from top to bottom. In this decade the orders progressed were fewer than in the previous ten years but, of the twenty three orders worked on, sixteen were naval and included twelve submarines (although three Vickers private venture submarines were cancelled) and one of two destroyers for the Imperial Iranian Navy. The submarines, all for the Royal Navy, included two "Resolution" class SSBNs, two "Oberon" class conventional submarines, two "Valiant" class and two "Improved Valiant" class fleet submarines and the first of the "Swiftsure" class fleet submarine HMS SWIFTSURE. The other naval order was for the engines for a "Leander" class frigate built at the Walker Yard on the Tyne. Orders from civil sources were fewer and included one LNG carrier and six oil tankers.

This picture has been laid out to be read in the form of a book – from left to right and from top to bottom and shows:

Yard No. 1068: The oil tanker MALWA. This ship was launched for Peninsular and Oriental Tankers Ltd. by Mrs J Houston Jackson – the wife of the Managing Director of P & O Tankers Ltd - on 30th May 1961. The ship, which was managed by Trident Tankers Ltd. of the P & O Group, is shown at sea with the P & O House Flag depicted above the funnel.

Yard No. 1058: The 42,495 ton oil tanker BRITISH PRESTIGE. Launched for the British Petroleum Tanker Co. Ltd on 28th July 1961, the tanker is shown underway at sea.

Yard No. 1067: The 52,323 ton oil tanker BRITISH GRENADIER was launched for the British Petroleum Tanker Co. Ltd on 16th August 1962. The tanker is shown at sea. Two flags are shown. On the left below the stern is the British Petroleum house flag and the Red Ensign (otherwise known as the 'Red Duster') – the ensign of the Merchant Navy - is shown above the bows.

Yard No. 1080: IINS ZAAL was a 1,265 ton Mark V destroyer launched for the Imperial Iranian Navy at Barrow by H.E. Abbas Aram (the Iranian Ambassador) who was deputising for HIH the Princess Shadokt Fatemah Pahlevi on 4th March 1969. A sister ship, IINS ROSTAM, was also launched for the Imperial Iranian Navy at the Swan Hunter Shipyard at Walker on the Tyne by H.E. Abbas Aram (the Iranian

Ambassador) on 4th March 1969. After launch the ship was towed to and fitted out at Barrow from March 1969. ZAAL was renamed IS ALBORZ following the Iranian Revolution and ROSTAM was renamed IS SALDANAH. The flag shown is the Iranian Ensign.

Yard No. 1063: The Type 81 "Tribal" class frigate HMS MOHAWK. The ship was launched for the Royal Navy by Mrs. J.M. Villiers on 5th April 1962 and the ship is shown in a pen and ink drawing – the flag is the Royal Navy White Ensign.

Yard No. 1071: METHANE PRINCESS was a specialised 20,300 ton Liquified Natural Gas Carrier launched by Mrs. William Wood Prince of Chicago for Conch Methane Tankers Ltd. on 22nd June 1963.

Yard No. 1069: The 100,000 ton Oil Tanker BRITISH ADMIRAL was launched by HM The Queen for the BP Tanker Co. Ltd. on 17th March 1965. This was the first European built 100,000 ton tanker and it replaced two 50,000 ton tankers previously ordered as Yard Nos. 1065 and 1070. Details relating to BRITISH ADMIRAL are shown in the lower half of the painting. On the left is the BRITISH ADMIRAL moving down the slipway into the Walney Channel where tugs are waiting to take the ship under tow to the deep water berths shown on the right hand side. The ship was too large to be taken into the Dock System for fitting out. Because of this the BRITISH ADMIRAL was completed on the slips with boilers, main engines and all other fittings ready to go to sea. Note the angle of the ship on the slipway, the drag chains starting to brake and slow the ship, the waves at the stern as she enters the water and the tugs blowing their steam whistles in salute. Superimposed on the hull of the ship is a panoramic view showing the slipways and the hammerhead cranes of the shipyard.

The view at the lower left shows BRITISH ADMIRAL being berthed at the deep water berth in the Walney Channel where she was prepared to go to sea with, amongst other work, the removal of the launch ways which were attached under the hull.

The upper mount shows the decade dates of '1961 to 1970'.

The lower mount shows a portrait, on the left hand side, of Sir Leonard 'Len' Redshaw who was the company Chairman during this decade, in the centre a view of the Vickers Shipyard from the Walney Channel where preparations are underway for the launch of a nuclear submarine and, on the right hand side, an aerial view of the Devonshire Dock and its surrounding areas as it was in 1969.

This painting was the second commissioned by Dez Northover. Dez is a member of the West of Scotland Branch of the Submariners Association. He served in the Royal Navy from 1970 to 1985 and as a WEM(O) and POWEM(O) in HM Submarines OPOSSUM, PORPOISE, SEALION, FINWHALE, REPULSE (Port), SOVEREIGN and OBERON. His sponsorship of this painting is a memory of his time serving at sea with his many friends in Submarines.

DECADE PAINTING
1971-1980

The Painting and the 1971 to 1980 Story

The years 1971 to 1980 saw only one merchant ship order progressed and this was for the passenger liner COPENHAGEN although, in the event, the ship was completed at Wallsend on the Tyne. Work at Barrow was predominantly naval with fifteen orders progressed and, of these, eleven were for submarines. The submarines included five "Swiftsure" class fleet submarines, three "Oberon" class submarines for the Brazilian Navy and three Type 540 "Gal" class submarines for the Israeli Navy. The surface ship orders included three "Type 42" destroyers – two for the Royal Navy and one for the Armada Argentina and a through-deck cruiser, HMS INVINCIBLE, for the Royal Navy.

This painting shows (from top left clockwise) some of the output of the Barrow Shipyard between 1971 and 1980:

Yard No. 1098: HMS INVINCIBLE. Originally designated a through deck cruiser this was a first of class aircraft carrier launched for the Royal Navy by HM The Queen on 3rd May 1977. HMS INVINCIBLE was part of the Task Force (Operation Corporate) sent to the South Atlantic to reclaim the Falkland Islands between April and June 1982. A British Aerospace Sea Harrier is shown flying from the carrier.

Yard No. 1102: HMS MANCHESTER was a 4,150 ton "Type 42" destroyer launched for the Royal Navy by Lady Cornford (wife of Sir Clifford Cornford – former Chief of Defence Procurement) on 24th November 1980. In the background are shown some shipyard cranes and the Submarine Machinery Installation and Test Establishment (SMITE).

The FH70 155-mm towed gun is an example of the output of the Gun Shop during this decade.

Yard Nos. 1093, 1094 and 1095: Israeli Navy Submarines GAL (Wave), TANIN (Crocodile) and RAHAV (Sea Monster) were launched on 2nd December 1975, 25th October 1976 and 8th May 1977 respectively. All three submarines were paid off around the start of the 21st Century and INS GAL is now on public display in Haifa.

Yard No. 1091: HMS CARDIFF was the third of the "Type 42" destroyers launched for the Royal Navy by Lady Gilmour (wife of Sir Ian Gilmour, Secretary of State for Defence) on 22nd February 1974. HMS CARDIFF was also deployed to the South Atlantic in April to June 1982.

Yard No. 1084: HMS SHEFFIELD: "Type 42" destroyer launched for the Royal Navy by HM The Queen on 10th June 1971. During Operation Corporate in 1982 HMS SHEFFIELD (Commander Sam Salt) was hit by an air-launched Exocet missile, badly damaged, and later sank.

Yard No. 1085: The passenger liner COPENHAGEN was launched for K/S Nordline by Mr. L. Michaelson (Director of Nordline) on 20th December 1972. The ship was later sold (July 1974) to Black Sea Shipping Company and renamed ODESSA.

The Main Machinery Raft for a "Swiftsure" class submarine is shown leaving SMITE on the transporter for installation into the submarine on the slipways.

Yard No. 1092: The "Swiftsure" class submarine HMS SCEPTRE leaving Barrow heading for the Clyde Submarine Base at Faslane for sea trials with Piel Island in the background. HMS SWIFTSURE was paid off in the 1990s and is currently (2017) laid up awaiting disposal at HM Naval Base Devonport.

Vickers Oceanics Ltd. support vessel VICKERS VENTURER is shown lowering the submersible VICKERS PISCES into the water. The logo 'Pisces' belongs to the Pisces submersible.

The upper mount shows the Vickers Limited logo (1957 to 1981).

The lower mount shows a view of the Vickers Shipyard (showing left to right) the New Assembly Shop, the SMITE Facility, the Fabrication Shop and some of the tower cranes. Also shown is a White Ensign with Bill Cole. Bill Cole – a long time Member of the Barrow-in-Furness Branch of the Submariners Association and his wife, Joan, were responsible for the idea of the Submarine Heritage Paintings Collection. The sketch is of the ADEB facility where nuclear submarine main machinery was built and tested at full power using steam supplied from a boiler plant – hence the tall Chimney.

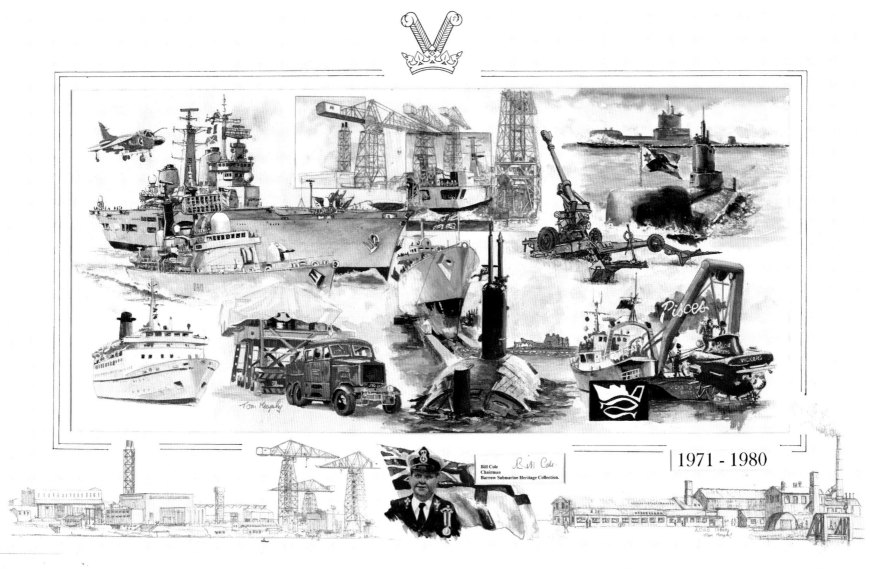

1971 - 1980

Bill Cole
Chairman
Barrow Submarine Heritage Collection.

This painting was jointly sponsored by Joan Cole (the wife of Bill Cole) one of the driving forces behind the Submarine Heritage Paintings Collection and Ian Edmondson – one of the major contributors to the authorship of the book. Bill Cole served in the "S" class submarine built in this decade.

DECADE PAINTING
1981-1990

The Painting and the 1981 to 1990 Story

This decade saw two new company names when the former Vickers Shipbuilding Group Limited became Vickers Shipbuilding and Engineering Limited in 1981 and then became VSEL in 1986. The change to VSEL also saw a new Chief Executive – Dr. Rodney Leach. Other changes in the decade saw the end of dynamic (slipway) launches for submarines (HMS TALENT was the last to be launched down a slipway) with the construction and opening of the Devonshire Dock Hall (DDH) by the Prime Minister Margaret Thatcher, MP on 3rd September 1986 on the same day as the keel laying ceremony took place in the DDH for the first of the "Vanguard" class SSBNs which were to replace the ageing "Resolution" class submarines. The first submarine to be built in the Devonshire Dock Hall was HMS TRIUMPH which was rolled out and launched via the shiplift on 16th February 1991. Shipbuilding during this decade was wholly submarine related.

The Painting shows from the top left clockwise:

A view of the start of the build of Devonshire Dock Hall – sketched by the artist on 1st January 1984.

Yard No. 1100: The first of class "Trafalgar" class submarine HMS TRAFALGAR was launched for the Royal Navy by the Lady Fieldhouse on 1st July 1981.

Yard No. 1106: The first of class "Upholder" class submarine HMS UPHOLDER is shown fitting out in the floating dock.

Yard No. 761: The previous "U" class submarine HMS UPHOLDER - launched for the Royal Navy on 8th July 1940 by Mrs Doris Thompson – wife of Mr Hubert Thompson – Special Director of Vickers Armstrong.

Yard No. 1106: HMS UPHOLDER was launched for the Royal Navy by HRH the Duchess of Kent on 2nd December 1986.

Early stages of construction of the Devonshire Dock Hall (DDH).

View of the north end of the Devonshire Dock Hall.

A view of the sandstone 'Wavy Wall' at the Dock Museum. This wall was designed by Julia Barton and was the winning design in a competition to create an attractive and appropriate boundary for the Dock Museum. The swirling design utilised reclaimed sandstone from the Dock Museum site and local limestone. Julia Barton was originally from South Lancashire but has lived and worked in Northumberland since 1981.

The remains of the railway bridge which separated the Devonshire Dock (now the site of the DDH) from the Walney Channel. Thr remains of the bridge were demolished in 2016 in preparation for an extension of the DDH.

Yard No. 1107: The "Trafalgar" class submarine HMS TALENT was launched for the Royal Navy by HRH The Princess Royal on 15th April 1988. This was the last traditional (dynamic) launch of a submarine down a slipway at Barrow.

A view of south end of the Devonshire Dock Hall showing the "Trafalgar" class submarine HMS TRIUMPH on the shiplift waiting to be lowered into Devonshire Dock. HMS TRIUMPH (Yard No. 1108) was the first submarine to be constructed in the Devonshire Dock Hall.

Self Propelled AS 90 guns.

Dr. Rodney Leach - Chief Executive of VSEL from 1986.

Yard No. 1107: HMS TALENT was launched on 15th April 1988 and is shown entering Barrow Docks on her way to her fitting out berth in the Devonshire Dock.

The Devonshire Dock Hall shiplift – the shiplift is used for lifting out and lowering submarines into the Devonshire Dock.

A gathering of spectators enjoying the launch of HMS TALENT.

The upper mount shows the logo of Vickers Shipbuilding & Engineering (1981-86), decade 1981 to 1990 and the logo of Vickers Shipbuilding and Engineering Limited (1986 to 1995).

The lower mount shows HMS UPHOLDER passing Piel Castle, the DDH and Ferry Beach, HMS UPHOLDER on shiplift and a "Trafalgar" class submarine.

The decade painting 1981 to 1990 was sponsored by Ron Hiseman – a Member of the Barrow-in-Furness Branch of the Submariners Association, former Branch Secretary and Branch Website Manager.

DECADE PAINTING
1991-2000

The Painting and the 1991 to 2000 Story

The Barrow shipyard completed both submarine and surface ship orders during this decade although the number of orders progressed was less than in previous decades. There were several changes of company name in the 1990s. In 1995 VSEL was bought by GEC Ltd and then became a Marconi Marine Company. The company then became Marconi Marine (VSEL) Ltd. and then Marconi Naval Systems. Finally, in 1999, the company was taken over by British Aerospace (BAe). Following on from the keel laying of HMS VANGUARD and HMS VICTORIOUS in the previous decade all four of the "Vanguard" class were rolled out, launched, completed and replaced the previous "Resolution" class SSBNs. In addition there were orders for both naval and merchant surface ships covering the fitting out of an amphibious helicopter carrier for the Royal Navy, completion of two fleet tankers for the Royal Fleet Auxiliary and three tankers for James Fisher Tankers Limited.

This picture shows (clockwise from the top left):

Yard No. 1114: Bow and stern views of the amphibious helicopter carrier HMS OCEAN (LPH01) which was launched for the Royal Navy at Kvaerner Govan (Clydeside) on 11th October 1995. This ship was towed to Barrow for fitting out and was completed in 1998. HMS OCEAN was named by HM The Queen at Barrow on 20th November 1998. The ship is to decommission in 2018.

The output of the Gun Shop in this decade included the 4.5-inch Mk 8 Mod 1 naval gun.

A front view of the Devonshire Dock Hall (DDH) where all submarines are constructed before rolling out to the shiplift for launching into Devonshire Dock.

Yard No. 1119: RFA WAVE KNIGHT - A389 - was a Fleet Tanker launched for the Royal Fleet Auxiliary on 29th September 2000 and completed on 15th October 2002. The picture is of the bow section shown on the slipway and alongside is the stern section being transported into place. A second ship of this class, RFA WAVE RULER - A390 - (Yard No. 1120) was completed at the Govan Yard on the Clyde on 30th October 2002.

Yard No. 1115: THAMES FISHER was launched for James Fisher Oil Tankers Limited in 1997.

Yard No. 1121: MERSEY FISHER was launched for James Fisher Oil Tankers Limited in 1997.

Yard No. 1116: HUMBER FISHER was launched for James Fisher Oil Tankers Limited in 1998.

Yard No. 1109: HMS VANGUARD (SSBN05) was the lead vessel of the "Vanguard" class. Rolled out and launched on 4th March 1992. She was commissioned on 14th August 1993. HMS VANGUARD was the first of four ballistic missile submarines built to replace the "Resolution" class SSBNs. She is the largest submarine ever launched for the Royal Navy and was still in service in 2017. The other three submarines of the "Vanguard" class (but not shown in the painting) were:

Yard No. 1110: HMS VICTORIOUS was rolled out and launched on 29th September 1993, commissioned on 7th January 1995 and was still in service in 2017.

Yard No. 1111: HMS VIGILANT was rolled out and launched on 14th October 1995 and commissioned in April 1997 and was still in service in 2017.

Yard No. 1112: HMS VENGEANCE was rolled out and launched on 19th September 1998 and commissioned in March 1999 and was still in service in 2017.

A stern view of RFA WAVE KNIGHT, an artist's impression of WAVE KNIGHT at sea and the launch of WAVE KNIGHT in September 2000.

The upper border shows the BAE Systems logo.

The lower border shows the logos of Marconi Naval Systems, GEC Marine and the Sponsors.

MARCONI
NAVAL SYSTEMS

1991 - 2000

ELECTRICAL
INSTALLATION
DEPARTMENT
1966 TO 2004
SOCIAL CLUB

GEC MARINE

This painting was sponsored by the Vickers Electrical Installation Department Social Club.

DECADE PAINTING
2001-2010

The Painting and the 2001 to 2010 Story

Orders progressed at Barrow in this decade were for submarines and surface ships. In addition to Yard No. 1122 the first of class submarine HMS ASTUTE (see below), HMS AMBUSH was rolled out and launched on 5 January 2011 and HMS ARTFUL was launched in May 2014. Work was authorised to progress the build of three further "Astute" class submarines these being HMS AUDACIOUS, HMS AGAMEMNON - the first steel for this submarine was cut in April 2010 - HMS ANSON – the 'go ahead for ordering long lead items for this submarine was given in March 2010 and an order was anticipated for a seventh submarine of the class - provisionally named HMS AJAX. A submarine contract was completed for the 'Reactivation' of four former Royal Navy "Upholder" class submarines (HM Submarines UPHOLDER, UNSEEN, URSULA and UNICORN) and their transfer to the Royal Canadian Navy as HMCS CHICOUTIMI, VICTORIA, CORNER BROOK and WINDSOR. The last of the four to be reactivated was HMCS CHICOUTIMI which left for Canada in 2004. One overseas submarine related order was received - the first since the Israeli Navy order for the three "Gal" class submarines in the 1970's. This order was from the Spanish Navy and was for the manufacture and delivery of forward and after domed bulkheads for a class of eight conventional submarines to the Navantia Yard in Spain – the first set delivered in April 2010 and the second in August 2010. The initial design work for a "Successor" class of SSBNs intended to replace the four "Vanguard" class SSBNs in the later years of the decade 2011 to 2020 was progressed in the last months of the decade. As a private venture concept design work has been progressed by BAe for submarines of the future and an artists impression is included in the painting.

Orders for the design and build of the 'Lower Block 3' sections of two 60,000 ton aircraft carriers were received but, in the event, these two orders were later changed to the 'design only' of the 'Lower Block 3' sections - with actual construction being transferred to Clyde shipyards allowing Barrow to concentrate on submarine orders. In anticipation of the associated ship building work, plans were made for the construction of a new 20,000 square metre preparation & assembly building on the site formerly occupied by the old central workshops, foundry and the boiler shop. These plans were scrapped with the loss of the aircraft carrier build contract.

Miscellaneous work in the yard in this decade included an order for the installation of self protection guns fitted on two nuclear waste transport ships for James Fisher and the repair of the main dock gate to the entrance lock to the Barrow Harbour Dock System - which had failed in 2009 – just prior to HMS ASTUTE leaving for sea trials.

This Picture shows – reading from left to right as if reading a book:

Yard Nos. 1117 and 1118: HMS ALBION and HMS BULWARK (Landing Platform Dock Ships) under construction on the Top Yard Slipways, the two ships shown alongside at the fitting out berths in Buccleuch Dock below the hammerhead crane and the launch of HMS ALBION,

with HMS BULWARK in the background against a panoramic view showing the new assembly sheds and the old shipwrights shop.

The rusting remains of one of the hammerhead cranes formerly sited on the slipways by the Walney Channel – now all demolished.

The innovative FH-777 lightweight air transportable 105-mm field gun, parts of which are manufactured by BAe Land Systems for the United States Armed Forces and the Canadian Army - this gun, uniquely, utilises large amounts of the metal titanium in its construction. The prototype TALISMAN remotely operated vehicle with 'stealth' characteristics developed by BAe Systems with the Royal Navy in mind - as seen on display at a Military Equipment Exhibition in the south of England and a Merlin helicopter which forms part of the capability of HM Ships ALBION and BULWARK.

Yard No. 1125: HMS QUEEN ELIZABETH – an artist's impression of the 60,000 ton aircraft carrier at sea from the starboard bow.

One of the LCU Mk10 landing craft provided for use with HM Ships ALBION and BULWARK.

Yard No. 1122: HMS ASTUTE – a view of the 7,400 ton "Astute" class attack submarine and the lead vessel of the class from the starboard bow. This was rolled out on 7th June 2008 in the presence of the Sponsor - Camilla, Duchess of Cornwall. HMS ASTUTE was launched from the ship lift a few days later on 14th June 2008.

Also shown is an artist's impression of submarine HMS ASTUTE at sea – dived.

Yard No. 1126: HMS PRINCE OF WALES. The picture shows an artist's impression of the aircraft carrier at sea viewed from the port quarter.

A former Royal Maritime Auxiliary Service fleet tender was converted into a Medical Support Ship for use on the Amazon River in Brazil following refitting at Barrow in 2007 and was renamed AMAZON HOPE II. The vessel is used to provide primary healthcare to communities along the length of the Amazon River.

The bottom row and the mount show the hammerhead crane at the fitting out berth in Buccleuch Dock with HMS ONYX in the foreground (sketched in August 2010) prior to the demolition of the hammerhead crane, a bow view of HMS BULWARK on the slipway above the battle honour boards of HMS QUEEN ELIZABETH and HMS PRINCE OF WALES, a pencil sketch of HMS BULWARK in the Walney Channel passing Piel Island and Roa Island above a pencil portrait of John Hudson –the Managing Director of BAe Submarine Solutions Ltd.

2010-date: The third Astute class submarine, HMS ARTFUL was launched on 17 May 2014 and work is underway to progress the build of four further "Astute" class submarines. HMS AUDACIOUS is scheduled to be launched in 2017. The remaining three HMS AGAMEMNON, HMS ANSON and the now unnamed seventh submarine, are all at various stages of construction within the DDH. HMS ASTUTE was commissioned in August 2010; HMS AMBUSH in March 2013 and HMS ARTFUL in March 2016.

This painting was commissioned by Dez Northover. Dez is a member of the West of Scotland Branch of the Submariners Association. He served in the Royal Navy from 1970 to 1985 and as a WEM(O) and POWEM(O) in HM Submarines OPOSSUM, PORPOISE, SEALION, FINWHALE, REPULSE (Port), SOVEREIGN and OBERON. His sponsorship of this painting is a memory of his time serving at sea with his many friends in submarines.

INDEX OF BARROW BUILT SHIPS NOT INCLUDED IN DECADE PAINTINGS

Note: Tonnage for Merchant Vessels is quoted as Gross Tonnage where 1 ton = 100 cubic feet of Ship's Capacity (100cu. ft = 2.83 m³). Tonnage for Naval Vessels is quoted as displacement tonnage i.e. the actual wieght of the completed vessel.

DECADE 1871 to 1900

Yard No.	Name	Launched	Ship Type/Tonnage	Comments
1	DUKE OF DEVONSHIRE	25 Jun 1873	Passenger Ship/3,001	Built for Eastern Steamship Co Ltd, Barrow. Scrapped Italy Sep 1903.
2	DUKE OF BUCCLEUGH	09 Oct 1873	Passenger Ship/3,005	Built for Eastern Steamship Co Ltd, Barrow. Sank 6th Mar 1889 off Brighton after a collision.
3	DUKE OF LANCASTER	18 May 1874	Passenger Ship/3,010	Built for Eastern Steamship Co Ltd., Barrow. Stranded and sank off Indian coast 11 Jul 1880.
4	ANCHORIA	27 Oct 1874	Passenger Ship/4,168	Built for Barrow Steamship Co Ltd, Also sailed for Anchor Line. Scrapped Germany 1922.
5	DUKE OF ARGYLL	Not known	Passenger Ship/3,013	Completed Glasgow 1873 for Eastern Steamship Co Ltd. Scrapped Genoa, Italy in Jul 1903.
6	DUKE OF SUTHERLAND	Not known	Passenger Ship/3,012	Completed in Glasgow Apr 1873 for Eastern Steamship Co. Ltd. Scrapped Danzig 1925.
7	DEVONIA	28 Mar 1877	Passenger Ship/4,270	Built for Barrow Steamship Co. Ltd. Scrapped Jul 1899 Hamburg, Germany.
8	CIRCASSIA	19 Mar 1878	Passenger Ship/4,270	Built for Barrow Steamship Co. Ltd. Scrapped at Hamburg Jun 1899.
12	ARIES	12 May 1873	Steam Yacht/145	First launch at Barrow. Built for Sir James Ramsden. Struck rocks off Holyhead. Sank Mar 1880.
13	APOLLO	02 Apr 1874	Not known/489	Various owners. Sold to Germany 1889. No further trace.
14	ACHILLES	18 Apr 1874	Not known/453	Various owners. Sold to Italy 1902. No further trace.
15	ADONIS	16 Feb 1874	Not known/406	Various owners. Sold to France 1877. No further trace.
16	LISMORE	02 Sep 1874	Not known/181	Various owners. Sold to Liverpool owners 1920. Still existing in 1923. No further trace.
17		26 Oct 1874	Dredger	Built for Furness Railway Co. No further details.
18	DUCHESS OF MARLBOROUGH	08 Nov1877	Not known/402	Built for James Little & Co Barrow. Sold to West India & Panama Telegraph Co Ltd, London 1880. No further trace.
19	BRITISH DUKE	21 Jan 1875	3 Masted Sailing Ship/1,464	Built for British Shipowners Co, Liverpool. Lost off Cape of Good Hope Nov 1888.
20	FALSTAFF	24 Feb 1875	3-Masted Sailing Ship/1,465	Built for James Beazley & Sons, Liverpool. Various owners. Used as coal hulk at Callao 1905. No further details.
21	DALECARLIA	20 May 1875	3-Masted Sailing Ship/1,488	Built for S. R. Greaves & Sons. No further details.

Yard No.	Name	Launched	Ship Type/Tonnage	Comments
22	BIRKER	08 Apr 1875	3-Masted Sailing Ship/1,042	Built for John Henry Bushby, Liverpool. Lost off Lobos de Tierra Island Jun 1895.
23	WESTERN MONARCH	21 Aug 1875	3-Masted Sailing Ship/1,385	Built for Royal Exchange Shipping Co., Liverpool. Various owners. Used as grain barge in Limerick 1957. No further details.
24	DUKE OF CONNAUGHT	21 Jul 1875	Paddle Steamer/1,082	Built for Lancashire & Yorkshire and London & Northwestern Railway Companies. Sold to Galbraith, Glasgow 1893. No further details.
25	BEN-MY-CHREE	06 May 1875	Paddle Steamer/1,031	Built for Isle of Man Steam Packet Co Ltd. Scrapped in Dec 1906 by Wards of Morecambe.
26	BRAMBLETYE	28 Jan 1876	Sailing Ship/1,544	Built for W. R. Price & Co., London. Scrapped in Rotterdam 1909.
27	TAURUS	27 Feb 1876	Steam Yacht/201	Built for Sir T. G. Hesketh Bt. Various owners until sold to Hugh Andrews, London in 1895. No further trace.
28	KENTS BANK	10 Aug 1876	Sailing Ship/1,040	Built for J. B. Sprott, Liverpool. No further trace.
29	LORD HOUGHTON	27 Apr 1876	Not known/790	Built for Goole Steam Shipping Co. Ltd., Goole. No further trace.
30	DREDGER No. 5 NEVA	25 May 1876	Dredger	Built for N Portleeov. No further details.
31	DREDGER No. 6 NEVA	25 May 1876	Dredger	Built for N. Portleeov. No further details.
32	YARKAND	29 Jan 1877	Sailing Ship/1,352	Built for E. Bates & Sons, Liverpool. Various owners. Last known as barge in New York in 1939.
33	HMS FOXHOUND	29 Jan 1877	2nd Class Gunboat/455	First Admiralty contract. Possibly existing in 1986 as a coal hulk on the Thames.
34	HMS FORWARD	29 Jan 1877	2nd Class Gunboat/455	Built for the Admiralty. Scrapped between 1889 and 1896.
35	FAIRY	10 Aug 1876	Not known/239	Built for East Coast Steam Ship Co. Ltd., Lynn. No further details.
36	DUNMORE	28 Apr 1877	Not known/1,269	Built for Wm & Co, Liverpool. Wrecked off Ushant Apr 1878.
37	MARGARET	14 Apr 1877	Steam Yacht/283	Built for Henry Jameson. Various other owners. Sold to France in 1886. No further details.
38	COMMANDER	27 Sep 1877	Not known/1,580	Built for T J Harrison, Liverpool. No further details.
39	CRUISER	06 Jun 1877	Wooden Schooner/226	Built for Earl of Eglington & Winton. Various other owners. Used as survey vessel in Australia. No later details.
40	BALCHARRES	16 Jun 1877	Not known/1,349	Built for Wigan Coal & Iron Co. In service in 1895. No further details.
41	BENDIGO	30 Jul 1877	Not known/1,414	Built for Joseph Hoult & Co., Liverpool. No further details.
42	GLENSANNOX	14 Jul 1877	Not known/922	Built for Wm Johnston & Co., Liverpool. In service in 1895. No further details.
43	GLENLOGAN	28 Aug 1877	Not known/925	Built for Wm Johnston & Co., Liverpool. No further details.
44	BALLINA	01 Jan 1878	Not known/284	Built for C. W. Polloxfew. No further details.
45	AMY	10 Jun 1877	Steam Yacht/288	Built for N. B. Stewart. Various owners. Sold to Greece 1919. No further details.

Yard No.	Name	Launched	Ship Type/Tonnage	Comments
46	EARL OF ULSTER	24 Nov 1878	Paddle Steamer/1,107	Built for a railway consortium. Sold to Ireland 1894. No further details.
47	TRUTHFUL	06 Nov 1878	Not known/956	Built for F. H. Powell & Co. In service 1895. No further details.
48	LASCELLES	27 Apr 1878	Passenger Ship/1,942	Built for Lord Cavendish & Sir James Ramsden. Various owners. Sunk by enemy action off Egypt Dec 1916.
49	MERLE	15 Aug 1878	Wooden Schooner/14	Built for William Pitt Miller, Lake Windermere. No further details.
50	PLINY	04 Mar 1878	Not known/1,671	Built for Lamport & Holt, Liverpool. Wrecked at Long Beach, NJ, USA May 1882.
51	RECOVERY	06 Feb 1878	Salvage Steamer/488	Built for Independence Marine Salvage & Steam Pump Co, Liverpool. In service 1895. No further details.
52	COUNTESS OF ABERDEEN	06 Feb 1878	Not known/600	Built for Aberdeen Steamship Co. Ltd. No further details.
53	STEAM FERRY No.1	05 Jan 1875	Steam Ferry	Built for Furness Railway Co, Barrow. Used as ferry across Walney Channel. Scrapped in 1902.
55	HMS MINER 6	16 May 1878	Torpedo Mooring Steamer	Built for the Admiralty. No further details.
56	MARGARET	16 May 1878	Not known/408	Built for the Carron Co, Grangemouth. Sold 1895. No further details.
57	CICERO	31 Jul 1878	Not known/1,588	Built for W. H. Dixon. In service 1895. No further details.
58	SEAWEED	17 May 1879	Wooden Yawl/17	Built for Samuel Taylor. Various owners. Taken to Australia in 1925. No further details.
59	BELGENLAND	24 Dec 1878	Passenger Ship/3,692	Built for S A de Nav Belge-Americaine, Antwerp. Various owners. Sold to Italy. Scrapped Genoa Sep 1905.
60	RHYNLAND	10 Mar 1879	Passenger Ship/3,692	Built for S A de Nav Belge-Americaine, Antwerp. Various owners. Sold to Italy. Scrapped Genoa Sep 1906.
61	DUKE OF BUCKINGHAM	1880	Not known/3,123	Built for Eastern Steamship Co. Ltd., Barrow. Various owners. Scrapped at Genoa Jul 1903.
62	TEAL	05 Jun 1879	Windermere Passenger Steamer/53	Built for Furness Railway Co. In 1923 transferred to L.M.S. Railway Co. Scrapped 1927.
63	CYGNET	22 May 1879	Windermere Passenger Steamer/53	Built for Furness Railway Co. Various owners. Sank in shallows Lake Windermere May 1962. Sold for scrap.
64		09 Apr 1880	Barge	Built for Furness Railway Co.
65		09 Apr 1880	Barge	Built for Furness Railway Co.
66	HMS MINER 11	28 Jan 1880	Torpedo Mooring Steamer	Built for Admiralty. No further details.
67	HMS MINER 12	28 Jan 1880	Torpedo Mooring Steamer	Built for Admiralty. No further details.
68	FURNESSIA	19 Oct 1880	Passenger Ship/5,495	Built for Barrow Steam Ship Co. Ltd. Sold and scrapped 1912.
69	HMS GRAPPLER	05 Oct 1880	Second Class Gunboat/465	Built for Admiralty. Sold for scrap at Garston May 1907.
70	HMS WRANGLER	05 Oct 1880	Second Class Gunboat/465	Built for Admiralty. Scrapped in Dover Dec 1919.

Yard No.	Name	Launched	Ship Type/Tonnage	Comments
71	HMS WASP	06 Oct 1880	Second Class Gunboat/465	Built for Admiralty. Wrecked on Tory Island Sep 1884. Sold and scrapped Nov 1910.
72	HMS BANTERER	02 Nov 1880	Second Class Gunboat/465	Built for Admiralty. Sold and scrapped at Bristol May 1907.
73	HMS ESPOIR	02 Nov 1880	Second Class Gunboat/465	Built for Admiralty. No further details.
74	ADELAIDE	08 May 1880	Paddle Steamer/969	1st steel sea-going ship built at Barrow. Built for Great Eastern Railway Co. Sold for scrap Jun 1897.
75	HMS MINER 14	10 Aug 1880	Torpedo Mooring Steamer	Built for Admiralty. No further details.
76	SEVERN	26 May 1881	Steam Yacht/186	Built for Earl Ducie. No further details.
77	CITY OF ROME	14 Jun 1881	Passenger Ship/8,415	Built for Inman Steamship Co. Ltd. Various owners. Sold and scrapped at Lenwerder, Germany Jan 1903.
78	CRAIGMORE	21 Aug 1880	Not known/1,536	Built for William Johnston & Co, Liverpool. Wrecked at Nicaria Feb 1907.
79	ENNISMORE	23 Oct 1880	Not known/1,560	Built for William Johnston & Co, Liverpool. Various owners. Torpedoed by U-boat off Girdleness Dec 1917.
80	LISMORE	25 Aug 1881	Not known/4,141	Built for William Johnston & Co., Liverpool. No further details.
81	ARIES	25 Nov 1881	Steam Yacht/186	Built for Sir James Ramsden. Various owners. Mined off Leathercoat Oct 1915 whilst serving as Armed Yacht for Admiralty.
82	NAVARRE	18 Jul 1881	Not known/4,137	Built for Soc. Generale des Transports Maritime, France. No further details.
83	STRABO	02 Apr 1881	Cargo Ship/1,959	Built for Lamport & Holt, Liverpool. Scrapped at Genoa Mar 1905.
84	BEARN	24 Oct 1881	Not known/4,134	Built for Soc. Generale des Transports Maritimes, France. Scrapped in France 1901.
85		19 Feb 1881	Dredger	Built for European Commission of the Danube. No further details.
86	GANGES	26 Oct 1881	Passenger Ship/4,168	Built for P & O Steam Navigation Co, London. Scrapped at Bombay 1898.
87	SUTLEJ	22 Dec 1881	Passenger Ship/4,168	Built for P & O. Steam Navigation Co. Scrapped in France 1901.
88	ROSSAL	30 Sep 1881	Barge/192	Built for Barrow Dredging Co. No further details.
89	HESPERIA	07 Feb 1882	Passenger Cargo Ship/3,037	Built for Barrow Steamship Co. Ltd. Sold to Italy and scrapped 1906.
90	JUSTITIA	06 May 1882	Passenger Cargo Ship/3,040	Built for Barrow Steamship Co. Ltd. Wrecked off Ceylon (Sri Lanka) Feb 1885.
92	DUKE OF WESTMINSTER	20 Apr 1882	Cargo Ship/3,726	Built for Eastern Steamship Co. Ltd., Barrow. Various owners. Sold to Italy and scrapped Sep 1903.
95	FENELLA	09 Jun 1881	Steam Ferry/564	Built for Isle of Man Steam Packet Co. Ltd. Scrapped 1929.
96	NESSMORE	20 May 1882	Cargo Ship/3,377	Built for Steamship Nessmore Ltd, Liverpool. Wrecked on Isle of Coll Nov 1885.
97	ORANMORE	04 Jul 1882	Cargo Ship/3,377	Built for Steamship Oranmore Ltd. Scrapped in Italy Mar 1904.
98	NORMANDIE	28 Oct 1882	Passenger Ship/6,283	Built for Cie Generale Transatlantique. Scrapped at Bo'ness, Scotland in 1912.
99	TAYGETE	31 Jul 1882	Not known/1,861	Built for Transmet & Co. No further details.
100	EDEN	12 Sep 1882	Passenger Ship/2,144	Built for Royal Mail Steam Packet Co. Sold and scrapped 1909.

Yard No.	Name	Launched	Ship Type/Tonnage	Comments
101	NAVARRO	23 Dec 1882	Not known/3,771	Built for T Glynn & Co. No further details.
102	ESK	11 Dec 1882	Passenger Ship/2,144	Built for Royal Mail Steam Packet Co. Sold for scrap 1910.
103	YOROUBA	10 Feb 1883	Not known/1,910	Built for Vermaine & Sons. No further details.
104	KOW-SHING	10 Mar 1883	Not known/2,134	Built for Indo-China Steam Nav. Co. Ltd. No further details.
105	PEMBROKE CASTLE	07 Jul 1883	Passenger Ship/3,946	Built for Castle Line. Sold to Turkey 1906. Sunk by Russians in Black Sea 1915.
106	MONARCH	08 May 1883	Steam Yacht/247	Built for Earl Ducie. No further details.
107	TAKAPUNA	05 Jun 1883	Passenger Ship/930	Built for Union Steam Ship Co, New Zealand. Lost in Cook Strait 1924.
108	ANNIE	23 Jun 1883	Not known/411	Built for J J Mack & Co, Liverpool. No further details.
109	ARGUS	03 Jul 1883	Not known/1,191	Built for Thomas Kish, Sunderland. Still in commission 1898. No further details.
110	BALBUS	20 Sep 1883	Not known/1,191	Built for Thomas Kish, Sunderland. No further details.
111	DELPHUS	15 Nov 1883	Not known/1,191	Built for Thomas Kish, Sunderland. Sold 1887. No further details.
112	MOUNT EDGECUMBE	21 Aug 1883	Not known/1,667	Built for Bellamy & Co. No further details.
113	EARL OF JERSEY	04 Oct 1883	4-Masted Barque/2,129	Built for the Earl Line. Stranded in Chittagong River 1887 becoming a total loss.
114	BORDERER	30 Jan 1884	Cargo Ship/4,740	Built for Stewart & Co., Liverpool. Sold to Spain 1900. No further details.
115	BEDLINGTON	15 Jan 1884	Cargo Ship/1,379	Built for Stewart & Co, Liverpool. No further details.
116	NORHAM	15 Feb 1884	Not known/1,091	Built for J Londen & Co. No further details.
118	COUNTY OF SALOP	29 Mar 1884	Not known/2,164	Built for Taylor, Abrahams & Co. No further details.
119	EUTERPE	15 Mar 1884	4 Masted Barque/2,129	Built for B. Wenke & Sons, Hamburg. Exploded west of Scilly Isles Sep 1902 being a total loss.
120	DOLLIE	01 Mar 1884	Not known/402	Built for J J Mack & Co, Liverpool. No further details.
121	PEVERIL	24 May 1884	Passenger CargoShip/561	Built for Isle of Man Steam Packet Co. Ltd. Lost in collision off Douglas, Isle of Man Sep 1899.
122	SOMBRALENSE	09 Aug 1884	Cargo Ship/1,982	Built for R Singlehurst & Co, Liverpool. Various owners. Mined and sunk off Port Arthur May 1905.
124	GANNET	06 Sep 1884	Paddle Tug/246	Built for Melbourne Harbour Commissioners, Australia. Still in service 1942. No further details.
125	COUNTY OF YORK	20 Sep 1884	Not known/2,282	Built for Taylor, Abrahams & Co. No further details.
126	ABERDEEN	19 Nov 1884	Hopper Barge/256	Built for Aberdeen Harbour Board. No further details.
127	EARL OF CHATHAM	20 Nov 1884	4-Masted Barque/2,141	Built for Earl Line. No further details.
128	DRUMCRAIG	19 Jan 1885	Sailing Ship/1,969	Built for Gillison & Chadwick, Liverpool. Disappeared without trace in the Pacific Ocean 1905.
129	HMS FEARLESS	20 Mar 1886	3rd Class Cruiser/1,580	Steel construction. Scrapped in 1907
130	MONA'S QUEEN	18 Apr 1885	Paddle Passenger Steamer/1,559	Built for the Isle of Man Steam Packet Co. Ltd. Sold and scrapped on the Clyde Oct 1929.

Yard No.	Name	Launched	Ship Type/Tonnage	Comments
132	ITUMBA	19 Feb 1885	Not known/273	Built for Hatton & Cookson. No further details.
133	COMO	16 May 1885	Not known/477	Built for Lamport & Holt, Liverpool. No further details.
137	PRINCE OF WALES	20 Feb 1886	Paddle Passenger Steamer/1,429	Built for London & Northwestern & Lancashire & Yorkshire Railway Cos. Sold Jun 1886. No further details.
138	ORIZABA	06 May 1886	Passenger Ship/6,077	Built for Pacific Steam Navigation Co. Wrecked near Fremantle, W. Australia Feb 1905.
139	OROYA	21 Aug 1886	Passenger Ship/6,077	Built for Pacific Steam Navigation Co. Scrapped in Italy 1908.
141	POWHATTON	19 Jun 1886	Passenger Ship/2,599	Built for Mediterranean & New York Steamship Co. Ltd. In service in 1902. No further details.
150	GOVERNOR MACLEAN	30 Oct 1886	Not known/285	Built for Gold Coast Government. No further details.
152	BAZALGETTE	25 May 1887	Sludge Vessel/990	Built for London County Council. No further details.
154	GRANGENSE	25 May 1887	Not known/420	Built for R. Singlehurst & Co, Liverpool. Sold to Brazil 1890. Scrapped 1922.
155	HAINAULT	03 Sep 1887	3-masted, full rigged Sailing Oil Tanker/1,760	Built for R. Speth & Co., Antwerp. Various owners. In service 1951. No further details.
161	EDITH AND ANNIE	Apr 1888	Lifeboat	Built for RNLI for Southport station. No further details.
162	FREDA	06 Jun 1888	Not known/498	Built for Lamport & Holt, Liverpool. No further details.
163	HENRY RICHARDSON	1888	Lifeboat	Built for RNLI for Brighton Station. No further details.
164	GERDA	28 Jun 1888	Not known/498	Built for Lamport & Holt, Liverpool. No further details.
165	ORUBA	20 Mar 1889	Passenger Ship/5,857	Built for Pacific Steam Navigation Co. Scuttled in Greece 1915.
166	OROTAVA	15 Jun 1889	Passenger Ship/5,857	Built for Pacific Steam Navigation Co. Bought by Admiralty 1914 as Armed Merchant Cruiser. Scrapped 1919.
167	SANTIAGO	10 Jul 1889	Passenger Ship/2,953	Built for Pacific Steam Navigation Co. Lost near Corral, S. America Jun 1907.
168	AREQUIPA	27 Sep 1889	Passenger Ship/2,953	Built for Pacific Steam Navigation Co. Lost off Chile Jun 1903.
169	BARKING	02 Mar 1889	Not known/1,106	Built for London County Council. No further details.
170	HILDA	30 May 1889	Not known/527	Built for Lamport & Holt, Liverpool. No further details.
171	BOMA	15 Aug 1889	Cargo Ship/2,510	Built for British & African Steam Navigation Co. Ltd. (later Elder Dempster Lines Ltd.). Torpedoed by U-boat off Bear Island Jun 1918.
172	MATADI	08 Oct 1889	Cargo Ship/2,510	Built for British & African Steam Navigation Co. Ltd. Destroyed by explosion at Boma Mar 1896.
173	SOUDAN	23 Nov 1889	Cargo Ship/2,625	Built for Elder Dempster & Co. Ltd., Liverpool. Sank after hitting rocks off Guinea Coast Jul 1891.
174	IDA	04 Oct 1889	Not known/561	Built for Lamport & Holt, Liverpool. No further details.
175	HMS LATONA	22 May 1890	'Apollo' Class Cruiser/3,400	Built for RN. Converted to Minelayer 1910. Sold to Malta and scrapped Dec 1920.
176	HMS MELAMPUS	02 Aug 1890	'Apollo' Class Cruiser/3,400	Built for RN. Scrapped at Felixstowe Jul 1910.

Yard No.	Name	Launched	Ship Type/Tonnage	Comments
177	HMS NAIAD	29 Nov 1890	'Apollo' Class Cruiser/3,400	Built for RN. Converted to minelayer 1910 Scrapped at Troon, Scotland Jun 1922.
178	COOMASSIE	22 Feb 1890	Heavy Cargo Ship/2,625	Built for British & African Steam Navigation Co. Ltd. Sold to various owners. Torpedoed in Channel May 1917.
179	EMPRESS OF INDIA	30 Aug 1890	Passenger Ship/3,210	Built for Canadian Pacific Railway Co. Converted to Auxiliary Cruiser 1914 then Hospital Ship. Various owners. Scrapped Bombay 1923.
180	EMPRESS OF JAPAN	13 Dec 1890	Passenger Ship/3,210	Built for Canadian Pacific Railway Co. Converted to Armed Merchant Cruiser 1914. Scrapped Vancouver 1926.
181	EMPRESS OF CHINA	25 Mar 1891	Passenger Ship/3,210	Built for Canadian Pacific Railway Co. Wrecked in Tokyo Bay Jul 1911. Scrapped at Yokohama 1912.
184	SIR CHARLES HARTLEY	20 Apr 1891	Dredger/300	Built for European Commission on the Danube. No further details.
185	BONNY	25 Apr 1891	Not known/2,702	Built for British & African Steam Navigation Co. Ltd. Torpedoed by U-boat off Tuskar Aug 1915.
186	LOANDA	23Jun 1891	Not known/2,702	Built for British & African Steam Navigation Co. Ltd. Sunk in collision in English Channel May 1908.
187	KWARRA	20Apr 1891	Not known/812	Built for African Steamship Co. Ltd., Liverpool. Sank at Forcados Dec 1908.
188	WEST INDIAN	27 Jun 1891	Cargo Ship/2,704	Built for West India & Pacific Steamship Co. Ltd, Liverpool. Various owners. Wrecked Hudson Bay Sep 1913.
189	INDIANAPOLIS	06 Jun 1891	Not known/2,464	Built for James W Little. Various owners. Sold to Italy 1912. No further details.
192	VOLTA	08 Aug 1891	Cargo Ship/2,702	Built for British & African Steam Navigation Co. Ltd, Liverpool. Scrapped in Holland. Jun 1924.
193	MEXICAN	19 Sep 1891	Cargo Ship/3,488	Built for West India & Pacific Steamship Co. Ltd., Liverpool. Torpedoed off Ushant Sep 1916.
194	CUBAN	20 Oct 1891	Cargo Ship/3,488	Built for West India & Pacific Steamship Co. Ltd., Liverpool. Wrecked off Cape Santa Marta Jul 1918.
195	MALACCA	30 Dec1891	Heavy Cargo Ship/5,900	Built for P & O Steam Nav. Co, London. Sold 1909. Scrapped Glasgow 1911.
196	FORMOSA	12 Mar 1892	Heavy Cargo Ship/5,900	Built for P & O Steam Nav. Co, London. Sold 1909. Scrapped Glasgow 1911.
198	HMS JASON	14 May 1892	'Alarm' Class Torpedo Gunboat/810	Mined off Isle of Coll, Western Scotland Apr 1917.
199	HMS JASEUR	24 Sep 1892	'Alarm' Class Torpedo Gunboat/810	Built for RN. Sold for scrap at Portsmouth Jul 1905.
200	HMS NIGER	17 Dec 1892	'Alarm' Class Torpedo Gunboat/810	Built for RN. Sunk by U-boat off Deal, Kent Nov 1914.
201	BINNIE	27 Feb 1892	Sludge Vessel/1,001	Built for London County Council. No further details.
204	JEANETTE	27 Feb 1892	Steam Yacht/182	Built for Frederick Platt of Newark. Various owners. No further details.
207	HURONA	07 Jul 1892	Cargo Ship/3,432	Built for London & Dundee Co. No further details.
208	ISIS	10 Aug 1892	Cargo Ship/2,505	Built for Aitken & Walker. No further details.

Yard No.	Name	Launched	Ship Type/Tonnage	Comments
209	UNIONEN	26 Aug 1892	3-Masted Barque Oil Tanker/1,730	Built for Vestendske Petroleum Co., Bergen. Various owners. No further details.
211	BARROW	23 Apr 1892	Sludge Vessel/1,001	Built for London County Council. No further details.
212	BELVEDERE	07 May 1892	Sludge Vessel/1,001	Built for London County Council. No further details.
213	BARBADIAN	19 Nov 1892	Cargo Ship/4,501	Built for West India & Pacific Steamship Co. Ltd., Liverpool. Various owners. Scrapped in Italy 1924.
214	JAMAICAN	31 Dec 1892	Cargo Ship/4,501	Built for West India & Pacific Steamship Co. Ltd., Liverpool. Scrapped in Italy 1914.
215	NORTHERN LIGHT	21 Jan 1893	Oil Tanker/3,893	Built for Lane & MacAndrew. No further details.
216	BLACK ROCK	10 Oct 1892	Not known/865	Built for Dublin & Mersey Steamship Co. Ltd. No further details.
217	WARREN HASTINGS	18 Apr 1893	Troopship/3,902	Built for Government of India. Sunk in Indian Ocean. No further details.
218	BRANCKER	04 Mar 1893	Sand Suction Dredger/2,511	Built for Mersey Docks & Harbour Board. No further details.
219	ACCRA	31 May 1893	Cargo Ship/2,808	Built for British & African Steam Navigation Co. Ltd., Liverpool. Scrapped at Bombay 1925.
220	BATHURST	15 Jul 1893	Cargo Ship/2,808	Built for British & African Steam Navigation Co. Ltd, Liverpool. Torpedoed off Bishop Rock May 1917.
221	VENETIA	18 May 1893	Steam Yacht/818	Built for Lord Ashburton. No further details.
222	BATANGA	12 Oct 1893	Cargo Ship/2,808	Built for British & African Steam Navigation Co. Ltd, Liverpool. Scrapped in Germany 1922.
225	INDRANI	24 Apr 1894	Cargo Ship/4,994	Built for T B Roygen & Co, Liverpool. Sold to Japan 1911. Sunk by Allied submarine Jun 1943.
226	LADY WOLSLEY	22 Mar 1894	Not known/1,449	Built for British & Irish Steam Packet Co. Ltd. sunk by gunfire from U-Boat in Aug 1915.
227	CLAN ROSS	07 Jun 1894	Cargo Ship 2,602	Built for Cayzer, Irvine & Co. (Clan Line). Sold to France 1925. Scrapped 1930.
228	CLAN CAMPBELL	03 Sep 1894	Cargo Ship/2,615	Built for Clan Line, London. Various owners. Lost during World War 2.
229	CLAN MACKAY	31 Oct 1894	Cargo Ship/2,615	Built for Clan Line, London. Various owners. Taken by Japanese 1941. No further details.
231	AXIM	04 Aug 1894	Cargo Ship/2,793	Built for British & African Steam Navigation Co. Ltd. Lost in Atlantic Dec 1910.
232	BAKANA	04 Jul 1894	Cargo Ship/2,793	Built for British & African Steam Navigation Co. Ltd. Stranded on Gold Coast Sep 1913.
233	HMS STURGEON	21 Jul 1894	'A' Class Destroyer/241	Built for RN. Sold for scrap in London May 1912.
234	HMS STARFISH	26 Jan 1895	'A' Class Destroyer/241	Built for RN. Sold for scrap in Preston May 1912.
235	HMS SKATE	13 Mar 1895	'A' Class Destroyer/241	Built for RN. Sold for scrap in Falmouth Apr 1907.
237	HMS POWERFUL	24 Jul 1895	Powerful Class Cruiser/14,200	Built for RN. Served in Far East. Returned UK. Reserve to 1913. Accommodation Ship. Scrapped Blyth 1929.

Yard No.	Name	Launched	Ship Type/Tonnage	Comments
238	No. 1 DREDGER	07 Jul 1894	Dredger/282	Built for Kingston Harbour Board, Jamaica. No further details.
239	HMS JUNO	16 Nov 1895	'Eclipse' Class Cruiser/5,600	Built for RN. Sold to Denmark 1920 for scrap.
240	HMS DORIS	03 Mar 1896	'Eclipse/ Class Cruiser/5,600	Built for RN. Sold to India for scrap Feb 1919.
241	BURNS	09 Mar 1895	Sludge Vessel/1,019	Built for London County Council. No further details.
242	No. 2 DREDGER	13 Mar 1895	Dredger/54	Built for Irish Board of Works. No further details.
243	DUKE OF LANCASTER	09 May 1895	Passenger Steamer/1,546	Built for London & North Western and Lancashire & Yorkshire Railway Companies. No further details.
244	G B CROW	07 Sep 1895	Sand Suction Dredger/2,383	Built for Mersey Docks Board. No further details.
245	CLAN MENZIES	01 Feb 1896	Cargo Ship/2,669	Built for Clan Line. Sold to Italy. Scrapped in 1928.
246	CLAN LINDSAY	02 Apr 1896	Cargo Ship/2,668	Built for Clan Line. Wrecked near East London, South Africa Mar 1898.
248	HMS NIOBE	20 Feb 1897	'Diadem' Class Cruiser/11,000	Built for RN. Spent most of commissions in Atlantic. Scrapped in USA 1922.
249	HMS AVON	10 Oct 1896	'C' Class Destroyer/313	Built for RN. Scrapped at Plymouth Feb 1923.
250	HMS BITTERN	01 Feb 1897	'C' Class Destroyer/313	Built for RN. Sunk after collision off Portland Bill Apr 1918.
252	CLAN SUTHERLAND	26 Sep 1896	Cargo Ship/2,820	Built for Clan Line. Sold to Japan 1921. Scrapped 1933.
253	HMS OTTER	23 Nov 1896	'C' Class Destroyer/313	Built for RN. Scrapped at Hong Kong 1916.
254	HMS LEOPARD	20 Mar 1897	'C' Class Destroyer/313	Built for RN. Sold for scrap Jun 1919.
255	DUCHESS OF DEVONSHIRE	21 Jan 1897	Passenger Ship/1,265	Built for Barrow Steam Navigation Co. Ltd. Various owners until 1928. No further details.
256	ROEBUCK	06 Mar 1897	Passenger Ship/1,281	Built for Great Western Railway Co. Torpedoed and sunk at Scapa Flow.
257	REINDEER	01 Apr 1898	Passenger Ship/1,281	Built for Great Western Railway Co. Scrapped in 1928.
258	HMS AMPHITRITE	05 Jan 1898	'Diadem' Class Cruiser/11,000	Built for RN. Served in Far East then Reserve UK. Converted to minelayer 1917. Scrapped Milford Haven 1920.
262	JOSEPH THOMPSON	17 Jul 1897	Dredger/995	Built for Manchester Council. No further details.
264	DUKE OF CORNWALL	23 Apr 1898	Passenger Ship/1,540	Built for Lancashire & Yorkshire* London & North Western Railway Cos. In service 1928. No further details.
265	HMS VENGEANCE	21 Aug 1898	'Canopus' Class Battleship/12,950	Built for RN. Various commissions. Depot Ship 1918. Scrapped Dover Jan 1922.
266	ANGLIA	20 Jun 1898	Cargo Ship/6,538	Built for Telegraph Construction & Main Co. Ltd. Torpedoed and sunk off Malta Dec 1916.
267	CLAN FERGUSON	04 Oct 1898	Cargo Ship/4,808	Built for Clan Line. Of 'turret design'. Torpedoed and sunk off Cape Spartel Sept 1917.
268	CLAN CUMMING	26 Jan 1899	Cargo Ship/4,808	Built for Clan Line. Of 'turret design' Sold to Italy 1925. Scrapped 1932.
269	JEANETTE	20 Apr 1898	Steam Yacht/217	Built for Frederick Platt of Newark. Various owners. Scrapped in Greece 1961.
270	SOKOTO	25 Feb 1899	Cargo Ship/3,080	Built for British & African Steam Navigation Co. Ltd. Sold to Spain 1919 and scrapped in 1925.

Yard No.	Name	Launched	Ship Type/Tonnage	Comments
271	BORNU	09 May 1899	Cargo Ship/3,238	Built for British & African Steam Navigation Co. Ltd. Foundered off Ushant Oct 1916.
272	ORTONA	10 Jul 1899	Passenger Ship/8,058	Built for Pacific Steam Navigation Co. Ltd. Torpedoed & sunk as troopship in Mediterranean Apr 1917.
273	HIJMS MIKASA	08 Nov 1900	Battleship/15,150	Built for Imperial Japanese Navy. Blown up by allied frogmen in WW2. Preserved as national monument Japan.
274	HMS HOGUE	11 Aug 1900	'Cressy' Class Cruiser/12,000	Built for RN. Commissioned into Channel Squadron. Torpedoed and sunk off Hook of Holland Sep 1914.
275	SABRINA	11 Feb 1899	Steam Yacht/379	Built for Sir W. H. Willis. No further details.
278	HMS VIXEN	29 May 1900	'C' Class Destroyer/104	Built for RN. Scrapped in Essex Mar 1921.

DECADE 1901 to 1910

Yard No.	Name	Launched	Ship Type/Tonnage	Comments
277	HMS KING ALFRED	28 Oct 1901	'Drake' Class Cruiser/14,100	Built for RN. Spent most of WW1 in the Atlantic. Sold to Holland and scrapped Mar 1920.
286	FRANCHE-COMTE	02 Oct 1902	Cargo Ship/7,078	Built for unknown owners. Sold to Russia. In service 1942. No further details.
290	HMS DOMINION	25 Aug 1903	'KE VII' Class Battleship/16,350	Built for RN. Served in home waters. Scrapped in Preston Oct 1924.
291	CORONATION	25 Apr 1903	Sand Hopper Dredger/3,044	Built for Mersey Docks & Harbour Board. Used as Anti-Aircraft vessel WW2. Sold 1947 No further details.
297	COLLEEN BAWN	12 Jun 1903	Passenger/Cattle Ship/1,204	Built for Lancashire & Yorkshire and London & Northwestern Railway Companies. No further details.
298	HMS SENTINEL	19 Apr 1904	'Sentinel' Class Scout/2,900	Built for RN. Unsuccessful design. Scrapped in Sunderland Jun 1923.
299	MELLIFONT	10 Sep 1903	Passenger/Cattle Ship/1,088	Built for Lancashire & Yorkshire and London & Northwestern Railway Companies. No further details.
301	ALEXANDRA	16 Apr 1904	Light Tender/618	Built for Commissioner of Lights, Liverpool. No further details.
302	HMS SKIRMISHER	07 Fe4 1905	'Sentinel' Class Scout/2,900	Built for RN. Scrapped in Preston Apr 1920.
314	DUFFERIN	14 Sep 1904	Troopship/280	Built for Indian Government. No further details.
315	MANXMAN	15 Jun 1904	Passenger Ship/2,174	Built for Midland Railway Co. Aux. Aircraft Carrier WW1. Troopship in WW2. Scrapped Sep 1949.
316	HMS NATAL	30 Sep 1905	'Warrior' Class Cruiser/12,660	Built for RN. Served in home waters. Blown up by internal explosion at Cromarty Firth Dec 1915.
317	CANADA	13 Jun 1904	Fisheries Protection Vessel/411	Built for Canadian Government. No further details.
330	LADY GREY	21 Aug 1906	Ice Breaker/ 733	Built for Canadian Government. Still in service 1951. No further details.

Yard No.	Name	Launched	Ship Type/Tonnage	Comments
331	ALMIRANTE GRAU	27 Mar 1906	Cruiser/3,200	Built for Peruvian government. In service 1907. Decommissioned on 24th Dec 1958 and stricken from Navy.
344	CORONEL BOLOGNESI	24 Sep 1906	Cruiser/3,180	Built for Peruvian Government In service 1907. Decommissioned on 24th Dec 1958 and stricken from Navy.
356	INVESTIGATOR	11 Jun 1907	Survey Ship/1,015	Built for Indian Government. No further details.
358	CARTMEL	13 Aug 1907	Tug/304	Built for Furness Railway Co. Ltd., Barrow. LMS Railway 1923. Redhead & Sons Tugs 1934 then Leith Salvage & Towage. Renamed BULLGER. Struck Mine and sank in Druridge Bay 14th Mar 1941.
359	GENERAL GUERRERO	23 Jan 1908	Cruiser Transport/1,880	Built for the Mexican Government. Renamed VINCENTE GUERRERO in 1918. Named after hero of War of Independence and Mexico's first African/Indian President.
360	SLIEVE BLOOM	05 Nov 1907	Twin Screw Cargo Vessel/1,116	Built for the Furness Railway Co. Ltd, Barrow. Sunk 1918 in collision with US warship off Anglesey.
361	SLIEVE GALLION	04 Dec 1907	Twin Screw Cargo Vessel/1,118	Built for the Furness Railway Co. Ltd, Barrow. Attacked by U-Boat Aug 1918 but torpedo missed. Sold to Arnott Young, Dalmuir, Mat 1937 and scrapped.
362	RATHMORE	03 Mar 1908	Passenger Ship/1,569	Built for London & Northwestern Railway Co. Ltd. No further details.
385	EARL GREY	18 Jun 1909	Vice Regal Yacht/ Icebreaker/2,357	Built for the Canadian Government. Sold to Russia 1915. Still in service in White Sea 1962. No further details.
386	JOSE MARQUES	09 Mar 1909	Ferry/87	Built for the Brazilian Government. No further details.
389	HMS LIVERPOOL	30 Oct 1909	'Bristol' Class Cruiser/4,800	Built for RN. Served Heligoland Bight 1914 then in Mediterranean from late 1915. Scrapped in Germany 1921.
400	ALFONSO PENNA	09 Jun 1910	Floating Dock	Built for Brazilian Government. Launched in 3 sections. Size increased 1913. No further details.
409	LAURINDO PITTA	20 Aug 1910	Tug/304	Built for the Brazilian Government. Still in service 1964. No further details.

DECADE 1911 to 1920

Yard No.	Name	Launched	Ship Type/Tonnage	Comments
402	HMS DARTMOUTH	14 Feb 1911	'Weymouth' Class Cruiser/5,250	Built for RN. Served in Indian and Atlantic Oceans. Sold for scrap 1930.
407	HMS PRINCESS ROYAL	29 Apr 1911	'Lion' Class Battle Cruiser/26,350	Built for RN. Served at Heligoland Bight and home waters. She was Flagship at Jutland 1916. Scrapped 1926.
410	YING SWEI	14 Jul 1911	Cruiser/2,750	Built for Chinese Navy. Used for training. Sunk by Japanese at Canton Sep 1937.
411	HMS PHOENIX	09 Oct 1911	'Admiralty' Class Destroyer/765	Built for RN. Torpedoed and sunk in Adriatic May 1918.

Yard No.	Name	Launched	Ship Type/Tonnage	Comments
412	SIR HUGH ALLAN	28 Apr 1911	Tug/354	Built for Montreal Harbour Commissioners. No further details.
414	HIJMS KONGO	18 May 1912	Battle Cruiser/27,500	Built for Imperial Japanese Navy. Torpedoed & sunk by American submarine off Formosa (Taiwan) Nov 1944.
424	GUARANY	18 Jun 1912	Tug/344	Built for Brazilian Government. No further details.
425	RESHADIEH	03 Sep 1913	Battleship/25,250	Built for Turkish Government. Completed for RN as HMS ERIN. Served at Jutland. Scrapped Queensborough Dec 1933.
429	HMS EMPEROR OF INDIA	27 Nov 1913	'Iron Duke' Class Battleship/25,000	Built for RN. Sunk as target Jul 1931. Raised and scrapped at Rosyth Feb 1932.
433	JAVERY	17 Jun 1913	River Monitor/1,250	Built for Brazil. Bought by RN as HMS HUMBER before completion. Served in Channel & Dardanelles. Sold for scrap 1920.
434	SOLIMOES	19 Aug 1913	River Monitor/1,250	Built for Brazil. Bought by RN as HMS SEVERN before completion. Served in East Africa. Sold for scrap 1921.
435	MADEIRA	30 Sep 1913	River Monitor/1,250	Built for Brazil. Bought by RN as HMS MERSEY before completion. Served in East Africa. Sold for scrap 1921.
443	HMS PENELOPE	25 Aug 1914	'Arethusa' Class Cruiser/3,512	Built for RN. Saw war service with the Grand Fleet. Sold for scrap 1924.
444	HMS PHAETON	21 Oct 1914	'Arethusa' Class Cruiser/3,512	Built for RN. Served with the Grand Fleet and at Jutland 1916. Sold for scrap 1923.
445	SANTA MARGHERITA	23 Oct 1915	Oil Tanker/7,496	Built for RN as Royal Fleet Auxiliary (RFA) vessel. Sold to Anglo-Saxon Petroleum Co. Ltd. During WW2 used as oil hulk in Africa. Sold for scrap at Rosyth 1951.
455	HMS REVENGE	29 May 1915	'Royal Sovereign' Class Battleship/31,250	Built for RN. Served in both World Wars. Scrapped at Inverkeithing Sep 1948.
486	HMS CASSANDRA	25 Nov 1916	'Caledon' Class Cruiser/4,120	Built for RN. Mined and sunk in Baltic Dec 1918.
493	SCYTHIA	23 Mar 1920	Passenger Liner/19,761	Built for Cunard White Star Ltd, Liverpool. Troopship during WW2 and after. Scrapped at Inverkeithing 1958.
497	HMS CURLEW	05 Jul 1917	'Ceres' Class Cruiser/4,190	Built for RN. Served with Home Fleet until sunk by bomb off Norway May 1940.
505	WAR MASTER	25 May 1918	Cargo Ship/5,175	Built for British Government. No further details.
506	WAR RULER	17 Dec 1918	Cargo Ship/5,175	Built for British Government. Sold to Belgium before completion. Various owners Sold to Japan 1951. No further details.
546	HMS CALCUTTA	09 Jul 1918	'Carlisle' Class Cruiser/4,290	Built for RN. Converted to Anti Aircraft Cruiser. Sunk by aircraft off Crete Jun 1941
562	HMS DIOMEDE	29 Apr 1919	'D' Class Cruiser/4,850	Built for RN. Served throughout WW2. Scrapped Dalmuir May 1946.
570	NARRAGANSETT	27 Nov 1919	Oil Tanker/6,889	Built for Anglo-American Oil Co. Ltd. Scrapped in 1934.
571	CORTONA	14 Sep 1920	Cargo Ship/7,093	Built for Donaldson Line Ltd., Glasgow. Torpedoed and sunk Jul 1942.

Yard No.	Name	Launched	Ship Type/Tonnage	Comments
579	SEMINOLE	11 Dec 1920	Oil Tanker/6,923	Built for Anglo-American Oil Co. Ltd. Scrapped 1935.

DECADE 1921 to 1930

Yard No.	Name	Launched	Ship Type/Tonnage	Comments
498	ANTONIA	11 Mar 1921	Passenger Liner/13,867	Built for Cunard White Star Ltd., Liverpool. Converted for war service 1939. Scrapped at Troon 1948.
573	MORETON BAY	23 Apr 1921	Passenger Liner/14,193	Built for Australian Commonwealth Government Line. Converted for war service 1940. Scrapped Barrow 1957.
574	HOBSONS BAY	04 Oct 1921	Passenger Liner/14,204	Built for Australian Commonwealth Government Line. Various owners. Converted for war service 1939. Scrapped Faslane 1955.
575	JERVIS BAY	17 Jan 1922	Passenger Liner/13,840	Built for Australian Commonwealth Government Line. Converted for war service 1939. Sunk by German Battleship ADMIRAL SCHEER Nov 1940.
580	SCOTTISH STANDARD	08 Apr 1921	Oil Tanker/6,999	Built for Tankers Ltd., London - subsidiary of BP. Torpedoed and sunk Feb 1941.
581	SCOTTISH MAIDEN	07 Jul 1921	Oil Tanker/6,999	Built for Tankers Ltd., London. Torpedoed and sunk in North Atlantic Nov 1940.
582	SCOTTISH MINSTREL	15 Nov 1921	Oil Tanker/6,999	Built for Tankers Ltd., London. Torpedoed and sunk in Western Approaches Jul 1940.
583	SCOTTISH MUSICIAN	14 Feb 1922	Oil Tanker/6,998	Built for Tankers Ltd., London. Various owners. Scrapped in Yugoslavia Jul 1960.
586	CARINTHIA	24 Feb 1925	Passenger Liner/20,277	Built for Cunard White Star Line Ltd., Liverpool. Converted for war service Jan 1940. Torpedoed west of Ireland Jun 1940.
591	SLIEVE DONARD	06 Oct 1921	Passenger-Cargo Ship/1,116	Built for London & Northwestern Railway Co. Scrapped 1954.
596	No. 2 STEAM BARGE	03 Nov 1922	Hopper Barge/505	Built for Furness Railway Co. Ltd. Various owners. No further details.
598	ORAMA	20 May 1924	Passenger Liner/19,777	Built for Orient Steam Navigation Co. Ltd. Shelled and sunk by German battleship ADMIRAL VON HIPPER off Scotland Jun 1940.
603	HELMWOOD	25 Sep 1923	Collier/2,156	Built for Wm. France, Fenwick & Co. Ltd., London. Various owners. Scrapped 1965
604	DASHWOOD	05 Feb 1924	Collier/2,154	Built for Wm. France, Fenwick & Co. Ltd., London. Sunk by air attack North Sea Jun 1941.
605	GERALDINE MARY	19 Aug 1924	Pulp & Timber Carrier/7,244	Built for Anglo-Newfoundland Shipping Co. Ltd. Torpedoed and sunk Aug 1940.
606	MOVERIA	10 Oct 1924	Passenger Cargo Ship/4,867	Built for Donaldson Line Ltd., Glasgow. No further details.
607	GLANRHYD	25 Mar 1924	Collier/1,590	Built for Harries Bros. Coal & Shipping Co. Ltd. No further details.
610	COLLIER No. 1	06 May 1924	Collier/1,858	Built for Canada Steamship Lines Ltd, Montreal. No further details.
611	DEARNE	18 Sep 1924	Coaster/1,037	Built for London, Midland & Scottish Railway Co, Goole. Various owners. Scrapped Tyne Feb 1957.

Yard No.	Name	Launched	Ship Type/Tonnage	Comments
612	DON	18 Sep 1924	Coaster/1,037	Built for London, Midland & Scottish Railway Co, Goole. Various owners. Scrapped Holland Nov 1958.
615	J H HUNTER	02 Oct 1924	Sludge Vessel/1,500	Built for London County Council. No further details.
616	G W HUMPHREYS	13 Nov 1924	Sludge Vessel/1,500	Built for London County Council. No further details.
617	NEWFOUNDLAND	24 Jan 1925	Passenger Cargo Ship/6,791	Built for Warren Line (Liverpool) Ltd. Converted to hospital ship Sep 1941. Bombed & sunk Salerno Sep 1943.
618	HMS CUMBERLAND	16 Mar 1926	'Kent' Class Cruiser/9,750	Built for RN. Scrapped at Newport, Wales Nov 1959.
619	OTRANTO	09 Jun 1925	Passenger Liner/20,026	Built for Orient Steam navigation Co. Ltd. Served as troopship during WW2. Scrapped at Faslane Jun 1957.
623	NOVA SCOTIA	29 Jan 1926	Passenger Cargo Ship/6,790	Built for Warren Line (Liverpool) Ltd. Converted to troopship Jan 1941. Torpedoed by Japanese submarine off East Africa Dec 1942.
626	MOLDAVIA	23 Sep 1926	Cargo Ship/4,858	Built for Donaldson Line. Torpedoed and sunk Feb 1943.
627	ORFORD	27 Sep 1927	Passenger Liner/19,941	Built for Orient Steam Navigation Co. Ltd. Bombed off Toulon. Beached and became a total loss May 1940.
628	KEDAH	16 Jul 1927	Feeder Passenger Ship/2,499	Built for Straits Steamship Co. Ltd., Singapore. Various owners. Scrapped at Newport, Wales Oct 1956.
636	HMS RESOURCE	27 Nov 1928	Fleet Repair Ship/12,300	Built for RN Scrapped at Inverkeithing Feb 1954
637	ORONTES	26 Feb 1929	Passenger Liner/20,097	Built for Orient Steam Navigation Co. Ltd. Served as troopship WW2. Scrapped in Valencia Mar 1962.
642	HMS ARROW	22 Aug 1929	'A' Class Destroyer/1,350	Built for RN. Scrapped at Taranto, Italy May 1949.
650	SUKHODOYA	19 Nov 1929	River Gunboat/645	Built for Siamese Navy. No further details.
652	ARAUCANO	22 Oct 1929	Submarine Depot Ship/9,000	Built for Chilean Navy. Still n service 1985. No further details.
656	HMS KEITH	10 Jul 1930	'B' Class Destroyer/1,400	Built for RN. Bombed and sunk off Dunkirk Jun 1940.
660	LADY OF MANN	04 Mar 1930	Passenger ship/3,104	Built for Isle of Man Steam Packet Co. Ltd. In service 1985. No further details.
661	OTAIO	26 Aug 1930	Passenger-Cargo Ship/10,298	Built for New Zealand Shipping Co. Ltd. Torpedoed and sunk west of Valentia Aug 1941.
662	MAYON	26 Jun 1930	Passenger-Cargo Ship/3,207	Built for Philippine-Inter Island Steamship Co. Served with US Navy. Sunk Philippine waters Jan 1942.

DECADE 1931 to 1940

Yard No.	Name	Launched	Ship Type/Tonnage	Comments
663	STRATHNAVER	05 Feb 1931	Passenger Liner/22,540	Built for P & O Steam Navigation Co., London. Sold to Hong Kong for scrap Apr 1962.

Yard No.	Name	Launched	Ship Type/Tonnage	Comments
664	STRATHAIRD	18 Jul 1931	Passenger Liner/22,550	Built for P & O Steam Navigation Co., London. Sold to Hong Kong for scrap Jul 1961.
667	HMS CYGNET	29 Sep 1931	'C' Class Destroyer/1375	Built for RN. Transferred to Canada as HMCS St LAURENT. Scrapped Nov 1945.
668	HMS CRESCENT	29 Sep 1931	'C' Class Destroyer/1375	Built for RN. Transferred to Canada as HMCS FRASER. Sunk after collision off Bordeaux Jun 1940.
670	RANGATIRA	16 Apr 1931	Passenger-Cargo Ship/6,152	Built for Union Steamship Co., New Zealand. Scrapped in Hong Kong Oct 1967.
674	HMS DEFENDER	07 Apr 1932	'D' Class Destroyer/1,375	Built for RN. Bombed and sunk off Sidi Barrani Jul 1941.
675	HMS DIAMOND	08 Apr 1932	'D' Class Destroyer/1,375	Built for RN. Bombed and sunk during evacuation of Greece Apr 1941.
681	QUEEN OF BERMUDA	02 Sep 1932	Passenger Liner/22,575	Built for Furness Withy & Co. Ltd. Converted for war service Oct 1939. Scrapped at Faslane 1966.
682	HMS AJAX	01 Mar 1934	Leander Class Cruiser/6,985	Built for RN. Served South Atlantic (River Plate) & Mediterranean. Scrapped at Newport, Wales Nov 1949.
688	ALMIRANTE SALDANHA	19 Dec 1933	Sail Training Ship/3,825	Built for Brazilian Navy. Still in service 1968. No further details.
691	HMS FARNE	28 Jun 1934	'F' Class Destroyer/2.060	Built for RN. Sold to Dominican Republic 1949. Still in service 1962. No further details.
692	HMS FIREDRAKE	28 Jun 1934	'F' Class Destroyer/2,060	Built for RN. Torpedoed and sunk in North Atlantic Dec 1942.
697	ORION	07 Dec 1934	Passenger Liner/23,371	Built for Orient Steam Navigation Co. Ltd. Converted for war service. Scrapped at Tamise Sep 1963.
698	STRATHMORE	04 Apr 1935	Passenger Liner/23,428	Built for P & O Steam Navigation Co., London. Hotel & Pilgrim ship 1963. Scrapped La Spezia Sep 1969.
699	HMS GREYHOUND	15 Aug 1935	'G' Class Destroyer/1,335	Built for RN. Bombed and sunk off Crete May 1941.
700	HMS GRIFFIN	15 Aug 1935	'G' Class Destroyer/1,335	Transferred to Canada as HMCS OTTAWA 1943. Placed on Disposal List Jan 1946. No further details.
707	AWATEA	25 Feb 1936	Passenger-Cargo Ship/13,482	Built for Union Steamship Co., New Zealand. Bombed and sunk at Algiers Nov 1942.
711	LA ARGENTINA	16 Mar 1937	Training Cruiser/7,610	Built for Argentine Navy. Still in service 1960. No further details.
712	ORCADES	07 Dec 1936	Passenger Liner/23,456	Built for Orient Steam Navigation Co. Ltd., London. Troopship WW2. Torpedoed off Capetown Oct 1942.
715	TEAL	04 Jul 1936	Passenger Ship/251	Built for London, Midland & Scottish Railway Co. Used on Lake Windermere service Still in service.
717	FENELLA	16 Dec 1936	Passenger Ship/2,376	Built for Isle of Man Steam Packet Co. Ltd. Sunk at Dunkirk May 1940
718	TYNWALD	16 Dec 1936	Passenger Ship/2,376	Built for Isle of Man Steam Packet Co. Ltd. Converted for war service Sep 1939. Sunk at Algiers Nov 1942.

Yard No.	Name	Launched	Ship Type/Tonnage	Comments
719	BUENOS AIRES	21 Sep 1937	Destroyer/1,375	Built for Argentine Navy. Entered service 1939. Decommissioned 1971
720	ENTRE RIOS	21 Sep 1937	Destroyer/1,375	Built for Argentine Navy. Entered service 1939. Decommissioned 1971
721	CORRIENTES	21 Sep 1937	Destroyer/1,375	Built for Argentine Navy. Sunk after collision with Cruiser ALMIRANTE BROWN in Oct 1941.
722	STRATHEDEN	10 Jun 1937	Passenger Liner/23,722	Built for P & O Steam Navigation Co, London. Various owners. Broken up at Spezia in 1969
723	STRATHALLAN	23 Sep 1937	Passenger Liner/23,722.	Built for P & O Steam Navigation Co., London. Torpedoed and sunk off North Africa Dec 1942.
726	SHOAL FISHER	16 Jan 1937	Coaster/698	Built for James Fisher & Sons Ltd., Barrow. Lost by enemy action Feb 1941.
732	HMS ILLUSTRIOUS	05 Apr 1939	Aircraft Carrier/23,000	Built for RN. Saw full war service. Scrapped at Faslane Nov 1956.
735	HMS INDOMITABLE	26 Mar 1940	Aircraft Carrier/23,000	Built for RN. Served in war from 1941. Scrapped at Faslane Sep 1955.
741	HMS HANDY	29 Sep 1939	Destroyer/1,375	Built for Brazil. Bought by RN before completion. Torpedoed and sunk in Western Approaches Mar 1943.
742	HMS HURRICANE	29 Sep 1939	Destroyer/1,375	Built for Brazil. Bought by RN before completion. Torpedoed and sunk in North Atlantic Dec 1943.
743	SWAN	10 Jun 1938	Passenger Ship/251	Built for London, Midland & Scottish Railway Co. Used on Lake Windermere. Still in service.
747	MUAVENET	15 Dec 1940	Destroyer/1,375	Built for Turkey. Bought by RN before completion. Renamed INCONSTANT. Returned to Turkey 1945. Scrapped 1960.
750	HMS JAMAICA	16 Nov 1940	'Fiji' Class Cruiser/8,000	Built for RN. Served in Home Fleet throughout the war. Scrapped at Dalmuir Dec 1960.

DECADE 1941 to 1950

Yard No.	Name	Launched	Ship Type/Tonnage	Comments
748	GAYRET	24 Feb 1941	Destroyer/1,375	Built for Turkey. Bought by RN before completion. Renamed HMS ITHURIEL. Damaged beyond repair 28 Nov 1942. Scrapped at Bo'ness from Nov 1945.
767	HMS SPARTAN	27 Aug 1942	'Dido' Class Cruiser/5,770	Built for RN. Served in Home Fleet and Mediterranean. Sunk by glider bomb off Anzio Jan 1944.
768	EMPIRE GALE	29 Apr 1941	Cargo Ship/7,089	Built for Ministry of War Transport. Sold to Greece 1953. In service 1964. No further details.
769	EMPIRE MORN	01 Jul 1941	Cargo Ship/7,089	Built for Ministry of War Transport. Sunk (mined) Mar 1943 in position 33°52' N 07°50W.
787	EMPIRE BAXTER	08 Oct 1941	Cargo Ship/7,089	Built for Ministry of War Transport. Survived the war. No further details.

Yard No.	Name	Launched	Ship Type/Tonnage	Comments
788	EMPIRE MARCH	20 Feb 1942	Cargo Ship/7,089	Built for Ministry of War Transport. Sold to Spain 1947. No further details.
793	HMS DERWENT	22 Aug 1941	Hunt Class Destroyer/1,087	Built for RN. Scrapped from Jan 1947.
794	HMS CATTERICK	22 Nov 1941	Hunt Class Destroyer/1,087	Built for RN. Transferred to Greece 1946 as RHN HASTINGS. No further details.
809	HMS PENYLAN	17 Mar 1942	Hunt Class Destroyer/1,087	Built for RN. Torpedoed and sunk by E-boat in English Channel Dec 1942.
810	HMS ROCKWOOD	13 Jun 1942	Hunt Class Destroyer/1,087	Built for RN. Scrapped at Gateshead Aug 1946.
827	EMPIRE NOBLE	13 Nov 1843	Cargo Ship/7,125	Built for Ministry of War Transport. Sold to Hong Kong 1963. No further details.
829	RIVER FISHER	27 Sep 1943	Coaster/734	Built for James Fisher & Sons Ltd., Barrow. Bought by Ministry of War Transport Before completion. Reverted to Fishers 1946. No further details.
856	EMPIRE ELAINE	22 Jul 1942	Cargo Ship/7,513	Built for Ministry of War Transport as Landing Ship Carrier. Several owners post war. Sold to Liberia. No further details.
857	EMPIRE CHARMIAN	25 Nov 1942	Cargo Ship/7,513	Built for Ministry of War Transport as Landing Ship Carrier. Sold to London owners in 1946. No further details.
858	EMPIRE VICEROY	08 Apr 1943	Cargo Ship/7,803	Built for Ministry of War Transport. Various owners post war. Sold to Panama 1954. No further details.
859	EMPIRE ADMIRAL	26 Mar 1945	Cargo Ship/7,842	Built for Ministry of War Transport. Various owners post war. No further details.
884	HMS PIONEER	28 May 1944	Aircraft Maint. Carrier/13,190	Built for RN. Served with the Pacific Fleet. Scrapped at Inverkeithing Sep 1954.
885	HMS MAJESTIC	28 Feb 1945	Aircraft Carrier/16,000	Built for RN. Work suspended 1945-49. Sold to Australia as HMAS MELBOURNE. Sank HMAS VOYAGER in collision 10th Feb 1964 and sank USS FRANK E EVANS in collision 3rd Jun 1969. Sold to China and broken up from 1985.
931-938	LCT 7082 – LCT 7089	Mar/Apr 1944	Tank Landing Craft/625	Built for RN. LCT 7089 was sunk in Boulogne harbour Dec 1944. No further details.
940	LST 3044 HMS NARVIK	29 Jul 1945	Landing Ship Tank/3,065	Built for RN. Renamed 1947. Later Submarine Accommodation Ship at Faslane. Broken up at Faslane in 1965.
941	LST 3045	24 Oct 1945	Landing Ship Tank/3,065	Contract cancelled after launch but before completion.
943	LST 3006		Landing Ship Tank/3,065	Completion of LST built at Harland & Wolff. Completed as TROMSO (1947) later EMPIRE GANNET (1956)
944	LST 3007		Landing Ship Tank/3,065	Completion of LST built at Harland & Wolff. Completed for Greek Navy as RHN AXIOS (1947).
945	HINEMOA	30 May 1946	Passenger Cargo Ship/6,911	Built for Union Steamship Co., New Zealand. No further details.
948	ACCRA	24 Feb 1947	Passenger Cargo Ship/11,644	Built for Elder Dempster Lines Ltd., Liverpool. Sold to Spain and scrapped Nov 1967.
949	APAPA	18 Aug 1947	Passenger Cargo Ship/11,651	Built for Elder Dempster Lines Ltd., Liverpool. Scrapped in China Feb 1975.
950	ORCADES	14 Oct 1947	Passenger Liner/28,396	Built for P & O Steam Navigation Co. Ltd., London. Sold and scrapped in Taiwan Feb 1973.

Yard No.	Name	Launched	Ship Type/Tonnage	Comments
951	HIMALAYA	05 Oct 1948	Passenger Liner/27,989	Built for P & O Steam navigation Co. Ltd., London. Broken up.
964	CHUSAN	28 Jun 1949	Passenger Liner/24,261	Built for P & O Steam Navigation Co. Ltd., London. Withdrawn from service 1973. Broken up at Kaohsiung, China from 1973.
969	PRESIDENTE PERON	03 Nov 1948	Passenger Cargo Ship/12,653	Built for Argentine government. Several Argentine owners. No further details.
970	EVA PERON	25 Aug 1949	Passenger Cargo Ship/12,627	Built for Argentine government. Various owners. No further details.
971	17 DE OCTUBRE	04 Apr 1950	Passenger Cargo Ship/12,653	Built for Argentine government. No further details.
976	ORONSAY	30 Jun 1950	Passenger Liner/27,632	Built for P & O Steam Navigation Co. Ltd., London. No further details.
994	BRITISH ADVENTURE	12 Dec 1950	Oil Tanker/18,492.	Built for B.P. Tanker Co. Ltd., London. No further details.

DECADE 1951 to 1960

Yard No.	Name	Launched	Ship Type/Tonnage	Comments
928	HMS HERMES	16 Feb 1953	Aircraft Carrier/23,000	Built for RN. Laid down 1944. Completion was delayed to 1959. flagship of the Falklands Task Force in 1982. Sold to India as INS in 1987 as INS VIRAAT. Decommissioned 2016.
1000	WORLD CONCORD	29 Jan 1952	Oil Tanker/21,101	Built for Niarchos Group of Companies, Greece. Vessel broke into two halves whilst under ballast in Irish Sea Feb 1954. Repaired and in service until 1974.
1008	CARL SCHMEDEMAN	12 May 1952	Ore Carrier/10,839	Built for Tropical Steamship Co. Ltd., Toronto.
1009	NUEVA ESPARTA	19 Nov 1952	Destroyer/2,600	Built for Venezuelan Navy. No further details.
1010	ZULIA	29 Jun 1953	Destroyer/2,600	Built for Venezuelan Navy. No further details.
1011	ESSO WESTMINSTER	24 Sep 1953	Oil Tanker/17,540	Built for Esso Petroleum Co. Ltd., London.
1012	ESSO CANTERBURY	19 Feb 1954	Oil Tanker/17,515	Built for Esso Petroleum Co. Ltd., London.
1019	BRITISH SOVEREIGN	11 Aug 1954	Oil Tanker/21,138	Built for B.P. Tanker Co. Ltd., London.
1020	BRITISH VICTORY	13 Dec 1954	Oil Tanker/21,153	Built for B.P. Tanker Co. Ltd., London.
1021	ORSOVA	14 May 1953	Passenger Liner/28,790	Built for Orient Steam Navigation Co. Ltd., London.
1026	HINDSIA	24 May 1955	Oil Tanker/12,212	Built for Shell Bermuda (Overseas) Ltd., Bermuda.
1027	HINEA	19 Aug 1955	Oil Tanker/12,212	Built for Shell Bermuda (Overseas) Ltd., Bermuda.
1032	SPYROS NIARCHOS	02 Dec 1955	Oil Tanker/30,159	Built for Neptune Tanker Corp., Liberia. This was a member of the Niarchos group. Largest tanker in world when built.
1033	EVGENIA NIARCHOS	08 Aug 1956	Oil Tanker/30,159	Built for Neptune Tanker Corp., Liberia.
1036	ARAGUA	27 Jan 1955	Destroyer/2,600	Built for Venezuelan Navy. No further details.
1040	SAN GREGORIO	26 Jul 1957	Oil Tanker/10,256	Built for Eagle Oil & Shipping Co. Ltd., London. Sold to Shell Tankers (UK) Ltd., London 1960.
1044	BRITISH GLORY	01 Feb 1957	Oil Tanker/21,001	Built for B.P. Tanker Co. Ltd., London.
1047	BRITISH FAITH	10 Dec 2957	Oil Tanker/21,000	Built for B.P. Tanker Co. Ltd., London.

Yard No.	Name	Launched	Ship Type/Tonnage	Comments
1055	ALMIRANTE WILLIAMS	05 May 1958	Destroyer/2,730	Built for Chilean Navy. No further details.
1056	ALMIRANTE RIVEROS	12 Dec 1958	Destroyer/2,730	Built for Chilean Navy. No further details.
1057	BRITISH AMBASSADOR	16 Aug 1958	Oil Tanker/27,506	Built for B.P. Tanker Co. Ltd., London.
1061	ORIANA	03 Nov 1959	Passenger Liner/41,923	Built for Orient Steam Navigation Co. Ltd., London.

DECADE 1961 to 1970

Yard No.	Name	Launched	Ship Type/Tonnage	Comments
1058	BRITISH PRESTIGE	28 Jul 1961	Oil Tanker/27,480	Built for B.P. Tanker Co. Ltd., London.
1063	HMS MOHAWK	05 Apr 1962	'Tribal' Class Frigate/2,300	Built for RN. Decommissioned 1979. Arrived Cairnryan for scrapping in 1982.
1067	BRITISH GRENADIER	16 Aug 1962	Oil Tanker/32,303	Built for B.P. Tanker Co. Ltd., London.
1068	MALWA	30 May 1961	Oil Tanker/24,266	Built for Charter Shipping Co. Ltd., London.
1069	BRITISH ADMIRAL	17 Mar 1956	Oil Tanker/100,000 dw	Built for B.P. Tanker Co. Ltd., London
1071	METHANE PRINCESS	22 Jun 1963	LNG Carrier/20,300	Built for Coch. Methane Tankers Ltd. Operated by Shell Tankers.
1079	ROSTAM	04 Mar 1969	Mark V Destroyer/1,265	Built for Iranian Navy. Launched at Swan Hunter on the Tyne and towed to Barrow for 'Fitting Out'. Renamed SABALAN after Iranian Revolution.
1080	ZAAL	04 Mar 1969	Mark V Destroyer/1,265	Built for Iranian Navy. Renamed after ALBORZ after Iranian Revolution.

DECADE 1971 to 1980

Yard No.	Name	Launched	Ship Type/Tonnage	Comments
1084	HMS SHEFFIELD	10 Jun 1971	Type 42 Destroyer/3,150	Built for RN. Sank following Exocet missile attack during 1982 Falklands War
1085	COPENHAGEN	20 Dec 1972	Passenger Liner/13,760	Built for Danish owners. Towed to Tyne for completion. Returned to Barrow for sale 1974. Sold to Black Sea Shipping Co. through Sudo Import, USSR. Renamed ODESSA. No further details.
1089	ARA HERCULES	24 Oct 1972	Type 42 Destroyer/3,150	Served in Falklands War in 1982. Major refit in 2000 to carry 240 Marines and 2 Sea King helos. Still In Service in 2017.
1091	HMS CARDIFF	22 Feb 1974	Type 42 Destroyer/3,150	Built for RN. Towed to Tyne for completion. Served in Falklands War 1982. Decommissioned in July 2005 and scrapped in Turkey.
1098	HMS INVINCIBLE	03 May 1977	Command Cruiser/19,810	Built for RN. Served in Falklands War 1982. Decommissioned in 2005. Scrapped in Turkey February 2011.
1102	HMS MANCHESTER	24 Nov 1980	Stretched Type 42 Destroyer	Built for RN. Decommissioned February 2011. Scrapped from November 2014.

Yard No.	Name	Launched	Ship Type/Tonnage	Comments

DECADE 1981 to 1990

No Surface Ship Orders received in this decade (1981 to 1990)

DECADE 1991 to 2000

Yard No.	Name	Launched	Ship Type/Tonnage	Comments
1113	HMS OCEAN	11 Oct 1995	Amphibious Helicopter Carrier	Built and Launched under sub contract at Kvaerner, Govan. Towed to Barrow. Superstructure and 'fitting out' completed at Barrow in 1998. Named by H.M. The Queen at Barrow 20 Nov 1998. Still in service but due to pay off 2018.
1114				Yard No. to cover work undertaken at Barrow on the Superstructure and installation of Combat Systems and Aviation Facilities to Yard No. 1113 (HMS OCEAN). In the event the number was withdrawn.
1115	THAMES FISHER	1997	Oil Tanker	Launched for James Fisher Tankers. Still in service 2017.
1116	HUMBER FISHER	1997	Oil Tanker	Launched for James Fisher Tankers. Still in service 2017.
1119	RFA WAVE KNIGHT	29 Sep 2000	Fleet Tanker Ship	Launched for the Royal Fleet Auxiliary on 30th Sep 2000. Still in service 2017.
1120	RFA WAVE RULER	9 Feb 2001	Fleet Tanker Ship	Launched for the Royal Fleet Auxiliary on 30th Sep 2000. Still in service 2017.
1121	MERSEY FISHER	1996	Oil Tanker	Launched for James Fisher Tankers. Still in service 2017.

DECADE 2001 to 2010

Yard No.	Name	Launched	Ship Type/Tonnage	Comments
1117	HMS ALBION	9 Mar 2001	Landing Ship (Dock)	Still in Service in 2017.
1118	HMS BULWARK	15 Nov 2001	Landing Ship (Dock)	Still in Service in 2017.
--	AMAZON HOPE		Former Fleet Tender	Conversion of former RMAS Fleet Tender for use as a Medical and Dental Support Vessel on the Amazon.
1125	HMS QUEEN ELIZABETH	17 Jul 2014	Aircraft Carrier/60,000	Design and build of Lower Block 3 of Future Carrier Type CVF. Build Contract cancelled - to be undertaken instead by BAE Systems Surface Ships, Govan. Yard No. changed to 'Design Contract' only.
1126	HMS PRINCE OF WALES		Aircraft Carrier/60,000	Design and build of Lower Block 3 of Future Carrier Type CVF. Build Contract cancelled - to be undertaken instead by BAE Systems Surface Ships, Govan. Yard No. changed to 'Design Contract' only.